UNDERSTANDING
POLICY
FIASCOES

UNDERSTANDING POLICY FIASCOES

MARK BOVENS
PAUL 'T HART

TRANSACTION PUBLISHERS
New Brunswick (U.S.A.) and London (U.K.)

Library of Congress Catalog Number: 95-9318
ISBN: 1-56000-214-X
Printed in the United States of America

Library of Congress Cataloging-in-Publication Data

Bovens, Mark.
    Understanding policy fiascoes / Mark Bovens, Paul 't Hart.
        p. cm.
    Includes bibliographical references and index.
    ISBN 1-56000-214-X (alk. paper)
    1. Policy sciences. I. Hart, Paul 't. II. Title.
H97.B68 1995
320'.6—dc20   95-9318
                                                                CIP

Contents

Preface

Our present state of knowledge is one of mitigated ignorance. In such situations, the honest enquirer always has one consolation — his blunders may be as instructive as his successes.

Alan Simpson[1]

The exact origins of a study are often obscure. They are easily lost sight of in the zig-zag process of developing and reconsidering ideas, considering potential research designs, and crafting texts. Heaps of files begin to obstruct rather than enhance one's command of the history of one's project. Many books therefore have no clear beginning and do not follow a linear path to completion; they just evolve. This book, at least, can be traced back to a well-defined date and place: Thursday May 5, 1988 at 1:30 PM when the authors met for the first time at the Leiden Institute for Law and Public Policy. In the late eighties our otherwise stable and well-reputed country was rocked by a series of highly publicized political controversies about mismanagement and fiascoes in the public sector. At that time, both authors had already, albeit from very different angles, been working on aspects of failures of governance. Paul 't Hart was completing a study on the groupthink phenomenon and its detrimental effects on the quality of governmental decision making. Mark Bovens was working on a study about the role and limits of accountability in preventing organizational deviance. This first meeting eventually set off a series of weekly discussions at work, in cafés, and at home. It was soon decided to join forces, and to concentrate on documenting and explaining the sudden increase in policy fiascoes in the Netherlands.

The original objective was to conduct a multi-case empirical study of policy fiascoes, designed to trace and to explain their common causes in a range of public sector domains. It was also clear that these policy fiascoes were not a typical Dutch problem but could also be found in many other Western countries. A comparative approach was therefore imperative. Case materials were being collected and the relevant literatures on policy and organizational failure, problems of public management, and policy analysis were digested. A selection was made of twenty-six cases of what we then believed were clear-cut policy fiascoes. The cases covered a broad range of Western liberal democracies and a variety of policy domains. The material was discussed intensively with graduate students, and eventually we started writing our own accounts.

Our idea was that by studying these fiascoes we could make an empirical contribution to the predominantly ideological debate about the future of "big government." Neoconservative critics of the public sector have argued time and again that in all but a limited range of tasks, government intervention in the economy and the delivery of public services is bound to fail. Looking at a controlled sample of the most dramatic failures of government, we wanted to know what causes them to happen, and to what extent these causes are inherent or remediable. If policy fiascoes turned out to be due to largely inherent, immutable problems of public administration, the neoconservative attack on government would gain strength. If fiascoes turned out to be more dependent on contextual, variable, and, in principle, remediable factors, however, this would provide some support for the less gloomy perspective maintained by liberal and social-democratic participants in the debate. In that case, moreover, studying policy fiascoes might provide us with leads to learn from past mistakes by "unlearning" faulty ways of organizing and conducting public policy, which is exactly what many contemporary students of politics, policy, and public administration call for.

Yet, the more we studied the evidence, the more and more complicated the questions we encountered became, and the more elusive the "answers" seemed to be. Even the basic question of definition, in other words how can we recognize a fiasco when we see one, became a major stumbling block. Likewise, the question of identifying recurrent causes proved debilitating.

Manuscripts came and manuscripts went. Grandiose theoretical frameworks and typologies were constructed, only to be discounted later because they did not lead anywhere or rested on untenable assumptions. Students, colleagues, and journal reviewers gave us a hard time. Gradually, we came to realize that a considerable part of the problem did not only lie with the complexity of the subject matter, but also with the ways in which we and other academic students of public policymaking have approached the notion of policy fiasco. The emerging literature on post-positivistic approaches to policy analysis and evaluation proved helpful in making sense of our experiences in developing a theory of policy fiascoes. In it, we found the clues for reformulating the aims and scope of the project. Instead of trying to explain the rise of policy fiascoes in terms of an objectivistic, general, or contingent causal theory, we tried to understand the notion of policy fiasco in order to make more sense of the difficult issues that surround the evaluation of policies that fall. This involved a switch in epistemology from a positivist concern with objectivity, causality, and generalization towards an interpretive approach emphasizing subjectivity, contextuality, and uniqueness. It also challenged us to face more squarely the political dimension of policymaking and evaluation, which in our original approach had become obscured from view by an emphasis on the managerial, technocratic dimension.

During the years of preparation, this book changed therefore from a theoretically informed empirical study to an empirically informed theoretical study. It became clear that our original impulse to do a large-scale comparative case study of policy fiascoes to illustrate or test a deductively derived theoretical framework was both impractical and unproductive. This was partly because of pragmatic reasons, such as the sheer costs associated with data gathering: to get to know "enough" about a single major historical policy fiasco to be able to systematically apply the numerous and complex theoretical categories and constructs we had in mind, would already have required a major research effort. To do this for twenty-six odd cases in different countries and policy sectors would be nightmarish. More importantly however, we found that much more work than originally expected was needed on the conceptual, philosophical, and theoretical side in order to be able to develop a coherent and relevant framework amenable to empirical research.

As observed many times by seasoned travellers, it is not so much any particular destination but the continuous process of moving from place to place which provides them with their greatest and most rewarding experiences. Accordingly, this book should be viewed as a kind of travelogue, a tale of two students on the road to an elusive goal. It relates in some detail issues we regard as fundamental in understanding and learning from policy fiascoes. They deal with seemingly simple questions. By what criteria should one judge the degree of success or failure of a policy's outcomes? How do we establish that these outcomes were in fact caused by the activities of policymakers and public agencies, rather than by other actors and circumstances beyond their control? Once we know which officials and agencies were the main forces contributing to a particular set of highly negative policy outcomes, how can we explain their behavior? How come they acted to create a situation which was not only harmful to many stakeholders or recipients of the policies concerned, but ultimately also to their own position and legitimacy? To what extent do they deserve blame for what they did?

This book could not have been written but for the insightful and selfless scholarship of a number of friends and colleagues with two or three decades more experience than we have in studying governance. They pointed out to us that we must not continue our struggle on the road to a comprehensive and empirically plausible theory of policy fiascoes, because it was like the quest for the Holy Grail: doomed to fail. They made us realize that the numerous problems we encountered would almost certainly be far more illuminating and useful for both students and practitioners of public policymaking. The fact that our struggles have resulted in a book at all, as well as the form which it has taken, is therefore due in many important ways to the advice and assistance of Yehezkel Dror, Alexander Kouzmin, Uriel Rosenthal, and the late Aaron Wildavsky. In addition, important comments and inputs to the manuscript at various stages of completion were made by other colleagues, including Rudy Andeweg, Hans Berg, Arjen Boin, Wim Derksen, Menno van Duin, Tom Eijsbouts, Alexander George, Robert Goodin, Tjeerd de Groot, Herman van Gunsteren, Joachim Jens Hesse, Alan Jarman, Marieke Kleiboer, Koen Koch, Ned Lebow, Bob Leivesley, Cynthia McSwain, Erwin Muller, Marc Otten, Ignace Snellen, Lucas van Spengler, Margo Trappenburg, Theo Toonen, Romke van der Veen, Henk Wagenaar, Orion White, Vincent Wright, and Dvora Yanow. We are grateful to all of them for their assistance.

We also benefitted from papers and comments by students in two consecutive series of graduate seminars on what we then called "Administrative Tragedies," at Leiden University. Chantal Hendriks, Digna van Herwaarden, and Marjan Schnetz efficiently traced all the readings we requested, however obscure. Henk Valk was of great assistance in the processing of the case studies and the final editing of the text.

Paul 't Hart's work on this project has been facilitated considerably by an extended postdoctoral fellowship from the Royal Dutch Academy of Sciences. Moreover, he has received hospitality at the Centre for European Studies, Nuffield College, Oxford and the Centre for Administrative Studies, Faculty of Management, University of Canberra, which provided congenial environments for working on this project. Jens Hesse's and Alexander Kouzmin's help in arranging these research visits and staff seminars during which we could present some of our thoughts, is gratefully acknowledged. Bengt Sundelius kindly arranged a useful seminar presentation at the Department of Political Science of the University of Stockholm.

Also at Kouzmin's invitation, Mark Bovens has enjoyed equally rewarding hospitality and financial support as a visiting research fellow at the Department of Management, Faculty of Commerce, University of Western Sydney. He would also like to thank Bob Goodin for inviting him to present the project at a research seminar at the Australian National University in Canberra, and to the participants at the seminar for their comments.

Finally, we have benefitted from the material, secretarial, and collegial support at the Department of Public Administration of Leiden University. Anne van der Zwalmen in particular has lended an artful and profession-al hand in preparing the manuscript for publication.

Note

1 *The wealth of the gentry, 1540–1660*, Chicago 1961, p.21, as quoted in D.H. Fischer (ed.), *Historians' fallacies: Towards a logic of historical thought*, London: Routledge 1970, p. xvii.

CHAPTER 1

Understanding Policy Fiascoes

Politics is the art of looking for trouble, finding it whether it exists or not, diagnosing it incorrectly, and applying the wrong remedy.

Sir Ernest Benn[1]

The Ubiquity of Failure

In many respects, the last decades of the twentieth century have had the air of a fin de siècle for the theory and practice of government. During the 1980s especially, the state of governance was paradoxical. Never before had the public sector been so big, never before had the impact of government decisions and activities on the daily lives of citizens been so diverse and comprehensive. Yet at the same time the idea of government as the primary institution for steering economy and society came under increasing attack. Neoconservative critics of government intervention in the economy rose to positions of political and bureaucratic power. The alleged excesses of the welfare state and its bureaucracy were heckled. The politically dominant view of government became a skeptical one: "the smaller, the better." Concerted attempts were made to limit government spending, to terminate programs, and to slim down the size of the bureaucracy – albeit with varying degrees of pugnacity and success.[2]

It was, in other words, a period in which what Hirschman calls a "rhetoric of reaction" prevailed.[3] While the unmitigated cynicism of Sir Ernest Benn's observation quoted above might have seemed too extreme to many, government itself and conventional politics and policymaking as its key constituent components, were definitely running out of favor among important bodies of public and expert opinion. The tide was turning sharply against the seemingly unstoppable expansion of the scope of public-sector intervention. Little good could be expected from it. It was portrayed as inefficient, slow, unresponsive, rigid, often rude, and very costly if not wasteful. Moreover, big government was said to have created a marked degree of apathy, cynicism, and irresponsibility among citizens. Negative stereotypes about government bureaucracies and bureaucrats reigned freely.[4]

Apart from relying on emerging economic doctrines and new formulations of old political ideologies, contemporary critics of big government claim to have "the facts" on their side. In particular, they have often pointed to various highly publicized instances of government failure: concrete and numerous cases of incompetence, red tape, fraud, waste, abuse, irrationality, and other serious deficiencies in government organization and the implementation of public programs. The specific cases referred to differed according to national experiences, but the seemingly endless stream of political scandals and policy fiascoes that burst into the open throughout the 1980s and 1990s seemed a clear indication of the idea that the public sector has grown out of hand and needs to be curbed drastically.

Examples from many different domains of public policy have been used to make this case. Especially popular have been alleged excesses of the welfare state, for example well-publicized failures in the administration of social security, health care, education, and public housing. Often, the acronyms that had been taken from the initials of the program or from the main actor involved have become local synonyms for fiascoes: CETA and HUD in the United States; RSV or WAO in the Netherlands; NHS in the United Kingdom.[5]

In addition many large-scale public works, vulnerable especially to cost escalations, corrupt practices, and emergent citizen protest, have been dismissed as "planning disasters."[6] Major public buildings (Sydney's opera house, Amsterdam's city hall and opera complex, Bonn's aborted new parliament house), nuclear energy installations and power plants (Washington State's aborted 5-reactor project, the aborted 3-country breeder reactor project at Kalkar, Germany) and airports (London, Tokyo, Frankfurt) have been notorious in this respect. More hesitantly during the Cold War but with increasing vigilance following its end, defense acquisition programs have come under attack. Specifically, various forms of political manipulation and waste and abuse of public funds were uncovered in the construction and acquisition of helicopters (United Kingdom), submarines (Netherlands), or high-tech weapon systems (United States).[7]

On top of that have come those traumatic cases where senior public authorities seemed to belie the public trust placed in them, engaging in secret and illegal practices and subsequently seeking to cover up their involvement after the events were publicly exposed. Following the Watergate prototype of the seventies, the eighties have given us some other "gates": Irangate in the United States (illegal arms for hostages deals with Khomeini's Iran), Belgranogate in the United Kingdom (a conspiracy to cover up the decision to sink a non-combatant Argentine vessel during the Falklands war), Recruitgate in Japan (secret corporate slush fund payments to senior Japanese politicians), and Boforsgate in Sweden (secret arms deals with India). In the nineties, major corruption scandals have rocked officials, government agencies, and political parties in countries like France, Belgium, and Spain, and have brought about a fundamental crisis of the political order in Italy.

The emergent social, political, if not moral, delegitimation of government and the increasing sense that many government policies are fundamentally flawed is not only a problem for modern states and their politicians and bureaucrats. The ubiquity of failure is also a profound challenge to those proponents of social science who have traditionally claimed to seek to understand and help improve the practice of government and public policymaking. While policymakers are facing a crisis of legitimacy as a result of the general mood of disappointment and skepticism towards politics and the state, policy scientists and students of public administration have been forced to reconsider the validity of their knowledge claims and the nature and extent of their impact on the practice of policymaking. Why have they not been able to help prevent major policy failures and scandals from happening? Why is it so difficult to explain the genesis of these failures more effectively, so as to facilitate policy learning and prevention? Is it because policy scientists are not listened to by policymakers, hence do we face a problem of knowledge dissemination and utilization? Or does the problem lie within policy science itself, that is, with its analytical tools for studying, comprehending, and in some cases predicting social and political processes? If so, what does this imply for its prescriptive aims and ambitions?

This *problematique*, the interrelated crises of policymaking and policy science, as dramatized especially by the stream of widely publicized and recurrent instances of major government failures – commonly referred to by observers and analysts as "policy fiascoes" – forms the background against which this book is written. Doing this research has taught us that the very questions we ask about government performance need to be sharpened and partially reframed. Policy "fiascoes" may seem concrete and ubiquituous, but to study them empirically and to learn the right lessons from them turns out to be very complex. This complexity has both intellectual and political components, that in combination tend to produce intractable and enduring public controversies about the interpretation of negative policy events. This book attempts to dissect the various dimensions of this complexity, and will challenge its readers to face up to the many conceptual, empirical, and normative dilemmas of contemporary policy evaluation and analysis, as it attempts to understand the public controversies through which policy fiascoes and their roots are constituted. Before we come to preview the book's design and content, let us first illustrate some major analytical challenges and dangers inherent in the study of policy fiascoes that prompted these questions.

The Relativity of Failure

The absence of fixed criteria for success and failure, which apply regardless of time and place, is a serious problem for anyone who wants to do a comparative study of major policy failures. Feldman's study of the politics of airport construction in London and Paris provides a wonderful illustration of this.[8] In the late fifties, a third airport in the London region was considered an essential requirement to accommodate the anticipated steep increase of air traffic to and from the British capital. An interdepartmental government committee was established which, in 1964, recommended to develop the former Stansted military airfield into London's third civilian airport. The report triggered local protests, new inquiries were held, and in the following years many other sites were considered and proposed in various reports issued by a number of official committees. Decades of public deliberation, extensive studies, and constant planning changes failed to result in any positive decision, let alone to construction activities. In the late eighties, Stansted was made London's third airport, but would operate on a small-scale basis for many years to come.

On the other side of the Channel, the French aviation authorities did much better apparently. Forecasts about the growth of air travel similar to those available to their British counterparts led the French to the same conclusion: by the end of the 1960s the Paris region would need a third airport in addition to Le Bourget and Orly. In contrast to their British colleagues, however, French planners operating in the more centralized French administrative system were able to move fast and rigorously. As early as 1957, a site north of Paris was chosen. Meanwhile, studies for the location of yet another, fourth airport were launched. By 1963, the master plan was ready, the site was officially announced, and land acquisition was started. The scope of the project was enormous. It was "the largest single construction project in France since the royal palace at Versailles."[9] Nonetheless, in 1974, only two years later than originally planned in the fifties, the new Charles de Gaulle Airport was officially opened.

British planners spent a great deal of money and effort yet clearly failed to accomplish their objective of building a third international airport. But should this be considered a policy fiasco or, in Hall's terminology, a "great planning disaster?"[10] Let us have a look at some of the policy outcomes in both cases. Air traffic indeed increased in the sixties and seventies, but certainly not to the extent predicted in the mid-fifties. The development of larger aircraft made it possible to carry more passengers on the same flight. Heathrow and Gatwick did become much more crowded, but new terminals and more efficient baggage-handling facilities made it possible to absorb the extra demand. In the end, the failure to develop a third airport did not greatly harm the overall objective of satisfying the air demand throughout the remainder of the twentieth century. On the contrary, it "may even have helped achieve the goal of serving the air-travelling public efficiently with minimal disruption to other services."[11]

On the other hand, the success of the French planners becomes much bleaker if looked upon from a broader socio-economic and political perspective. The plans for Charles de Gaulle Airport were developed in great secrecy and implemented in a highly centrist, almost autocratic fashion. Participation in decision making by local groups and authorities was denied. As a consequence, their interests and viewpoints were plainly ignored. Moreover, the development of the airport resulted in the forced evacuation and destruction of the nearby town of Rossy-en-France and to severe noise pollution and traffic nuisances for the remaining villages. In addition, the airport itself turned out to be costly and inefficient. Many of the major airlines complained about it and would have preferred extra terminals at Orly. Most importantly and as explained above, the number of flights did not expand as steeply as expected, leaving the Paris region with three seriously underutilized international airports. As Feldman concludes:

> The building of Charles de Gaulle Airport can no more be called a "success" than the nonconstruction of a third international airport for London can be termed a "failure." Aéroport de Paris accomplished its objective of building a technologically sophisticated airport able to absorb all traffic through Paris for the foreseeable future, but it failed to provide adequate access, satisfied clients (the airlines), or contented neighbours. It did not rationalize services with a second Paris international airport, and because it did not do so it may have contributed to a decline in the region's traffic; nor did it stimulate major economic growth. The goal, therefore that of assuring Paris its place as the premier air facility attraction in Europe may have been sacrificed to the narrow objective.[12]

This brief case comparison highlights the proposition that judgments about the success and failure of public policies are, first of all, a matter of perspective. From a technocratic, planning perspective, Charles de Gaulle Airport was a success and the nondevelopment of Stansted or any of the competing options a failure. The French planners reached their operational objective of building a new airport without too much delay or cost esca-

lations. Yet a convincing case can be made that the British were more successful. They succeeded in meeting the common strategic goal of accom-
modating the growth of air traffic at far lower financial and social costs
than their colleagues in France. Moreover, this was the result of a process
which left room for a variety of interested parties to state their case and
exert influence in a pluralistic process of partisan analysis and political
debate.

Secondly, the analysis suggests that failure and success are also a matter of time. De Gaulle Airport was initially considered a success: at first
most policymakers and observers focused on the remarkable feat that the
planners had succeeded in getting the job of building such a major infrastructural facility done pretty much as scheduled many years before. It
took a few years before the airport's structural underutilization and
"hidden" social costs became evident. Similarly, however, during the
long years of upgrading the existing facilities there, many regular users of
Heathrow would have disputed the more positive assessment of British
policies made above. Nowadays the benefits of concentration might have
become more apparent. Ironically, the temporal dynamics of evaluating
major policy ventures are such that in ten more years or so, a comparative
judgment on both cases might need to be readjusted once again. A sudden sharp rise in air traffic in the twenty-first century can be absorbed
much more easily in the Paris region, thanks to its current overcapacity.
Meanwhile, London planners have succeeded in the late eighties in reviv-
ing the Stansted option in a small-scale fashion, but might experience
great difficulties in expanding it further to accommodate Heathrow's sat-
uration over the next decades.

The Inevitability of Failure

What would have happened to the plan to attempt a military rescue operation for Americans held hostage in Iran if, during the final meeting of the
National Security Council on the issue, Admiral Stansfield Turner had
brought out for discussion the highly critical CIA estimates he had recently received, which predicted that even in the best of circumstances a significant number of Americans would die? What would have happened to
the building of the Sydney Opera House if the 1965 elections in New
South Wales had not brought to office a new minister for public works
less likely to give carte blanche to architect Utzon in supervising the construction process? What would have happened to the Space Shuttle
Challenger if the temperatures would have been just a few degrees higher at the time it was launched?

It is only when we start wondering what might have been that we fully realize that what in fact has happened need not have. It makes sense to do this kind of wondering especially when studying momentous historical events and highly controversial policy episodes. Often it seems the difference between what became stigmatized as a policy fiasco and what went unnoticed as a "nonevent" or was hailed as a major policy success, was extremely thin, trivial even. The more one knows about the intricacies of the actions and events that shaped a particular policy's fate, the more important small details seem to be in determining the collective appreciation of it. Change some of these details, and one could have changed the course of history.[13] If A had only talked to B earlier; if C had been a more forceful personality; if D had lived longer; if group X had been composed a little differently; if the weather had been different; if this distracting side event had not happened at that point in time; if that verification procedure had not been routinely ignored in organization Y; if party Z had just obtained one more seat in parliament than it did; if there had been no previous success to serve as a reference point; if ...

These counterfactual questions are often asked by both the victims and some of the perpetrators of major failures and disasters. They are part of the trauma caused by these events. On quite another level, they make for intriguing novels and movie scripts. In some cases, these questions are pointless because they refer to "might have beens" that were highly implausible in the given situation. But in many other cases, the cruel fact is that the course of history could indeed easily have taken another, less fateful turn.

This point easily gets lost on outsiders looking back at these events from a distance. In their quest for coherent explanations of what happened and why, they may easily overlook the vagaries and indeterminate nature of the situation as it unfolded. In the case of policy fiascoes, this may propel observers towards oversimplified and unnecessarily harsh judgments about the quality of policymaking. In fact, speaking about specific historical fiascoes some commentators even go as far as to conclude that the act of government, by its very nature, numbs the intellect, induces irrationalities, and generally brings out the worst in people. For example, after a devastating critique of Western political leadership, ranging from Priam, the king of Troy, to postwar American presidents, the historian Barbara Tuchman concludes that:

> Absence of intelligent thinking in rulership is another of the universals, and raises the question whether in modern states there is something about political and bureaucratic life that subdues the functioning of intellect in favor of "working the levers" without regard to rational expectations. This would seem to be an ongoing prospect.[14]

She puts forward a straightforward and parsimonious explanation for policy fiascoes:

> Mankind, it seems, makes a poorer performance of government than of almost any other human activity. In this sphere, wisdom, which may be defined as the exercise of judgment acting on experience, common sense and available information, is less operative than it should be.[15]

It follows that many policy fiascoes are caused by plain political or managerial folly. To Tuchman folly has several faces. It can manifest itself as overreacting, as the illusion of omnipotence or the illusion of invulnerability, as "wooden-headedness" and cognitive dissonance, or as "working the levers," the absence of reflective thought.[16]

Tuchman's book is a prime example of a brand of political analysis quite common amongst intellectuals, both in journalism and academia. Standing at the side line, and with the benefit of hindsight, policy errors and fiascoes seem easily identified and readily explainable. They were caused by greed, by the lust for power, by laziness, and, most of all, by cognitive arrogance and information pathologies. The American involvement in Vietnam for example, the analysis of which takes up almost half of her book, is described by Tuchman as one long march of folly, all the way from the first involvements under Truman in 1945 until the signing of the Paris peace treaty by Nixon in 1973.

We certainly do not want to dispute the disastrous character of the American involvement in Vietnam, but we do want to suggest that mere "folly" is not a very convincing and fruitful analysis of its causes. What Tuchman fails to explain is how it could happen that five successive presidents, from two different parties, with different characters and experiences, and equipped with large staffs of the best and the brightest people in one of the richest countries on earth, could all have behaved so foolishly over such a long period of time.[17]

In a review of Tuchman's book, Wagenaar has argued convincingly that she has become the victim of what we might call "the wisdom after the event trap."[18] Psychological experiments show that people's calculations of the likelihood of the possible outcomes of historical decisions are strongly biased by their knowledge of the actual events. For those who know the outcome, the unfolding of events seems much more logical and inevitable than for those who had no foreknowledge. They just "knew it would happen." However, as Wagenaar argues, "the subjectively perceived inevitability of events in the past is an ex-post reconstruction."[19] People tend to underestimate systematically the complexity of issues, the inconclusiveness of information and the general uncertainty which is caused by strategic interaction, once they know what actually happened.

Wagenaar makes clear that many of the crucial decisions facing Kennedy, Johnson, or Nixon during the course of the conflict in Vietnam had to be made on the basis of discussions and reports which involved at least two, often mutually exclusive points of view which were supported by extensive and rational, but in the end inconclusive arguments. What appears with hindsight as a folly, presented itself as a lack of adequate and conclusive information, as institutional or intellectual stalemate, and, eventually, as "fuzzy gambling" to the actual policymakers.[20]

The wisdom after the event trap makes one aware of the limited validity of deterministic and monocausal explanations of the evolution of policy episodes, including policy fiascoes. When interpreted in terms of a slightly different historical, institutional, and political perspective, many policy "fiascoes" could easily have turned out quite differently. The fact that these policy episodes have unfolded in the ways they did, does not mean they were inevitable.

Understanding Policy Fiascoes

Another reason why it is so difficult to make sense of policy fiascoes is the very notion of "policy fiasco" itself. It is not just another "essentially contested" concept, it is also a semantic tool used in political contestation and public debates about controversial policy episodes. These two contestational properties infuse discussions about policy fiascoes with value judgments in more than one sense. First, as many other concepts in social science, the concept of fiascoes is essentially contested as its content is not fixed but subject to constant debate and reformulation. Second, despite this indeterminacy, the concept of "fiasco" is also, and often predominantly, used to make a statement about affairs. To call something a fiasco is to impress on it a powerful negative label, and effectively to engage in an act of allegation. Labelling a set of actions and events as a fiasco may serve to contest claims, to diminish power, and to weaken positions. Likewise, characterizing a certain episode as a "fiasco" conveys a strongly negative impression of the officials concerned, the agencies responsible, or indeed the regime at large. This being the case, the term is bound to be used as a rather loose symbol or metaphor in mass media or political discourse. The same goes for related terms such as "crisis," "disaster," "affair," and "scandal."[21]

Policy fiascoes do not stand out as readily recognizable phenomena. At one level, they refer to events that affect what goes on in the real world: talk, decisions, actions or lack of them on the part of government officials, public agencies and other parties influencing a community's well-being. At another level, they refer to a rhetorical and political process of interpreting and evaluating these events and their effects. Departing as we do from an interpretive orientation towards policy analysis, it becomes impossible to keep these two dimensions separated. In fact, from an inter- pretivist point of view the former dimension is not knowable in any other way than through a version of the latter. In other words: policy events only assume significance when people perceive them and attribute mean- ing to them. Whenever individuals engage in these perceptions and attri- butions, they do so by taking into account a variety of cues from their social environment: shared norms, values, and symbols. In the special case of policy fiascoes, this process of cue-taking and meaning-making will be intensely, if not always overtly, political. This is because the course and outcomes of this process at the level of the community as a whole may have important consequences for those whose talk, decisions, and actions are being interpreted and assessed, and ultimately for the ways in which people relate to the political and bureaucratic system of the state as a whole.

In this book, we shall attempt to understand policy fiascoes by analyz- ing what happens when people label events as fiascoes, speculate about their causes, and draw lessons from them. Whenever a policy fiasco is "discovered," many different kinds of people engage in the meaning- making that produces it: citizens, stakeholders, journalists and other observers, politicians, and the policymakers and agencies most directly concerned. Professional, academically trained policy analysts do likewise, but many of them claim they do so more rigorously, independently, and reliably than everyone else. To back up this claim they have developed elaborate procedures for collecting and intepreting information about policymaking and its effects, and for making verifiable value judgments. We do not want to enter the debate of whether such claims can ultimate- ly be upheld in the emerging era of postpositivist social science.[22] For our purposes it suffices to observe that policy scientists too engage in mean- ing-making when they study policy events, and that the social and polit- ical context in which this meaning-making occurs is highly charged when policy fiascoes are at stake. Accepting the view that policy analysis, like the general public and political debate about policy events, is a form of argument, we may therefore examine both types of argument as they jointly affect the construction of policy fiascoes.

A useful starting point in doing so is to map out the different layers of meaning that are associated with fiasco as a social construct. We discern four such layers which are interrelated. In other words, whenever a stake- holder, professional evaluator, or other observer labels a particular gov- ernment decision, program, or set of actions as a policy fiasco, she makes a fourfold judgment. The four layers of this judgment are seldom fully articulated when this labelling takes place, but they are implied or taken for granted. Each of these acts of judgment is, as we shall demonstrate throughout this book, essentially contestable; and each is subject to, or plays a part in, a political process of competing interpretations of ambiguous events. Given the political nature of the process, the substantive issues and claims at stake in each layer may at the same time be objects and instruments of contestation.

Assessing Events: How Bad is Bad?

The concept of fiasco can only be appropriately applied to negatively valued situations. Some events must have happened or some series of actions must have occurred that somehow arouse or upset a certain number of people to a sufficient extent for them to seek to describe their feelings by means of such a strongly negative concept. The first question in fiasco analysis therefore is: what events are at stake, how bad are they perceived to be, by whom, and according to what standards? In other words, what damage has been experienced? This damage may be physical or psychological, such as the loss of lives and limbs, damage to public health, or an upsurge in collective stress and anxiety within a particular community. Damage can also be ecological, involving harm to the environment or to animal life. It can be financial or economic, taking the form of a marked decline in individual or collective incomes, major harm to a community's economic infrastructure, or unusually steep losses of private property. But damage can also be predominantly political, involving a decline of political or agency legitimacy or a major dent in the international reputation of a particular country. Identifying and assesssing the damage associated with a policy decision or a set of actions on the part of government agencies requires a great deal of subjective intepretation of the part of the observer or evaluator, no matter how sophisticated the registration procedures employed. The concept of net damage is important here. As pointed out by Wildavsky there are always two sides to risks or benefits.[23] How to balance the most relevant and reasonably detectable benefits and losses? These equations, especially when it comes to comparing nonmonetary costs and benefits defy the limits of empirical precision and economic sophistication. It follows that the very foundation for calling a decision or a set of actions a fiasco, for example, the occurrence of "negative events" can already become the subject of an intractable debate.

Let us use a relatively simple example to illustrate this first layer of contestation. During a long and hot summer an extraordinary amount of algal growth occurs in a large fresh water lake. Large clouds of algae take away the sunlight causing substantial parts of the underwater vegetation to die. Subsequently, the combination of rotting plants and algae results in a serious lack of oxygen and a massive rise in fish mortality. Is this a negative event? Professional fishermen or harnessed environmentalists will probably affirm this. Others, such as marine biologists for example, might point to the cyclical nature of algal growth and to the resilience of the lake's ecosystem. Plagues such as these have happened in the past without too many long term effects on the size of the fish population.

Identifying Agents: Who or What Brought this About?

Having established that something negative has happened that goes beyond the normal "zones of tolerance" of the society in question, the observer seeking to interpet its nature and significance faces a second layer implicit in the fiasco label. This layer has to do with the question of causation. If negative events are seen as outcomes of certain developments or actions, exactly what developments and whose actions have brought about these outcomes? Is it possible to establish a relation between the alleged negative event and some behavior on the part of human or organizational actors? Can the negative event be viewed as a consequence of certain well-defined acts or omissions by people responsible or was it due to a conflux of larger, impersonal forces, such as a stroke of nature? In short, is the negative effect the result of an act of man or is it to be considered an act of God? Applying the fiasco label to a situation implies that the observer holds that the events in question were caused in no small part by human agents. It is only when one accepts that human intervention (could have) made a crucial difference in producing the damage that one labels the episode in such an accusatory manner. In our example the key question to ask at this stage would be: how did the sudden growth of the algae that created the damage come about? Was it caused by the long and hot summer, or was it also, if only partially, due to an eutrophication of the lake caused by phosphates from detergents and fertilizers used by households and farmers in the area? If so, what does that tell us about the role of local water authorities and environmental agencies?

Explaining Agents' Behavior: What Prompted Their Actions?

Let's presume we have established that a negative event has occurred and that it has been caused at least partly by human, organizational, and in particular, governmental decisions and actions. Then the third crucial layer of the labelling process comes into play, which involves an assessment of the rationale of these behaviors. It is one thing to say that the actions of official X or agency Y caused the negative event, it is quite another thing to claim that these actions constituted avoidable failures. Yet that is exactly what the policy fiasco label implies. The third layer, therefore, involves a search for explanations of the policy processes which produced the negative event. This may cover many different attributes of these processes. To name but a few which are often mentioned as prime causes of failure: the composition of the policymaking arena, the allocation of political or agency attention, the gathering and processing of information, the recognition and resolution of value conflicts, the distribution of power among key stakeholders in the arena, the decision rules guiding the selection of actions, the organization of implementation, and the degree of political control over the actions of lower-level operatives. The key question governing this combined process of reconstruction and attribution is: how can we explain why they did not perform adequately? In other words, how can we identify the roots of failure in the policy process? In terms of our example: if the lake was in danger of becoming eutrophied, why did the local water boards fail to purify the waste water that enters the lake from the sewage system? And why did the local or even national environmental and agricultural agencies fail to limit the use of harmful fertilizers in area of the lake?

Evaluating Agents' Behavior: Who is to Blame?

The fourth layer deals with the pivotal normative and most explicitly political dimension of labelling policy events as fiascoes: the allocation of blame. The negative event may very well have become commonly construed as an outcome of a particular set of failures on the part of a human or organizational actor, but it only becomes a proper fiasco when a successful claim is made that these failures were both serious and avoidable. The fourth layer involves an assessment of who is to blame for what. This requires looking at the claims of the accusors, as well as at the excuses and justifications brought forward by the agents and their supporters. Each of these parties is likely to be attuned to different representations of the policy process. The accusors are typically interested in raising questions that imply a voluntaristic view of policymaking: did policymakers fail to see the problem developing, did they deliberately ignore it, did they choose the wrong way of dealing with the problem? Alternatively, defenders are likely to scan the process for factors that exonerate policymakers. They can do so by putting forward a more deterministic interpretation of policymakers' actions, which highlighs the power of external constraints on human choice and organizational action. The physical or technical impossibility of performing key functions constitutes one such set of constraints, but there are many others. In our example, for instance, the failure to prevent the algic bloom disaster may be due to a critical lack of political power on the part of the water authorities vis à vis the lobbies of farmers and industrialists, the absence of an appropriate regulatory regime, or significant shortages of personnel and other resources essential for monitoring and enforcing compliance with pollution laws.

None of these assertions can be established authoritatively by dispassionate, objective analysis. All of them require an assessment against a certain set of norms and values, and all of them are dependent upon the way in which the facts of the situation are represented. It would, however, be naive to think that each and every act of labelling controversial policy episodes is a product of such a complex reasoning process. Labelling events as fiascoes represents a short and potentially powerful way of subsuming all of these issues into a condensatory symbol. In most instances, one or more layers remain implicit or are subsumed under another that the person in question regards as more essential. For example, some people will never wonder whether events are caused by choice, chance, or circumstance; they simply assume governments should be able to prevent most forms of social damage from occurring, and will therefore automatically conclude that some failure must have occurred whenever such damage does occur. They do not accept the notion that some events "just happen." Other people may be more inclined to collapse the third and the fourth layers of meaning-making. In their view culpability is self-evident whenever it becomes apparent that failures have been made in the policy process. They may be sensitive to the idea that some negative events may be caused by uncontrollable forces, but if they are convinced that human action did help bring about the negative events in any given case, they will want to see those responsible pay. In their minds failure can never be excusable.

Even if most people do not recognize these four layers in the construction of policy fiascoes, viewing the process in these terms is useful as an analytical tool given the purposes of this book. It enables us to dissect the various dimensions of the claims made in public debates and scholarly writings about controversial policy episodes, and to examine these critically.

A Note about Terms and Concepts

This is a book about a subject that many people have strong views on. This is not surpising, since erratic courses and outcomes of public policy tend to affect large numbers of people in unpleasant ways. Furthermore we have mentioned earlier that these alleged failures of governance and policymaking have become an item in bigger ideological debates about how societies should and should not be run. Precisely because of this intensity of feeling and debate, those who want to study the dynamics of policy fiascoes face a semantic and normative minefield. It makes sense therefore to be quite specific about some of the key terms to be used in this book.

The central term and the focal point of our study is policy fiasco, which we define as follows: A *policy fiasco* is a negative event that is perceived by a socially and politically significant group of people in the community to be at least partially caused by avoidable and blameworthy failures of public policymakers. This definition highlights both the socially constructed and the political nature of policy fiascoes, and encompasses the various layers of the phenomenon outlined above. There is one complication to be noted here. This definition represents our notion of what a policy fiasco is, but, as will be amply demonstrated in the book, the term fiasco is used in different ways by citizens, journalists, political fora, and other participants in debates about negative events and controversial policy episodes. Many of them apply it in a more objectivistic way, in other words to characterize the quality of "the" decisions and actions taken by policymakers. Also, in taking this approach some people focus solely on the social outcomes of policymakers' activities, while others emphasize the linkage between certain types of social outcomes and the behaviors which allegedly produced these outcomes. To avoid confusion, we shall try to use the term policy fiasco only in our own definition; when we refer to other people's usage of the term we will mark it as "fiasco."

Furthermore, to avoid too much repetition and because they too are used very often in public discourse, we will use the terms "failure," "policy failure," and "government failure," in the colloquial sense, as a more generic way of expressing a discrepancy between what is or was and what should have been, for example, to indicate any kind of performance defect. This may pertain to individual "human error" on the part of policymakers or executive officials, but it may also refer to various forms of collective and institutional performance shortfalls. For example, countless numbers of program evaluation studies conducted in the sixties and seventies showed that most government programs "fail." In this context failure most often refers to the fact that the results of the program did not match social expectations, official objectives, or a certain set of performance standards chosen by the evaluators. Very few of these programs have become policy fiascoes, however. Failure therefore differs from fiasco in that the former refers to performance defects of any size or seriousness, which may or may not be politicized, whereas fiasco only refers to situations of: (a) subjectively significant social damage, that (b) are highly politicized.

The emphasis in this book is on policy fiascoes. Much is made in the evaluation literature about the definition of policy and about the differences between policies, programs, and projects. For our purposes, however, such debates are less important. Our focus lies with concrete negative events that are more or less circumscribed in terms of time and space, which somehow have become associated with the activities of policymakers and/or public agencies. These negative events may be associated with what evaluators would call a "program," such as a nationwide scheme to provide primary education to immigrants' children. They may follow from a more adhoc kind of government "project," for instance the construction of a hydroelectric dam. Alternatively, they may be connected to a more comprehensive set of ideas and activities called a "policy," for example a policy to maintain neutrality in the face of a conflict between two neighbouring countries, a notion which requires a more comprehensive and coordinated set of political, economic, diplomatic, and perhaps military activities. All of these levels and forms of government activity may become the locus of fiasco as defined above. They only differ in scope, importance, and complexity, not in kind.

In this study, the adjective "policy" in policy fiasco should be viewed as an equivalent for "government" or "public sector." It is merely added to denote that we are not interested in corporate, intra-organizational events and debates, but in public ones, those that pertain to the activities of governments. Our focus is on public rather than business adminstration, governmental rather than corporate politics, and politicians and government bureaucrats rather than CEO's and other corporate executives and personnel. This broad locus of study – and the conceptual skating it allows – is warranted given the fact that this project is not designed to arrive at detailed empirical statements about the ways in which these activities proceed and the results they bring. Instead it focuses on understanding how people perceive and evaluate these processes and outcomes. As yet, there is no reason to suggest that this process of meaning-making proceeds differently for programs, projects, policies, or whichever other class of government activities that policy scientists and evaluators generally distinguish.

We use the term "policy analysis" to refer to any form of professional, research-driven argument about policymaking, and "policy analysts" to anyone producing it. These may be policy scientists and other scholars employed by academic institutions who are driven by traditional academic concerns, or academically trained analysts working in government or other institutions with a stake in the policies concerned who are engaged in what is commonly referred to as "partisan analysis." Both groups participate in debates about policy failures and the construction of policy fiascoes. From an interpretive, argumentative perspective on policy analysis and policymaking, there is no prima facie reason for treating the two groups and their contributions to the debate in different ways.

Finally, a note not about terminology but about scope. Our observations remain limited to liberal-democratic political-administrative systems. It is clear that in non-democratic countries debates about negative events and their causes are highly constrained and set in a radically different institutional and cultural contexts. Also, strictly political disasters unrelated to the process and substance of public policy as such, for example the unfortunate end of a political career or the scandalous demise of a cabinet, will not be considered. Finally, we focus on policy fiascoes as forms of institutional action. This implies that we limit ourselves to collective behavior on the part of actors and officials in and around public agencies directly engaged in policymaking activities. In other words, we do not take into account micro-level administrative failures of a primarily technical-administrative kind. Nor does our analysis pertain to cases of individual corruption and petty crime. Likewise, we exclude from consideration debates about macro-level creeping policy problems with fiasco potential such as "the degradation of the environment" or "the ozone layer problem."

A Note about Aims and Audiences

Since policy fiascoes are such elusive yet ubiquitous phenomena that conjure up so many questions about politics, culture, management, and social science, it is important to state clearly our objectives with this book. Let us begin by saying what it is not. It is not a book for people who, in the tradition of Taylor, Gulick, and their contemporary "management guru" equivalents look for proverbs and formulas on how to prevent policy fiascoes, or, better still, to achieve major policy successes. The book does not claim to develop a managerial perspective on failure-causation and failure-avoidance in public policymaking. Also, it is not a systematic empirical study of policymakers, public agencies, or case episodes, designed to uncover perhaps not timeless proverbs but contingent generalizations about how and why things go wrong in public policymaking.

What this study seeks to do is to shed light on the ways in which people and societies come to terms with highly negative events, and to what extent and how they associate this with the actions and policies of their governments. The book looks at this process as it takes place in the political arena, as well as in the more confined setting of professional policy analysis. The basic assumption behind this is that by looking at how we make sense of policy fiascoes, and by uncovering certain patterns in this sense-making, we may learn more about what we expect from those who govern us, what we value in them, and what we loathe and fear in the conduct of the public business. Based on this, we may also learn more about the kinds of lessons that different groups of people – citizens, politicians, scholars – may draw from these negative experiences.

We hope that both policy practitioners as well as scholars and students of public policymaking will find something useful in this book. The former may see it as a catalogue of expectations, norms, and claims they may have to reckon with in designing policy proposals and justifying their past and future actions. The book may help them to provide somewhat more substance and structure to the cliché that others may not see the world in the same terms as they do and are therefore likely to evaluate situations and behaviors in different ways. Since in dealing with negative events and controversial policy episodes policymakers in most cases cannot afford to ignore these "others," it may be useful for them to have some idea of the types of claims these others may make.

As far as academic audiences are concerned, this study seeks to make two main contributions. First, it can be seen as an application of some of the basic tenets of what has been called "the interpretive turn" in policy analysis to a class of situations often shunned by professional evaluators. Even though it provides no new methodology or tests of well-defined theories and propositions, it shows in great detail how not only "partisan" but also "scientific" discourse on policy events contains many biases that guide towards certain intepretations and conclusions and eschew others. If one shares our view of policy analysis and policy science as essentially a process of argumentation, it is important to learn to understand how these biases follow from more deep-seated, mostly implicit, ontological, epistemological, and normative assumptions. This is what the present book seeks to do in the context of policy fiascoes.

Second, this book seeks to add force to the argument that professional policy evaluation takes place in the context of political processes of judgment and reckoning, which it may influence but by which it can also be influenced in important ways. Policy fiascoes provide a class of situations in which both patterns of influence can be quite marked: professional evaluations are permeated by political biases, and their results are used by different parties as ammunition in ongoing political struggles to assign and escape blame for what happened. A key challenge for evaluators is to make sure that these political dynamics of evaluating policy and constructing fiascoes do not overwhelm them, and jeopardize the soundness and impact of their work.

A Preview

The book roughly follows the four layers in the process of fiasco construction described above. The first layer concerns the assessment of negative events. Chapter 2 illustrates the relativity of judgments about the nature and value of policy outcomes. It documents the social and political biases

analysts and other observers may encounter when they seek to assess policy outcomes, especially in the case of controversial policy episodes.
Many of them are well-known in the evaluation literature, but seldom are
all of these biases grouped together. Also, the discussion is focused specifically on the effects of these biases in the charged context of negative
events and "fiascoes."

The second layer of meaning-making in fiasco construction, the identification of agents, is dealt with in chapters 3 and 4. A key issue here is
the competing notions of voluntarism and determinism in accounting for
policy outcomes. Focusing on the third layer of fiasco construction, chapters 5 shows how difficult it is to explain the behavior of policymakers
and institutions which is assumed to have brought about the negatively
valued outcomes. Existing theories and explanations for failures in policymaking produce very different explanations because they depart from
different, but virtually always implicit sets of assumptions about the
essence of policymaking.

The final layer, concerning the political dimensions of evaluating policymaking and assigning blame for failure, is dealt with in chapter 6. Here
we look at the politics of accusing and excusing as they are played out in
investigations and debates following controversial policy episodes.
Finally, chapter 7 reflects on the consequences of this analysis for the art
and science of policy evaluation and the practice of policymaking.

Notes

1 As quoted in R. Austin, P. Larkey, The unintended consequences of micromanagement,
  Policy Sciences, 25, 1, 1992, p. 19.
2 C.C. Hood, A. Dunsire, *Cutback management in public bureaucracies*, Cambridge:
  Cambridge UP 1989.
3 A.O. Hirschman, *The rhetoric of reaction: Perversity, futility, jeopardy*, Cambridge: Belknap
  Harvard UP 1991.
4 An overview of, and a spirited defense against, these stereotypes can be found in
  C. Goodsell, *The case for bureaucracy: A public administration polemic*, Chatham: Chatham
  House 1983.
5 CETA = Comprehensive Employment and Training Act, discussed further in chapter 2;
  HUD = Department of Housing and Urban Development, the scene of a series of scams
  and spending abuses (see I. Welfeld, *HUD Scandals: Howling headlines and silent fiascoes*,
  New Brunswick: Transaction 1992); RSV = Rijn-Schelde Verolme, the name of a Dutch
  shipbuilding conglomerate which received hundreds of millions in government support
  but went bankrupt nevertheless, discussed further in chapter 2; WAO = Wet Arbeids-
  ongeschiktheid, the Dutch worker's disability act, the costs of which soared through the
  roof in the early nineties, triggering a parliamentary enquiry report that was highly critical about its implementation; NHS = the British National Health Service, object of bitter criticism, ridicule and ideologically motivated political debates concerning its costs
  and quality of service-delivery,

6   See P. Hall, *Great planning disasters*, Berkeley: California UP 1982 (also: London: Weidenfled and Nicolson 1980).

7   See, for example, A. Fitzgerald, *The Pentagonists: An insider's view of waste, mismanagement, and fraud in defense spending*, Boston: Houghton Mifflin 1989, as well as the theme issue "Perspectives on Defense Acquisition" of *Policy Sciences*, 25, 1, 1992.

8   See for this case E.J. Feldman, *Concorde and dissent: Explaining high technology project failures in Britain and France*, Cambridge: Cambridge UP 1985; Hall (1982), op. cit. and the sources cited there.

9   Feldman (1985), op. cit., p. 47.

10 As it was labelled by Hall, basically for the reason that so much time and effort was spend producing nothing. Hall (1982), *op. cit.*, p. 15.

11 Feldman (1985), *op. cit.*, p. 84.

12 Feldman (1985), *op. cit.*, p. 83.

13 This is the central thesis in an emerging literature which develops counterfactual analyses of historical events and political crises, partly inspired by chaos theory. For an overview, see P.E. Tetlock, A. Belkin, Counterfactual thought epxeriments in world politics: Logical, methodological, and psychological perspectives, Conference Paper University of California, Berkeley January 1995 (*mimeo*).

14 B.W. Tuchman, *The march of folly: From Troy to Vietnam*, London: Cardinal/Sphere Books 1990 (first ed. 1984), p. 473.

15 Tuchman (1984), *op. cit.*, p. 2.

16 Tuchman (1984), *op. cit.*, pp. 470-473.

17 Compare, L.H. Gelb, R.K. Betts, *The irony of Vietnam: The system worked*, Washington: Brookings 1979.

18 W.A. Wagenaar, Wat dwaasheid heet, is wijsheid achteraf, *Psychologie*, 8, 1987, pp. 48–52 (in Dutch).

19 Wagenaar (1987), *op. cit.*, p. 51.

20 The term is borrowed from Y. Dror, *Policymaking under adversity*, New Brunswick: Transaction 1986.

21 On the semantics and symbolism of the concept of crisis, see M. Edelman, *Political language: words that succeed and policies that fail*, New York: Academic Press 1977. On the semantics of scandals, see A.S. Markovits, M. Silverstein (eds.), *The politics of scandal: Power and process in liberal democracies*, New York: Holmes and Meier 1988 and the sources cited in the introductory essay by the editors. Some episodes that we, using our definition to be explained later in this chapter, would regard as policy fiascoes have obviously been labelled differently by different commentators and analysts using different frames of reference. The crisis concept is probably somewhat different from the others in that it has symbolic and normative connotations similar to those evoked by terms like fiasco and scandal, but also has a managerial connotation, e.g. as a special kind of situational challenge facing policymakers. This managerial notion of crisis has, in fact, generated a massive amount of research, particular research on individual, organizational and political decision making during crisis situations, broadly defined as situations in which decision makers perceive a high threat, pervasive uncertainty and/or surprise, and high time pressure. See U. Rosenthal, P. 't Hart and M.T. Charles, The world of crises and crisis management, in: U. Rosenthal, M.T. Charles, P. 't Hart (eds.), *Coping with crises: The management of disasters, riots, and terrorism*, Springfield: Charles Thomas 1989. Ironically, some policy episodes assume a crisis character precisely because they become labelled as a policy fiasco becomes apparent (e.g., are being "scandalized"), since authorities may then be forced to engage in damage control under severe public and political pressure, placing them in a crisis-like predicament.

22 See, F. Fischer, *Politics, values and public policy: The problem of methodology*, Boulder: Westview 1980; F. Fischer, J. Forester (eds.), *Confronting values in policy analysis*, Newbury Park: Sage 1987.

23 A. Wildavsky, *Searching for safety*, New Brunswick: Transaction Books 1988.

CHAPTER 2

Assessing Policy Outcomes: Social and Political Biases

In the polis, then, problem definition is never simply a matter of defining goals and measuring our distance from them. It is rather the strategic representation of situations.

Deborah Stone[1]

Policy Failures as Artifacts

What prompts people to view the outcomes of certain policy episodes as failures or disasters, while playing down others, which may be perceived by some to be equally harmful or debatable? Why do many people (and policy analysts) regard President Ford's massive inoculation program against what he was told might be a new and serious swine flu epidemic as a "fiasco?" One could also view it with good reason as nothing more than an example of a somewhat overzealous "caring government." Why, for many years, was the Sydney Opera House regarded as a classic planning disaster when much larger budget escalations occurring some years later during the construction of Australia's New Parliament House failed to tarnish that project's image as an astounding success?

To pose these questions already suggests the answer: judgments about the failure or success of public policies or programs are highly malleable. Failure is not inherent in policy events themselves. "Failure" is a judgment about events.[2] The thing about cases such as the swine flu inoculation program and the Sydney Opera House is that people often disagree in their judgments about them. Whether certain policy episodes are judged to be major failures strongly depends on who are doing the judging, what yardsticks they use, when they do it, and on the basis of what information. In chapter 1, we have tried to facilitate the task of analysts and commentators by making a distinction between four "layers" of meaning-making involved in the notion of policy fiascoes: The assesment of outcomes, the identification of agency, the explanation of agents' behavior, and the evaluation of agents' behavior. At first sight the importance of normative judgment gradually increases with each step or layer. The assessment of outcomes in terms of damage seems a rather technical affair, in which the core of the debate is about accounting procedures, the sophistication of standards, and the methodology of registration and measurement. In contrast, the evaluation of behavior, dealing explicitly with the question of who is to blame, seems a matter of full-fledged value judgments.

Unfortunately perhaps, things are not that simple. In fact, the very first layer in our conceptual scheme, the assessment of the outcomes of a certain policy episode, presupposes many value judgments. The very decision of what effects to register, when to register them, and by what means reflects the analyst's implicit or explicit biases and strongly predisposes his or her final evaluation of these policies. This may sound like a cliché, and perhaps it is, but the implications of this cliché for the debate about highly controversial policy episodes can easily be underestimated. The problem is not merely one of research methodology; it is predominantly a problem of conceptualization and value selection. Standards of evaluation insensitive to, for example, time, institutional context, and local culture are not likely to come to be regarded as authoritative yardsticks by all stakeholders in the debate about a controversial policy episode. Transnational discussions of policy fiascoes will easily turn into into *dialogues des sourds* if cultural differences in the ways people interpet social and political events are not taken into account. In this chapter, we shall first discuss three major types of biases that stem from the social context in which policy events are inevitably embedded and evaluated: biases of time, space, and culture.[3] The second part of the chapter will deal with another group of assessment biases, that is, those that originate in the political context in which policy evaluation inevitably takes place.

Policy Horizons: The Time Bias

In assessing policy outcomes, where one stands often depends upon when one looks, and with what kind of temporal perspective in mind.[4] Time is said to heal many wounds, and it can certainly alter the perceptions of the outcome of a public policy or project. A case in point is the construction of the Sydney Opera House (1954–1973).[5] During the conflict-ridden and traumatic implementation phase of this highly adventurous architectural project, it was considered a major fiasco. Construction took ten years longer than initially planned and the costs exploded from the 1954 tender of 7 million A$ to well over 100 million A$ upon completion in 1973. Significantly, the architect had walked out in midcourse following a series of confrontations with an increasingly skeptical client, the minister of public works whose party had won the New South Wales election which that year was virtually dominated by the Opera House issue. Yet this image of failure was not to last. During the late seventies and the eighties the Opera House became a major tourist attraction and symbol of Australian prowess. The original budget overruns came to be viewed in a different light. It was stressed more forcefully that most of the money for the building had not come from the public purse at all, but from a series of public lotteries. To complicate things further, in the early nineties yet another revision of judgments has been emerging as major maintenance and repair work to the building are required, the costs of which may turn out to exceed those of the original construction. Ironically, the very architectonic sophistication and innovativeness in the design and use of special forms and materials that made the building's reputation once again may compromise it. Moreover, this time it is probably not going to be public lotteries that will pay for the bills.

A prime source of analytical biases therefore involves the varieties of possible time horizons and the registration of the various effects policies have over time. The objectives of policies may vary in terms of their temporal scope (in economic policy planning, a differentiation between short-term, medium-term, and long-term policies is quite common) and temporal quality (unique/non-recurrent versus permanent/iterative policies). This affects the timing and nature of assessments about their effects when implemented. Policymakers are in fact continuously vacillating between different time horizons in setting priorities, allocating budgets, and making decisions. At the same time, many elected officials and others subject to the vagaries of the electoral cycle will be predisposed to judge policy proposals or feedback about past policies first and foremost in terms of their short-term political implications.[6]

Short-term effects are also more easy to register than long-term effects, which are likely to become intertwined with other phenomena in complex and often unintended ways. Moreover, short-term and long-term effects may in some cases be at odds with one another, the latter reversing or neutralizing the former. In general, the longer the time frame used for the assessment of policy outcomes the bigger the scope for controversy about their meaning and evaluation is likely to be. Similarly, policies aiming at nonrecurrent outcomes (such as the construction of a building, the liberation of hostages, or the policing of a soccer match) tend to be more easy to monitor than policies with iterative objectives that are constantly being renegotiated and adapted by different participants and in the face of changing circumstances (for example maintaining the territorial integrity of Israel, France, or the Netherlands, the production and distribution of affordable energy, and the maintenance of public health).

For many policies an exclusive reliance on short-term and quantifiable indicators to measure their impact is likely to result in negative evaluations: "[In] evaluating efforts to significantly change the behavior of large numbers of people, a limited time frame is inappropriate because it neglects both the severity of the initial administrative problems and the possibility of learning by doing."[7] For example, Roosevelt's resettlement program for black agricultural laborers failed to meet its short-term political objectives, yet had the latent effect of generating a black middle class which later would become the backbone of the civil rights movement.[8] Also, when judged from a short-run perspective, government reorganization programs are almost always judged to be failures. Yet a considerably better achievement record appears when analysts adopt a long-run perspective more capable of detecting and appreciating the latent functions and long-term effects of these reorganizations.[9] Similarly, an emphasis on short-term goals of policies leads people to regard as failures programs whose implementation has met with delays, even though these delays can be perfectly reasonable or hardly damaging to the long-term impact of these programs. Talking about a job creation program in Oakland targeted at the black youths and in part aimed to prevent a much-feared recurrence of ghetto riots, Pressman and Wildavsky observe that "[In] the light of this high standard – the creation of jobs for black people now – delay constitutes failure. But others may reasonably argue the maxim 'Better late than never.'"[10]

In addition, the intended and actual lifetime of a policy or program may come to diverge.[11] It often happens that policies aimed at short-term effects are continued beyond their originally term of operation. This may have various reasons. Implementation may be slow, clients may have become used to them, or the policy in question may have become embraced by powerful institutional interests.[12] In any case, it requires analysts to go beyond the original mission statements of policymakers and continue to monitor the policy's effects. Ingram and Mann give the example of the American energy policy, which shows yet another way in which time horizons can considerably change the evaluation of outcomes. In many respects the American energy policy was very successful in the 1960s. Through price controls, allocation schemes and the noninclusion of external costs, consumers were provided with inexpensive petroleum products. But seen from a longer-term perspective, the picture becomes less sanguine:

> These benefits created incentives to rely on the automobile for transportation, and oil and natural gas for heating, while ignoring mass transit and coal. The success of one policy has now led to the realisation of its harmful consequences: a nation shackled to oil and natural gas and unprepared to pay the real costs

that such dependence demands, i.e. subservience to foreign producers and the costs they impose.[13]

This is also an instance of what Wildavsky calls the "Paradox of Time": past successes lead to future failures. To illustrate it, he provides the example of the ironies of achieving success in public health care which come to haunt policymakers a decade or so later. The essay's title reflects the sense of despair policymakers may feel when they understand the paradox of time. It is called "doing better and feeling worse":

> As life expectancy increases and as formerly disabling diseases are conquered, medicine is faced with an older population whose disabilities are more difficult to defeat. The cost of cure is higher, both because the easier ills have already been dealt with, and because the patients to be treated are older. Each increment of knowledge is harder won; each improvement in health is more expensive. Thus time converts one decade's achievements into the next decade's dilemmas.[14]

In many of the cases we studied, time-related problems of evaluation manifested themselves also in another major way: a discrepancy in the time perspective of key policymakers and the dominant time frame of the people and institutions evaluating their actions. One example can be found in the case of the so-called RSV affair in the Netherlands, which reached its political peak in 1983–84. It evolved around the failure of an extensive, and in many people's opinion excessive, flow of government subsidies to the RSV shipbuilding conglomerate. The aim was to keep this vital part of Dutch manufacturing industry alive in the face of ever increasing international competititon. The "blank check" thus granted by the government to what turned out to be an internally weak, badly mismanaged set of firms which it had previously had pressured into merging, became the subject of the first formal parliamentary inquiry held in the Netherlands since the end of the Second World War. This produced a dramatic and televised spectacle in which successive ministers for economic affairs and senior civil servants from that ministry were called to testify before a special parliamentary committee.

In this context, it is interesting to note that the overriding consideration on the part of the Dutch minister for economic affairs and his key departmental advisors in continuing to allocate subsidies to RSV seems to have been their desire to counter the short-term threat of a possible RSV bankruptcy. This would have meant instant unemployment for several thousand workers. The center-right coalition government at the time (1977–81) was politically committed to bringing unemployment down. The considerable increase in the number of unemployed resulting from

RSV's collapse (which in itself would be of considerable symbolic significance) would be a major blow to its prestige. At the same time, the social-democratic opposition in parliament was also pressing for the subsidies to RSV because it was committed to saving the jobs of its working-class electorate. At that point in time, taking the long-term view and making a cold-blooded analysis of the prospects for long-term survival of the Dutch shipbuilding industry was politically inopportune and perhaps cognitively infeasible to key players on both ends of the political spectrum. Yet when the chickens came home to roost and RSV went bankrupt nevertheless, parliament responded in 1983 by the dramatic gesture of holding a special inquiry. The special parliamentary committee ended up severely criticizing the policy of the ministry for ignoring long-term issues and failing to take more stringent measures to improve RSV's capability to continue without further public subsidies. Furthermore the minister for economic affairs came under attack for witholding parliament crucial information about the true extent of RSV's problems.

There was undoubtedly a degree of hypocrisy or at least inconsistency involved in parliament's rapid turnabout with respect to RSV and the government's policy of subsidizing troubled industries. Its ultimate assessment was that the policy of granting what had amounted over the years to no less than 2.5 billion guilders (1 billion U.S. $, at the time) in subsidies to a badly managed conglomerate in an industry experiencing structural decline was misguided. But when the case is put in its historic context one is able to see the prominent role parliament itself played subscribing to the same kind of time frame that drove government policy. For many years, parliament itself had taken a short-term perspective and supported subsidies to save jobs at RSV. Only when that policy was collapsing did parliament take a broader time perspective. From that moment on, the frames of reference of government and parliament started to diverge.

In other words, what happened was that parliament's standards for judging the outcomes of policy gradually altered as the process unfolded.[15] At the time the RSV subsidies were investigated the political agenda had changed considerably. The new cabinet had introduced a very strict financial policy which led to substantial cuts in subsidies, welfare benefits, and salaries. Virtues like frugality, efficiency, and restraint had risen to prominence in the political debates and the idea of full employment slowly had been given up. The credibility of the new budgetary policy would have been damaged severely if the allegations about financial waste had gone unscrutinized. Many of the major actors in the RSV case thus found to their unpleasant surprise that they were judged in the early 1980s by different standards than those they had acted upon in the late 1970s.

Collective mood changes thus affect not only the relative success of particular problem definitions and policy alternatives, but also the kinds of standards people use to evaluate the conduct of public officials and agencies. It has been observed, for example that "all scandals are to some extent time-bound: what shocks in one era produces barely a ripple in another."[16] Apparently, policymakers who fail to grasp the current and future dynamics of "the public mood" about what is and what should be the substance and form of public affairs, are likely to run into serious problems.

Policy Scope: The Spatial Bias

Temporal complexities in policy evaluation are matched by spatial ones. Here the key problem is one of delineating the geographical or social system boundaries in determining and assessing the outcomes of public policies. The spatial distribution of the costs and benefits of a policy or project generates controversy and highly "localized" judgments about its success or failure. This spatial dimension is particularly acute in the design and evaluation of regional economic policies and large-scale public projects. The very decision by a central government body to select a particular community as a special economic zone or as a target for sustained central government or supranational economic support may in itself be a source of considerable controversy. The same goes for the designation of sites for major public projects, such as the construction of ports, railways, roads, plants, museums, and government buildings. In some cases, the source of conflict is competition for the expected benefits, but in many the spatial distribution of risk and harm is at stake.

A good example concerns the siting of high-tech facilities with negative side-effects, such as airports (noise and pollution) and nuclear power stations (waste disposal and disaster potential). Conflicts over the siting of the new airports in the London and Paris regions discussed in chapter 1 took the form of community administrators and citizens protesting against regional or central government airport construction plans on or near their territories. In the French case of Charles de Gaulle Airport, such local-level protests were quashed by a powerful central government, and the airport was built. In the London region, local-level veto power in combination with other factors succeeded in getting the construction plans shelved. From a spatial point of view, multiple evaluations of these different cases are possible, depending most literally on "where one sits."[17]

A more complex case presents itself when a national policy with international implications has to be evaluated. A case in point is the Japanese procrastination in revaluating the yen when the Bretton Woods international monetary system was on the verge of collapse and Japanese dollar holdings and economic strength were skyrocketing (1969–71).[18] Japanese policymakers delayed revaluation for two main reasons. Firstly, accustomed to years of postwar economic hardship and tight-belted monetary policies, Japanese politicians and Ministry of Finance bureaucrats were slow to publicly recognize that the Japanese economic resurgence of the late sixties was structural and not ephemeral. Secondly, they were afraid that any rumor of an impending Japanese revaluation to save the ailing U.S. dollar and the international monetary system based on it, would encourage runaway speculation and severely hurt the Japanese monetary position and the national economy. Makeshift policies to steer some kind of middle course were failing and the crisis atmosphere, both within Japan and internationally, was mounting. When U.S. president Nixon – frustrated with the Japanese attitude and seeing no other way out to save the dollar – announced his decision to let the dollar float on August 15, 1971, the Japanese were taken by surprise. In a crisis atmosphere prompted by the rapid devaluation of the value of the massive Japanese dollar holdings, it was eventually decided to float the yen as well. Japan's central bank sustained a considerable loss as a result of this policy, but the policymakers' fears of severe economic consequences of the yen's de facto revaluation never materialized. After the initial turbulences caused by the rapid developments, the international monetary system entered into a new stage without too many difficulties. However, Japan's international monetary reputation had suffered dearly as a result of the crisis and of the general perception that Japanese policy had been both self-seeking and ill-guided.

How to judge this episode? Again, location, or in this case perhaps more appropriately level of aggregation, is quite important. First of all, it is extremely difficult to pinpoint exactly who suffered from what in this case. Partly as a result of Japanese intransigence, the international monetary system went through a highly turbulent and traumatic period from 1969 to late 1971. Internationally, many individuals, organizations, and countries lost out when Nixon devaluated and a flurry of speculation followed his announcement. But who these people and groups were and how great their losses were is almost impossible to tell. Taking a national perspective, the Japanese economy itself became highly volatile because of the continued speculations and the apparent inability of the government to put and end to them. Speculation and signs of panic took a certain toll for which the government's policy can be held directly responsible. At the same time, however, the policymakers' strategy was directed to prevent what they saw as a worst-case outcome: a restabilization of the Bretton-Woods system at the price of a Japanese recession caused by the revaluation of the yen. The assessment of the policy outcomes in this case strongly depends on whether one takes a Japanese or a global perspective.

Policy Cultures: The Ethnocentrism Bias

The third category of social biases in assessing negative events as policy outcomes originates in cultural frames and the social expectations about government conduct that come with these frames. What classifies as a negative policy outcome and as a policy fiasco is inextricably embedded in the social "milieus" in which particular events occur, and the standards of accountability they espouse. As observed by students of political scandal, "what is a political scandal in a liberal democracy is often business as usual in other political systems."[19] For that reason, a certain element of ethnocentrism is always looming in debates about policy fiascoes, particularly when comparisons between different types of episodes are made in forming or legitimating assessments. In fact, cultural biases can easily turn a comparative conference on policy fiascoes into a scholarly Tower of Babel. These cultural biases operate both between but also within nations.

First of all, the assessment of the extent or nature of the failure of a project or policy can be biased by differences in national policy cultures. The very concept of policy or organizational failure is culturally loaded. Even within the contemporary Western liberal democracies, significant cross-cultural variations can be detected in people's judgments about the performance of their rulers. In shorthand: British "quiet desperation," Belgian mockery and cynicism, Dutch Calvinism, or American puritanism, for example, make for quite different bases of judging policy events.

An illuminating example is the Rainbow Warrior affair. In 1985, the French secret service, in an attempt to keep Greenpeace from protesting against the nuclear tests at Mururoa, bombed and sank its flagship, the Rainbow Warrior, in the harbor of Auckland, New Zealand, thereby killing a Dutch photographer.[20] If one compares the evaluations of this action in the three countries, important differences become visible. In Holland and New Zealand, the action was considered a major failure in moral terms. In both countries, but with particular ferocity in New Zealand, the illegal and illegitimate nature of the operation were stressed. In France, on the contrary, the action was also considered a failure, but for quite different reasons. The legitimacy of the operation was hardly questioned, but many observers and politicians felt embarrassed about the awkward, incompetent way in which the operation had been carried out, leading to its exposure and the resultant international outrage that hurt France's national interests. Nevertheless, the responsible minister Hernu whose position was compromised under international pressure and who thereupon resigned was wildly cheered at the conference of his ruling Socialist Party for having stood up for the *force de frappe*.

Secondly, cultural frames can strongly bias the assessment of outcomes even within one political system. Anthropologists tell us that cultural pluralism is a feature of all social situations. Different cultural biases may therefore also manifest themselves within the context of a superficially homogenous organizational or political culture. In fact, this cultural prism works both ways; what people identify as policy failure or success will also say something about the way they see the world and the institutions they live with.[21]

This more subtle shape of the ethnocentrism trap can be illustrated with the help of cultural theory as developed by Thompson, Ellis, and Wildavsky, using the work of Mary Douglas.[22] They emphasize that in every community of some size elements of at least four different cultural ideal types can be found. At the core of this cultural theory lies the grid-group typology developed by Douglas. The group dimension refers to members' experience of the group as tightly versus loosely bounded. High-group cultures thus have strong boundaries, endure through time, and have internal, group-based forms of structuring. The grid dimension refers to the number and salience of the kinds of rules and social categories people use to control behavior. Combining the two dimensions yields four ideal types: hierarchy (high group, high grid), individualist (low, high); egalitarianism (high, low); fatalism (low, low).

Various authors have applied this cultural theory framework to the domain of policy debates about technology and the environment, and institutional reactions to technological failures and accidents. They have argued persuasively that people intuitively select the risks they face, the dangers they are concerned about, and the criteria by which they judge government performance in dealing with these risks.[23] Schwarz and Thompson formulate it as follows:

> Our policy-analytic approach is premised on the idea of a small number of competing and culturally-dependent selection biases. Each distinct cultural orientation is seen to involve an appropriate way of selecting and vindicating how a policy issue is defined, what options and consequences are taken into account, and which evaluative criteria are to be seen as credible.[24]

Cultural theory can be applied usefully to illustrate how people with different sets of values are likely to call different kinds of events "failures," and how they tend to view and evaluate a single set of events in different ways.

In evaluating public policies, individualists will tend to focus on economy and efficiency. They will approve of whatever policy they feel contributes to the efficient allocation of societal resources. In many cases, this would be policies that minimize the extent of government intervention in social affairs, but individualists would also applaud policy initiatives that entail efficient and competitive public-service delivery. As a consequence, when asked to identify policy failures, they are most likely to point to cases of inappropriate government intervention, waste of resources, and bureaucratism (red tape, inflexibility).

In contrast, people inclined towards hierarchy, emphasizing the importance of detailed rules for achieving social order, will be particularly keen to ensure government operates in accordance with legal norms and organizational rules. The hierarchs tend to focus less on fundamental questions about the proper ends (and limits) of governance, as on the proper discharge of politically validated duties. They are troubled most by cases where officials deviate from accepted standards of political and administrative conduct, and compromise the public trust vested in them and their offices. When called to identify failures, hierarchs will be likely to focus primarily on instances of unlawfulness, insubordination, and other forms of disruption of bureaucratic routine and predictability.

Egalitarians will eschew both the archetypes of big government and market-oriented government and will instead seek a just government, one that protects the collectivity against the multiple and universal risks that threaten it, and offers equal outcomes to all. They will find failure most of all in cases where government fails to live up to its protective role, as in technological accidents, economic breakdowns, and natural disasters, as well as in cases where government policies condone or contribute to extreme inequalities.

Fatalists, finally, are the odd people out. Their preoccupation with fate and luck will lead them to consider the question of judging success and failure of governance largely as irrelevant. For them policy fiascoes are just another unalterable fact of life.

It should be noted that, to some extent, one cultural cluster's failures are the other's successes. This is particularly so for egalitarians versus individualists. For example, the swine flu program of the Ford administration discussed earlier would presumably trouble individualists most. They would regard it as an example of overzealous government protectiveness, implemented in a heavy-handed and overly bureaucratized way. They would have wanted to wait with any measures until the existence of a serious epidemic could be confirmed with greater certainty and then take swift action in response. Hierarchs would probably support the spirit of the program but would be troubled by the bureaucratic politics that surrounded it, the politicization of scientific expertise it entailed, and the fact that the president's decisions – misguided or not – were not

implemented more effectively. Egalitarians would probably be supportive of the program's objectives, which reflected a sense of public responsibility to protect the population nationwide against danger from illness.
If anything, they would be concerned about the dominant role of epidem-
iological experts in the development of the program.

It follows from this differentiation in cultural types evaluating the
succes and failure of public policies, that the specific normative "label"
which a particular policy episode eventually acquires in the political
system, may depend on the particular configuration of cultural biases in
that system. Whether, to what extent, and for what reasons a policy episode becomes viewed as a failure is a matter of a political process of attribution and blaming in which cultural biases compete and sometimes
amalgamate.

This brings us to the second category of biases that may affect the ways in
which we look at and assess policy outcomes. Assessing the outcomes of
a policy episode in terms of failure or success does not only reflect temporal, spatial, or cultural perspectives, it is also, and perhaps predominantly, a political matter. Labelling policy outcomes as negative events is
never done in a vacuum. To understand why key institutions and forces
in the political system come to view a policy episode as a failure, one
needs to take into account the political dynamics that give rise to these
judgments and the political context in which they are made.[25] Public policymaking is a form of political action, conducted by office-holders, be
they elected legislators or appointed administrators, operating in the context of large-scale, complex bureaucracies, in interaction with other public and private interest groups. In these political and institutional arenas,
stakeholders with different interests and perspectives meet and interact.
Conflict, whether overt or implied, is part and parcel of the politics of policymaking. Especially when a policy episode has generated a certain
amount of controversy along the way, the evaluation process tends to
take the form of a struggle about what is to become the dominant interpretation and assessment of the policy's results. This produces a context
for policy evaluation that harbors not only social but also distinctly political sources of bias.

Public Perception Biases

Peter Hall, in his book on what he calls "great planning disasters," used
public perception as a measuring rod in the selection of his case studies.[26]
He considered a planning disaster "any planning process that is perceived by many people to have gone wrong" (later he adds that a great

disaster is one that "cost a lot of money by almost anyone's standards").[27] This a simple and straightforward, but in the end equivocal criterion. Public perception, which is a direct function of the extent and nature of media coverage of certain policy episodes, can be a highly partisan guide. First of all, some negative effects of programs or policies may never make it to the public agenda at all because widely accepted ideological premises prevent their recognition, because appropriate conceptual categories to identify them are lacking, or because dominant political coalitions have an interest in framing the issue in a different way. For example, in many countries the negative effects of certain agricultural policies and major infrastructural projects on the environment and wildlife have only recently come to be noticed as a legitimate cause for concern.

An example of this is the reinforcement of the river dikes in the Netherlands in the eighties and nineties. This is a mammoth project of fortifying and heightening hundreds of miles of river dikes to guarantee maximum security from flooding. It was initiated by the powerful national agency for waterworks on the basis of its new flood protection standards. At first, the project was perceived as a politically unproblematic and primarily technical issue – the long tradition of fighting floods and claiming land in this country that partly lies below sea level has virtually assured popular support for any kind of waterworks. It nevertheless became clear after some years and many miles of new dikes, that the safety-first approach of the agency resulted in the complete destruction of the landscape, fauna, and culture that had developed around the existing small, dwindling river dikes. Many ancient houses, sometimes entire townships, and many habitats for rare plants and animals were replaced, or are about to be replaced, by huge concrete dikes coming straight off the safety designers' drawing boards, not allowing for any vegetation or dwellings. These cultural and environmental effects had never been taken into account in the decision making and evaluation processes. The key government agency, Rijkswaterstaat, a stronghold of engineers within the Dutch ministry of transport with a multimillion dollar budget, as well as regional actors in the political arena had simply framed the issue, often probably even unconsciously, as one of flood protection full stop. The design process was therefore governed only by the trade-off between the desire for appropriate safety and the financial costs of achieving that. Only recently, and not without slow but increasingly fierce political infighting, have local and environmental groups managed to swing parts of public opinion towards the idea that other legitimate values and concerns are at stake too. If one takes these into consideration, these groups have shown, the current mode of implementing the anti-flooding policy produces catastrophic results. As a result of this maneuvering, a compulsory environmental audit has now been included into the decisionmaking and planning procedures for those stretches that have not been reinforced yet.

Political maneuvering and competing evaluation frames do not remain confined to cases of unintended effects and hidden tragedies. Even those "fiascoes" that from the first instance indeed are "perceived by many people to have gone wrong" can be the product of political expediencies or media distortions. In fact, many public and political scandals do not originate in failures of policymaking as defined in this book. Many of them have little to do with public policymaking but evolve around the faux pas and indiscretions of individual politicians and bureaucrats. A recent major reference compendium on political scandals since 1945 is filled to a large extent with cases of extramarital affairs, espionage, obscure deaths, and many instances of corruption.[28] Individual tragedies usually make for better newspaper reading than the technical and intricate details of policy processes that might have gone astray.[29] Media attention in general is often biased towards the spectacular cases, preferrably those that can be personalized.

Moreover, the accounts of those policymaking episodes that do reach the front pages and the nine o'clock news are often strongly biased. Much public attention depends on how these events become labelled in the press and by political opinion leaders, who, in turn, are influenced by vested interests and political expediencies. In other words, to paraphrase Edelman, a policy failure, like all news developments, is a creation of the language used to depict it; its identification is a political act, not a recognition of a fact.[30]

Consequently, whether an episode of problematic policymaking appears on the political agenda and turns into an "affair" does not only depend on the nature and extent of the damage done, but more predominantly on the political situation in which several actors might find it opportune to label a situation as a failure and expose it to the press.[31] Scandalogy, that is, research into the genesis of "affairs" and scandals, is therefore first of all a matter for rhetoricians and political sociologists.[32] The danger here is that policy analysts and other observers unwittingly allow their initial and subsequent assessment of policies to be biased by media-amplified criticisms and condemnations of policymakers voiced by politically interested parties and actors. By the same token, political mythologies about seemingly successful policies – for example about the "Swedish model" of running an economically strong welfare state or the "Japanese model" of industrial harmony and efficiency – may desensitize observers and analysts to their drawbacks and darker sides.

Political Failures Versus Program Failures

Important in securing political support for policy programs is the degree to which policymakers succeed in making the program look good. They must seek to provide different political stakeholders with such information, and present the information in such a way as to secure their support. This means that the political fate of a policy or program depends not only on its substance but also upon its appearance. Political judgments about the success or failure of a policy are mostly made on the basis of impressions about the effects and costs of the program, that is, predominantly on images and symbols.[33] These images might, but need not reflect the program's substance and operational reality as experienced by those directly involved with it. To put it bluntly: when a policy is judged to be a failure, this may reflect a failure of public relations as much as a failure to deliver the goods.

An example of this is U.S. postwar unemployment policy. Its image was distorted by its interference with preexisting and ongoing political games, institutional arrangements, and policy initiatives – in particular those that arose from the War on Poverty. Both policies were developed and administered by a myriad of public agencies, and were subject to complex political maneuverings within and between the White House and Congress. The main result was that both policies suffered from a lack of coherence, which resulted in a lack of coordination between various initiatives. In some cases, different programs were administered simultaneously, working at cross-purposes. In other cases, the multitude of agencies and programs competing for political support and budgetary appropriations led to a shortage of "critical mass" necessary to be able to achieve the original ends. Due to institutional fragmentation and the vagaries of the political process, these social programs intended to be sweeping in scope and speed began to "incrementalize" and ultimately generated disenchantment.[34] The sense of urgency which prompted the unemployment policy got lost in the legislative and administrative morass, as did its coherence. But does this mean it should be regarded as a failure?

Mucciaroni, who analyzed this policy episode, argues it is necessary to distinguish between political failures and program failures. A program is a political failure when it lacks political support and momentum necessary for its survival as a prioritized area of government activity. A program failure occurs when the program fails to have an impact on target populations, or produces unintended and unwanted effects. Hence programs that do have a certain positive social impact may still be labelled failures by many observers using a predominantly political success/failure criterion. Many of them will look at the political and administrative process rather than at the substantive outcomes of a policy in forming their impressions of it, even though the two might not necessarily be closely related:

> [T]he reality and perception of failure have had more to do with program design, administration, and service delivery than they have with the substantive impacts on the targeted populations. Thus, performance is important in understanding the political failure of employment policy, but performance mainly in the sense of how employment policy was conducted rather than what it accomplished.[35]

Mucciaroni then explains that the perception of failure was mainly focused on the many adjustments in the program's design and implementation that were required to keep it afloat in a very complex and conflict-ridden social and institutional environment:

> Policy has shifted from social to economic goals, from training to job creation, from efforts to assist the long-term unemployed living in the nation's cities to the cyclically unemployed and those displaced by structural economic change. Administrative arrangements have alternated from centralization, to decentralization, to a reassertion of centralization, before giving way most recently to another attempt at decentralization. Funding has risen and fallen less in response to any policy rationale than in reaction to economic crises and shifting political winds.[36]

It then becomes ironic to observe that the same political actors and institutions which have contributed to these displacement effects and continuous adjustments of means and ends, have come to judge the policy a failure precisely for that reason! It seems the roots of the problem lie as much within the political process itself as within the program and its achievements. To be sure, employment policy's achievement record was not splendid. But it was certainly not as bad as the widespread perception of it as a failure seemed to suggest:

> More than any other domestic program of the 1970's, CETA [the Comprehensive Employment and Training Act, as key program designed to integrate and administer the various components of employment policy, MB/PtH] came to symbolize the exhaustion of the liberal agenda and the corruption of its activities... [But] the CETA story is one not so much about the failure of a program as it is about a set of political institutions. It should not be confused with the notion that CETA failed to achieve, to one degree or another, several of its substantive objectives. While few of its programs were undisputed and overwhelming successes, few were abject failures. The gap between

actual results and the dismal perceptions of performance suggests that the place to look for the sources of CETA's difficulties is not in its statistical evaluations but in its political-institutional framework.[37]

The underlying cause of CETA's problems appears to lie in the fact that in the crisis-ridden atmosphere of the 1973–74 economic downturn, it became a kind of garbage can for all kinds of short-term initiatives and programs addressing various of the baffling problems that Washington policymakers suddenly saw themselves confronted with. Lacking an adequate understanding of emerging phenomena such as stagflation, policymakers went into a burst of activity and kept piling new programs on top of CETA's already overpopulated landscape.

Mucciaroni's distinction between political and program failures enables one to see further shades and biases in the assessment of outcomes of policies and programs. A failure in political terms does not necessarily stand for a failure in terms of the program's objectives (even though political failures may erode the political support for a program and may thus in the long run cause a program to fail). Vice versa, failures to reach substantive objectives need not necessarily result in political failures.

The Political Paradox of Achievement

Judgments of success and failure are directly related to the expectations people use to judge programs, policymakers, and institutions of governance. There is a case to be made that in the first three decades since the Second World War, societal expectations about governance and its benefits have increased sharply in many Western countries. In many cases, governments have actively promoted these rising ambitions, perhaps without realizing that they also entailed increasingly high and stringent standards for judging their actual performance. From the mid-sixties onwards, many governments were confronted with the effects of the growing discrepancies between societal demands and expectations on the one hand, and the limits of progressive government on the other. Political observers of many ideological persuasions have coined this development in different ways, for example as the crisis of the welfare state, government overload, or as a legitimation crisis. Seen from this perspective, modern government is destined to "fail" in many of its reformist and redistributive activities:

> One result of the social activism of the 1960s was that Americans grew disillusioned with government. As criticism of social conditions rose, so did the level

of government activity; but regardless of how much government had achieved in the way of social improvement, it had led the public to expect more. The more government tried to do, the plainer became its inability to do very much, or at least all that its leaders said it would. Both the right and the left attacked it for failing to fulfill its promises.[38]

Inevitably, this general disenchantment with government shapes people's judgments about specific policies or programs. Cynicism about politics and bureaucracy – tellingly defined by one of its most prominent students as a type of organization unable to learn from its mistakes – among citizens and policy evaluators alike does little to offset this.[39] This combination of the rise of government activity and a growing disenchantment with it, constitutes what one might call a "paradox of achievement." This paradox is, again, best captured in Wildavsky's observation about the medical sector: "doing better, feeling worse."[40]

To make things worse, government agencies in many areas of public policy are faced with conflicting demands. Patients, medical professionals, and other lobbies demand sophisticated and costly health programs which cover many illnesses and defects that hitherto had been considered a stroke of bad luck. At the same time and sometimes even by the same persons, the government in general is expected to balance and preferably to reduce its budget. Similarly, governments currently are pressed to reduce acid rain and other forms of environmental pollution. Yet simultaneously, in a different arena, other powerful interests argue against a levy on energy or any other burdens that might reduce the competitiveness of national industries or increase the costs of living. As policy spaces become denser, "as more and more policies aim to solve more and more difficult problems, the consequences become harder to predict and the chances for failure increase."[41]

Thus progressive ideals and/or rationalist standards concerning government planning and policymaking can only produce predictably gloomy evaluations of overwhelmingly incrementalist planning and policy realities. The day-to-day reality of public policymaking is one in which the objectives of programs are continuously modified to accomodate the limitations of the available means and the impact of multiple social constraints that become apparent during program implementation.[42] In the political world of public policymaking problems are not so much solved as they are elaborated, redefined, and superseded.[43] Why then do so many observers and analysts continue to adhere to standards that are clearly beyond the grasp of even the most sophisticated and powerful policymakers? At one level, this may be a function of a professional role conception as critics of the powers that be. But as we have tried to show, many of these biases may go unrecognized by all concerned. Part of the explanation then can also be found in the following paradox: The logic of democratic electoral politics appears to dictate that policymakers themselves are in many ways actively involved in raising expectations and espousing myths of rational, just, and omnipotent governance that help to create the conditions for their own political failure.

Goal-Based Biases

One way to circumvent at least part of the paradox of achievement is by simply evaluating government by its self-confessed standards, namely the official goals of policies and programs as contained in policy documents and other authoritative written or verbal statements of purpose. Using official goals as standards not only allows for a convenient anchor for assessing policy effectiveness and efficiency, it can also be viewed as a form of democratic control. It is a way of taking government at its word.[44] Accordingly, goal-based assessments of program effectiveness have constituted an important if not the dominant current of public policy evaluation studies. Of these, the great majority were critical, and revealed many discrepancies between policy-as-planned and policy-as-implemented.[45]

In response to these findings, questions have been raised about their significance: do they tell us that most of the time government does not work as it should even by its own standards, or do they reflect the inherent limitations of this type of methodology of outcome assessment? This has led to a debate about the strengths and weaknesses of goal-based versus goal-free evaluation.[46] In this respect, an important issue concerns the linkages between goals and values. Goals and goal-related evaluation criteria are always based on underlying social and political values. In many societies a plurality of value systems exists (one might call them ideologies or cultural biases), which could make for quite different expectations and specifications of the goals of public policies. Which values, and perhaps more acutely, whose values, in fact come to guide the official goals of a policy, depends partly on the differential appeal of the various value sets to individuals and groups in society, and partly on the structure and process of political power in that society. Should this process of selective value articulation be taken for granted by fiasco researchers, or should it in itself be a topic for evaluation and reflection? This touches upon one of the most difficult normative issues in contemporary policy analysis.[47] In addition, the observer should be aware that the particular set of values that drives the official policy goals need not be the same as those dominating the post-hoc societal and political assessment of the outcomes of the policy, as we have seen earlier in this chapter.

From a political perspective on public policy, several other well-known and important limitations of goal-based evaluation stand out. The common denominator among them is that, for various reasons inherent in the complex organizational and political nature of contemporary governance, official goals have little of the normative or precriptive strength imputed to them by most goal-based evaluation researchers: "the goals of policy are often not what they seem to be, and it is a mistake to take stated purposes too literally."[48] It follows that official goals cannot easily be translated into a reliable and relevant standard to base evaluations on. Analysts who overlook the complex and ambiguous character of goal-based policy evaluation fall victim to the "official objectives bias," and produce analytically coherent but politically naive and bureaucratically irrelevant assessments of past policies. The following complications should be taken into account.

First, policy goals are often vague. They allow for multiple interpretations and, consequently, for different operational standards of evaluation. As observed by Stone: "The inescapable ambiguity of political goals means that they are more like moving targets than fixed standards."[49] From a political perspective, such ambiguity makes sense. It dampens controversy and allows various internal and external stakeholders the flexibility to present favorable interpretations of what the official policy is going to be to their different constituencies, while at the same time providing a semblance of coherence in government policy. From the perspective of assessing policy outcomes, however, ambiguous goals are not a facility but a problem.

Second, seen from the perspective of technical feasibility, policy goals often appear to be set unrealistically high or low. Agency myths and highly ambitious policy statements often do not take into account the costs and limitations of implementation. But this in itself is no reason to fault them, because their main rationale tends to be not substantive but symbolic. They often fulfill the strategic function of mobilizing broad support and the symbolic function of providing a vision for the future, projecting a leader's commitment, or indicating the general thrust of the government's direction.[50] Sometimes laws are enacted and policies endorsed which clearly will never be able to reach their stated objectives. But this does not turn them into instant failures. They can be meant to convey a message to particular groups and interests, to take the pressure off a particular issue, to delineate boundaries, or to instigate a change of social attitudes. Anti-discrimination policies, equal protection clauses, and environmental laws often fall into this category. In contrast, excessively modest goals are usually formulated in a more defensive spirit: in anticipation of political criticism or to prevent making commitments that may come to haunt the policymakers. In both cases the stated goals in all probability do not reflect the actual policies of the government.

Third, policymakers pursue many types of goals, either simultaneous-ly, or, as revealed by Cyert and March's studies of strategic decision mak-ing, sequentially.[51] But the various goals and subgoals they pursue may well be at odds with one another. Classic examples include the police or the corrections system. The police are continuously confronted with com-peting demands on their limited resources and conflicting policy impera-tives:

- which types of crimes to "go after" in force and which ones to treat in a low-key manner;
- enforcing the law or keeping the peace;
- trying to prevent crime and trying to control it;
- working to bring down actual levels of victimization or seeking to reduce the public's fear of becoming victimized (the two turn out to be at best only indirectly related);
- focusing on crime alone or taking a more broad perspective of com-munity service.

Selecting a profile implies trading off some concerns against others.[52] Perhaps even more acutely problematic, managers of a corrections system need both to incarcerate and rehabilitate convicted and often seasoned criminals. This they have to do amidst growing public concerns about crime and safety, disenchantment with the performance of the criminal justice system, and competing pressure groups for and against liberal cor-rections philosophies.[53] Task structures like these harbor inherent goal conflicts. Moreover, different stakeholders within these systems may pur-sue different (sets of) goals. As a consequence, the formulation of agency objectives and program principles involves a major political and bureau-cratic balancing act, which is bound to be vulnerable to political if not substantive failure.[54]

A fourth and final major problem with goal-based evaluation is that it assumes that policy goals remain stable throughout the policy process. This assumption is inaccurate at best. A number of detailed studies of decision making and policy implementation show that goals are highly dynamic properties. In fact, there is much to be said for a view of public policymaking as a continuous process of adjustment in which goals are discovered, specified, modified, and subsequently abandoned in favor of new ones. The more sophisticated empirical theories of the policy process all share a view of goals as dynamic rather than static.[55] For this reason, these theorists argue against any rigid prior specification of criteria for policy effectiveness and related specification of evaluation procedures.[56] Brewer and DeLeon argue that programs can rarely be developed with complete foreknowledge of their eventual outcomes and effects. To maintain this fiction and to impose "neatly prespecified criteria" may, in fact, be counterproductive and act as a deterrent to learning and good policy. They quote March:

> The prior specification of criteria and the prior specification of evaluational procedures that depend on such criteria are common presumptions in contemporary social policymaking. They are presumptions that inhibit the serendipitous discovery of new criteria. Experience should be used explicitly as an occasion for evaluating our values as well as our actions.[57]

All of this complicates the task of goal-based evaluation in various ways. The official goals may be a tenuous political and bureaucratic compromise among policymakers faced with conflicting yet politically equally inevitable tasks and claims. In many cases, the official goals constitute a tactical façade for hidden goals that cannot be articulated openly, for the very fact of their publication may diminish their chances of being attained. Also, substantive goals may be less important than symbolic ones; the same goes for long-term and unspecified versus short-term and explicit goals.

The Anglo-French Concorde project constitutes one example of how the acknowledgement that policymakers may have been striving after long-term, latent goals even at immense short-term costs, alters the overall assessment of a policy episode. In 1962, the British and French governments signed a treaty for the joint design, development, and manufacture of a commercially viable supersonic airliner, the Concorde. This official objective was never fully reached. The Concorde was taken into production, but at great cost to the British and French taxpayer. It is currently being operated only halfheartedly by two government-backed airlines, British Airways and Air France. No other airlines have bought Concordes and the planes have not been allowed to fly outside of very narrow, transatlantic routes. Many airlines and airport authorities have been reluctant to embrace Concorde because of the noise produced by its flying at great speed. Many studies of the Concorde project have emphasized these points and have consequently condemend it as a monumental failure.

And indeed, in a narrow sense, the project has failed. A number of key objectives internal to the project have not been met. However, the assessment of the Concorde project begins to change for the better if one takes into account that both the French and the British governments adopted the project pursuing not only the commercial goals of the project itself, but also, and perhaps much more strongly so, a number of indirect, strategic political goals.[58] The French wished to reestablish and modernize their ailing aircraft industry and needed access to the state-of-the-art technology that was being successfully developed and exploited by the then superior British aircraft industry. For their part, the British were perfectly happy to accomodate the French in this respect even though it meant doing a risky joint project and, in time, helping one's own future competitors. They were after something far greater: proving their willingness and ability to be a reliable partner in transnational ventures in order to get the French to lift their veto against a British entry to the European Community. Seen from this broader angle, it can be argued that both governments managed to acomplish these latent goals by initiating and continuing against the odds with the Concorde project.

The point here is not to argue that goal-based evaluation is useless and should be abandoned. Rather, we have sought to illustrate that goal-based outcome assessment cannot be taken for granted as an unproblematic, neutral, and static methodology for policy evaluation. Using it to evaluate complex and controversial policy episodes is insufficient in itself to properly negotiate the cognitive and value complexities inherent in the task. We have pointed out that underneath the seemingly simple procedure of comparing outcomes to preestablished goals, there remain multiple ways of identifying and weighing official policy goals, each of which may generate quite different assessments. Just as with any other method of outcome assessment and policy evaluation, goal-based analysis needs to be contextualized in order to be useful. Failure to put the results of goal-based assessments into a proper institutional and contingent perspective implies a serious underestimation of the degree to which the selective articulation of policy goals is an integral part of the politics of policymaking.

Action-Oriented Biases

In labelling a particular policy episode as a failure, investigators or evaluation researchers may fail to reflect on what outcomes might have resulted had other courses of action been followed. This constitutes what might be called the "neglected alternatives bias." It is a bias because by failing to assess – even if this can usually only be done counterfactually – the consequences of alternative options, the analyst may not fully appreciate and discount the ambiguities and dilemmas the policymakers were facing at the time they had to make a decisions. The analyst may be quite pervasive in arguing that the policy that was pursued had highly negative effects. But in this he or she may have failed to consider fairly the possibility that any other course of action than the one actually selected by policymakers would have resulted in consequences that were even worse. Or, to recapitulate terminology used in the previous chapter, the analyst evaluates the present without reference to a number of other possible presents. As we will argue in chapter 4, in some cases an argument can be made that policymakers found themselves in a situation of "tragic choice" in which either of the choices they had would result in a significant amount of social harm. If this is the case, and even though the policy outcomes were highly negative, it would be misleading to label these episodes in terms of failure.

Secondly, a related phenomenon is what one might call the "action onus bias." This bias comprises two tendencies: one entailing selective attention and the other selective judgment. The dimension of selective attention refers to the tendency for analysts to focus on policies that imply proactive intervention and expansion of governmental activities, and to pay less attention to policies of nonintervention and contraction.[59] Activities seem to be much more visible than nonactivities or contraction-based policies. Who ever seriously evaluates cutbacks and terminations but opposition parties? Which policy analysts challenge the predominantly financial and economic rationales of deficit reduction from which they derive both their impetus and legitimation? These policies are, in essence, chiefly inward-oriented (putting the government household back in order), and it is suggested that they should be evaluated in these same inward-looking terms. By doing so, the indirect external, social consequences of these cutbacks and terminations are often overlooked. The policies are couched in technical jargon and presented with an air of necessity that few tend to take issue with. Contrast this with the amount of critical analytical attention paid to interventionist infrastructural, social, and environmental programs. These programs are outward looking. They are designed to effect social changes and their potential successes and failures in doing so generally stand out much more clearly. The social, political, and ecological rationales underlying them tend to be a far better and less "technical" subject for analytical scrutiny as well as public and political debate.

The dimension of selective judgment in the action onus bias stems from cultural predispositions of many people in Western societies to valuate action as opposed to abstinention. Policymakers who try but fail tend to be judged less harshly than policymakers who are seen to have failed to try. In other words, errors of omission – though they are less frequently noted by the operation of selective attention – tend to count for more than errors of commission. Perhaps anticipating this bias, U.S. health officials confronted with scanty information about a possible new swine flu epidemea were keen to pursue a nation-wide inoculation program as soon as possible. They feared that if they would decide to adopt a conservative policy of "sit and wait" now, this could be construed as negligence if the epidemic would assume major proportions later.[60]

A nice illustration of this general phenomenon of differential action-oriented valuation comes from Feldman and Milch's study of airport construction projects. It is worth quoting them in full:

> There are two distinct levels at which different outcomes, however temporary they may be, must be assessed. Decision makers everywhere wanted to build. According to their criteria, authorities in Dallas-Fort Worth, Paris and Montreal were successful, whereas their counterparts elsewhere failed to achieve their objectives.
>
> The adoption of these criteria reflected a commitment to the fulfillment of strategies. The strategy chosen everywhere for solving the problem of anticipated air travel demand was the construction of civil aviation infrastructure. The intermediate goal of construction effectively supplanted the long-term goal of meeting demand; alternative solutions, therefore, could not be considered until and unless there would be no construction. Success was measured by building infrastructure, not by success in meeting travel demand.
>
> The second level appropriate to a judgment of policy success involves the consequences of government accomplishment and the fulfillment, in the most efficient and just manner, of the original goal. According to these criteria, success and failure must be reversed. The long-term goal, to meet the demands of the travelling public for the rest of the twentieth century, has not been compromised in the cities where construction has not taken place.[61]

Their analysis shows not only the biases at work in evaluating nonevents and negative decisions, but also highlights some of the limitations of framing outcome assessments in terms of the official goals of policymakers discussed earlier. It is interesting to see how the political dynamics of evaluation produced a differential assessment of the costs and benefits of "positive" versus "negative" outcomes. In those cases where the original construction plans were called off, the opportunity costs and alleged destruction of capital investments were highlighted and considered a main reason for calling these episodes failures. At the same time, far less attention tended to be paid to the construction costs of those airports that did get built, and the considerable efficiency losses resulting from operating multiple airport facilities in one region. Upon closer inspection, it might be argued that in each of the three cases studied by Feldman and Milch where construction went ahead as planned, the negative outcomes and costs overshadowed the benefits.[62]

Challenges for Understanding Policy Fiascoes

Important as these various types of social and political biases are in shaping judgments about policy events, the challenge they pose to under-standing policy fiascoes is ambiguous. One may, for example, view these biases as distortions of what ought to be a proper, balanced assessment of social events as policy outcomes. It follows from this view that what we need is a form of policy evaluation which skirts around or transcends these biases. Implicit in this position is a role conception of policy evalu-ation as an arbiter: a neutral, rule-driven, expert authority able to adjudi-cate various competing claims about how to evaluate the outcomes of cer-tain policy episodes. The main challenge to policy analysis then becomes to find ways to perform this role adequately, which means a need to develop systematic approaches to outcome assessment enabling the ana-lyst to stand aloof from, but at the same time understand, the social and political context of the events that are being assessed.

At the other end of the spectrum lies the extreme relativist position. This would argue that these biases are inherent to any kind of claim about the nature of social and political reality, and that they are particularly marked in normative claims purporting to evaluate that reality against a certain set of criteria. In this view, policy evaluators, like other partici-pants in debates about social and political events, are inevitably affected by these biases. These pervade the kinds of questions they ask, the selec-tion of what are taken to be the relevant facts, and the choice and priorit-ization of norms and standards they use in evaluation. Since no one can completely divorce himself from the social environment in which knowl-edge is gained and judgments are formed, policy scientists and evaluators – whether they acknowledge it or not – play a role as advocates. They can-not aspire to be the kind of "legitimate value judges" that traditional sci-ence models suggests they should. The methodological apparatus of modern science can at best be used only to explicitize not transcend the social biases they bring to bear in assessing policy outcomes. In practice it is often used to obscure them, in order to preserve special status.

Underlying these different perspectives on how to interpret the chal-lenge posed by these social and political biases in outcomes assessment are epistemological differences. The former position fits in with a positi-vist, the latter with an interpretivist epistemology. However, each of these epistemologies can be interpreted with different degrees of orthodoxy. This is fortunate because neither extreme outlined above seems to offer a promising way forward. The former provides us with an ideal that fewer and fewer students of evaluation see as realistic, while the latter may lead us to wonder why we should bother at all.

As suggested in chapter 1, we find ourselves most comfortable with a modified-interpretive position which basically argues that all knowledge about social affairs is based on limited information and social construc-tions. It accepts that public policymaking is a particularly complex object of inquiry which at best allows only for highly contextual and contingent generalizations, let alone predictions. Policy science is conceived of here as a set of conventions designed to generate and continually reassess more or less systematic and verifiable knowledge about public policy. It is taken to be one among other forms of making sense of complex and controversial policy episodes, one that like all the others is pervaded by both epistemological assumptions and social and political values.[63] For that reason, policy analysis that rests on these conventions of science is not superior to other forms of sense-making.[64] Yet its single most important asset, and in it also the key to its practical relevance, lies, we believe, in its institutionalized commitment to facilitate enlightenment, reflection, and dialogue.

From this perspective on policy evaluation, the social and political biases identified in this chapter are indeed challenges. They challenge us to continually reexamine the basis of our reality claims and normative judgments. They imply that meaning-making about policy events may slip into myth-making if we forget that the initial judgments we form about events and policymakers are likely to take a narrow, contemporaneous and politically opportune time perspective. These initial judgments tend to guide the socially organized process of remembering and forgetting that we call history-making. The biases also imply that the same set of events can be assessed very differently, and legitimately so, from different cultural, spatial, and institutional positions.

Slowly we are beginning to come to terms with these challenges. Contemporary historians, for example, are building up a tradition of revisiting momentous, controversial, and conventionally regarded as politically catastrophic policy events such as the Munich agreements of 1939 and the Suez crisis of 1956. Benefitting from hitherto classified new archival materials, they ask poignant questions about these events, including what has become the dominant political and/or historical appreciation of these episodes. Benefitting also from the passage of time, they are naturally better able to assess the events in question from a more balanced temporal perspective, differentiating more sharply between short-term and longer-term effects.[65] Benefitting also from the fact that time heals many wounds, both historians and political scientists have set about bringing together key players or scholars from opposing sides in historical confrontations such as the Cuban missile crisis, in order to get a sharper feel for the differential effects of space and culture in evaluating these events.[66] Also, political scientists are beginning to explore the importance of temporal dynamics in constraining the performance of policymakers as well as in shaping the kinds of social expectations and values that their contemporaries are likely to employ in judging their success or failure.[67] Policy scientists are beginning to take cultural pluralism as a

starting point in developing conceptual frameworks for policy evaluation.[68] And finally, policy analysts themselves become increasingly aware
of the need for them to be politically astute, both in avoiding being used
politically when shaping their analysis and in making sure the results of
their work become politically relevant.[69] In the concluding chapter we
will return to these emerging ways of coping with social and political
biases in assessing policy outcomes, and try to reflect on what they may
offer in the way of helping us to better understand the contextuality and
the institutional dynamics of policy fiascoes.

Notes

1　D.A. Stone, *Policy paradox and political reason*, Glenview: Scott, Foresman and Company 1988, p. 106.
2　C. Hyatt, L. Gottlieb, *When smart people fail*, Harmondsworth: Penguin 1988, p. 20 and pp. 31-33.
3　Compare for example D. Elazar, *The American mosaic: The impact of time, space, and culture on American politics*, Boulder: Westview 1993.
4　An important preliminary distinction in these matters is between clock time and social time: these are different entities and may diverge considerably. See R.H. Lauer, *Temporal man: the meaning and uses of social time*, New York: Praeger 1981, who observes that planning and policymaking can be viewed as attempts to bring the drifts of social time under a form of rational control – and who may use time factors and timing as important instruments of such control (pp.113–117). For an elaboration of this point, see: Y. Dror, *Policymaking under adversity*, New Brunswick: Transaction 1986, pp. 5–7, 35–37, and 174–175; also: P. A. Sabatier, What can we learn from implementation research?, in: F. X. Kaufmann, G. Majone and V. Ostrom (eds.), *Guidance, control and evaluation in the public sector*, Berlin: De Gruyter 1986, pp. 318–319.
5　J. Baume, *The Sydney Opera House affair*, Sydney: Halstead Press 1967; P. Hall, *Great planning disasters*, London: Weidenfeld and Nicolson 1980; A. Kouzmin, Building the New Parliament House: An Opera House revisited?, in: G. Hawker (ed.), *Working papers on parliament*, Canberra: Canberra Case Series in Administrative Studies, Canberra College of Advanced Education 1979; J. Yeomans, *The other Taj Mahal: What happened to the Sydney Opera House*, London: Longman 1968.
6　R.A. Hays, Perceptions of success or failure in program implementation: The "feedback loop" in public policy decisions, *Policy Studies Review*, 5, 1985, 51–67, in particular p. 57.
7　G. Majone, *Evidence, argument, and persuasion in the policy process*, New Haven: Yale 1989, p. 182.
8　L.M. Salomon, The time dimension in policy evaluation, in: *Public Policy*, 27, 1979, 121–153.
9　Compare J.G. March, J.P. Olsen, *Rediscovering institutions*, New York: Free Press 1989, pp. 53-116.
10　J.L. Pressman, A. Wildavsky, *Implementation: How great expectations in Washington are dashed in Oakland*, Berkeley: University of California Press (3d ed.) 1984, p. 123.
11　A. Hoogerwerf, Policy and time: Consequences of time perspectives for the contents, processes and effects of public policies, *International Review of Administrative Sciences*, 56, 4, 1990, 671–692.
12　See, for example, H. Kaufman, *Are government organizations immortal?* Washington:

Brookings Institution 1976; B. Hogwood, B. Guy Peters, *The pathology of public policy*, Oxford: Clarendon Press 1985.

13 H.M. Ingram, D.E. Mann (eds.), *Why policies succeed or fail*, Beverly Hills: Sage 1980, p. 14.

14 A. Wildavsky, *Speaking truth to power: The art and craft of policy analysis*, New Brunswick: Transaction Books 1987, p. 283.

15 See also K.S. Cameron, D.A. Whetten, Organizational effectiveness: One model or several?, in: K.S. Cameron, D.A. Whetten (eds.), *Organizational effectiveness: A comparison of multiple models*, Orlando: Academic Press 1983, p. 13.

16 A. Kuntz, From Spiegel to Flick: The maturation of the West German Parteienstaat, in: A.S. Markovits, M. Silverstein (eds.), *The politics of scandal: power and process in liberal democracies*, New York: Holmes and Maier 1988, p. 151.

17 Referring to Miles's Law: "where you stand depends on where you sit", made famous by Allison as a key proposition of his paradigm of governmental politics. G.T. Allison, *Essence of decision: Explaining the Cuban missile crisis*, Boston: Little, Brown 1971.

18 R.C. Angel, *Explaining economic policy failure: Japan and the international monetary crisis of 1969–1971*, New York: Columbia UP 1991.

19 A.S. Markovits, M. Silverstein, Introduction: Power and process in liberal democracies, in: Markovits and Silverstein (eds. 1988), *op. cit.*, p. 9.

20 See R. Shears, I. Gidley, *The Rainbow Warrior*, Sydney: Sphere Books 1985.

21 Compare also March and Olsen (1989), *op. cit.*

22 M. Douglas & A. Wildavsky, *Risk and culture: An essay on the selection of environmental dangers*, Berkeley: University of California Press 1982; M. Thompson, R. Ellis, and A. Wildavsky, *Cultural theory*, Boulder: Westview Press 1990.

23 For a detailed empirical case study, see R.P. Gephart Jr., L. Steier, and T. Lawrence, Cultural rationalities in crisis sensemaking: A study of a public inquiry into a major industrial accident, *Industrial Crisis Quarterly*, 4, 1990, pp. 27–48. See also M. Schwarz, M. Thompson, *Divided we stand: Redefining technology, politics and social choice*, London: Wheatsheaf 1990.

24 Schwarz and Thompson (1990), *op. cit.*, p. 62.

25 See P. Bachrach, M.S. Baratz, *Power and poverty: Theory and practice*, New York: Oxford UP 1970.

26 Hall, (1982), *op. cit.*,.

27 Hall (1982), *op. cit.*, pp. 1–2.

28 L. Allen et.al. *Political scandals and causes célèbres since 1945: A reference compendium*, Harlow: Longman 1990.

29 See M. Edelman, *Constructing the political spectacle*, Chicago: Chicago UP 1988, chapter 5.

30 Edelman (1988), *op.cit.*, p. 31.

31 On the political functions of labelling policy events as successes or crises, see M. Edelman, *Political language: Words that succeed and policies that fail*, New York: Academic Press 1977.

32 See W. Klose, *Skandal und Politik: Ein Kapitel negativer Demokratie*, Tübingen: Katzmann 1971; M. Schmitz, *Theorie und Praxis des politischen Skandals*, Frankfurt: Campus 1981; and Markovits, Silverstein (eds. 1988), *op. cit.*

33 Compare Stone (1988), *op. cit.*

34 See P. Schulman, *Large-scale policymaking*, New York: Elsevier 1980.

35 G. Mucciaroni, *The political failure of employment policy, 1945–1982*, Pittsburgh: Pittsburgh UP 1990, p. 12.

36 Mucciaroni (1990), *op. cit.*, p.12.

37 Mucciaroni (1990), *op. cit.*, p. 185.

38 M. Derthick, *New towns in town: Why a federal program failed*, Washington: Brookings Institution 1972, p.XIII.

39 The definition is from Michel Crozier, *The bureaucratic phenomenon*, Chicago: Chicago UP 1964.

40 Wildavsky (1987), *op. cit.*
41 Ingram and Mann (eds. 1980), *op. cit.*, p. 18.
42 H. van Gunsteren, *The quest for control: A critique of the rational-central rule approach*, New York: Wiley 1976.
43 Wildavsky (1987), *op. cit.*, p. 57ff.
44 A. Hoogerwerf (ed.), *Succes en falen van overheidsbeleid* [Succes and failure of public policy], Alphen: Samsom 1983.
45 Ingram, Mann (eds., 1980), *op. cit.*; Hoogerwerf (ed., 1983), *op. cit.*
46 See M. Scriven, Goal-free evaluation. In: E.R. House (ed.), *School evaluation: The politics and process*, Berkeley: McCutchan 1973, pp. 319-328. See also the highly informative discussion by W.R. Shadish, jr., T.D. Cook, and L.C. Leviton, *Foundations of program evaluation: Theories of practice*, Newbury Park: Sage 1991, pp. 73–118.
47 See, for example, F. Fischer, *Politics, values and public policy*, Boulder: Westview 1980 and E.B. Portis, M.B. Levy (eds.), *Handbook of political theory and policy science*, Westport: Greenwood 1988. Shadish, Cook, and Leviton (1991), *op. cit.*, pp. 46–52; 455–463 discuss this issue in terms of a challenge for evaluators to develop coherent theories of valuing.
48 Ingram, Mann (eds., 1980), *op. cit.*, p. 20; See G.D. Brewer, P. DeLeon, *The foundations of policy analysis*, Homewood: Dorsey Press 1983, pp. 328 ff; H. Bressers, Analyse en evaluatie van beleidseffecten [Analysis and evaluation of policy outcomes], in: H. Blommesteijn, H. Bressers, and A. Hoogerwerf (red.), *Handboek beleidsevaluatie* [Policy evaluation handbook], Alphen: Samsom 1984, specifically pp. 127–130; B.Hogwood, L. Gunn, *Policy analysis for the real world*, Oxford: Oxford UP 1984, pp. 150-169 for critiques.
49 Stone (1988), *op. cit.*, p. 195.
50 Y. Dror, Visionary political leadership: On improving a risky requisite, *International Political Science Review*, 9, 1988, pp. 7–22.
51 R.T. Cyert, J.G. March, *A behavioral theory of the firm*, Englewood Cliffs: Prentice Hall 1963.
52 M.H. Moore, Police leadership: the impossible dream? In: E.C. Hargrove and J.C. Glidewell (eds.), *Impossible jobs in public management*, Lawrence: Kansas UP 1990, pp. 72–102.
53 E.C. Hargrove, J.C. Glidewell (eds., 1990), *op. cit.*, p. 3.
54 Partly for that reason, running a police department or a corrections system have figured prominently in a comparative analysis of "impossible jobs" in public administration. E. Hargrove, J.C. Glidewell (eds. 1990), *op. cit.* Others include the management of mental health and social security systems, as well as the management of the AIDS epidemic.
55 See, for example, M.D. Cohen, J.G. March and J.P. Olsen, A garbage-can model of organizational choice, *Administrative Science Quarterly*, 17, 1972, 1–25; Pressman and Wildavsky (1984), *op. cit.* Brewer and DeLeon (1983), *op. cit.*; D. Hickson, R.J. Butler, D. Cray, G.R. Mallory, D.C. Wilson, *Top decisions*, Oxford: Blackwell 1986.
56 For example, Brewer, DeLeon (1983), *op. cit.*, p. 332.
57 J.G. March, Model bias in social action, *Review of Educational Research*, February 1972, pp. 413-29, as quoted in Brewer and DeLeon (1983), *op. cit.*, p. 332.
58 See, for example, E.J. Feldman, *Concorde and dissent*, Cambridge: Cambridge UP 1985; P.W.G. Morris and G.H. Hough, *The anatomy of major projects: A study of the reality of project management*, New York: Wiley 1987, pp. 195–197.
59 See however, for example, C.C. Hood, A. Dunsire, *Cutback management in public bureaucracies*, Cambridge: Cambridge UP 1989.
60 A.M. Silverstein, *Pure politics and impure science: The Swine Flu affair*, Baltimore: Johns Hopkins UP 1981, chapter 3.
61 E.J. Feldman, J. Milch, *Technocracy versus democracy: The comparative politics of international airports*, Boston: Auburn House 1982, p. 117.
62 Feldman and Milch (1982), *op. cit.*, pp.118–122. As the authors point out themselves, and

as argued at length in chapter 2, this assessment might shift again if one extends the time frame used for evaluation. Air travel did reach new hights during the eighties, and pressures on the London, Toronto and other regions where building plans were stalled did increase, while in the other three cases, passenger increases were easily absorbed and even viewed with great relief.

63 R.A. Heineman, W.T. Bluhm, S.A. Peterson, E.N. Kearny, *The world of the policy analyst: Rationality, values, and politics*, Chatham, NJ: Chatham House 1990, pp. 1–6.

64 See, for example, D.K. Cohen, C.E. Lindblom, *Usable knowledge: Social science and social problem solving*, New Haven: Yale UP 1977; Majone (1989), *op. cit.*; R. Tong, *Ethics in public policy*, Englewood Cliffs: Prentice Hall 1986.

65 W.R. Louis, R. Owen (eds.), *Suez 1956: The crisis and its consequences*, Oxford: Clarendon Press 1989.

66 J.G. Blight, D.A. Welch, *On the brink: Americans and Soviets reexamine the Cuban missile crisis*, New York: Hill and Wang 1989; for a pointed piece of revisionism about the same crisis, which was long held to be a policy fiasco for the Soviets, see R.N. Lebow, J. Gross Stein, *We all lost the cold war*, Princeton: Princeton UP 1994.

67 S. Skowronek, *The politics presidents make: Leadership from John Adams to George Bush*, Cambridge, Mass: Belknap Press of Harvard UP 1993.

68 C.C. Hood, A public management for all seasons? *Public Administration*, 69, 1991, pp. 3–19. See also R. Hoppe, A. Peterse, *Handling frozen fire: Political culture and risk management*, Boulder: Westview Press 1993.

69 Compare, for example, Heineman, Bluhm, Peterson, and Kearny, (1990), *op. cit.*, pp. 63–64; 113–118; 173–174.

CHAPTER 3

Identifying Agents:
The Ontology of Policymaking

History isn't the account of all that happpened, but the reconstruction of what someone decides is significant

Sayles[1]

The Black Box of Policymaking

Thus far, we have talked about identifying fiascoes solely on the basis of judgments about policy outcomes, as if these are made independently of how people view the ways in which these outcomes have come about. This distinction is legitimate and useful for analytical reasons, but hardly tenable when studying actual controversies about past policies. Most of the stakeholders as well as the legal and political fora that evaluate the outcomes of certain policies, projects, or programs will also take the policymaking process into account. They will only consider a negative event to be a problem of policy if it involved well-recognized failures of policymakers. The crucial question that is being asked is: Did the policymakers contribute to the occurrence of these negative outcomes, or could this pernicious state of affairs have been prevented by them? If the answer is yes, the chance that some event will be labelled as a fiasco is far bigger than if both questions are answered negatively.

Compare, for example, the Heysel and Hillsborough soccer stadium disasters, two events that by all standards were very negative.[2] On May 29th 1985, 39 people died and 450 were left wounded following a confrontation between rival groups of supporters which triggered a severe crowd crush in the Brussels Heysel Stadium. Four years later, at Sheffield no less than 95 people were crushed to death and 400 wounded when a large crowd was allowed into the already overcrowded stands of Hillsborough Stadium. In the Heysel case, media reports, parliamentary, and judicial investigations suggested that the disaster was due to major flaws in the way police and soccer authorities had prepared for and handled crowd control. Consequently, the case became widely labelled as a major fiasco. Surprisingly given the fact that the number of fatalities was far greater, the Hillsborough disaster was portrayed differently. In his report on the events Lord Justice Taylor observed that in the years prior to the disaster a considerable effort had been made by both police and stadium officials to improve the stadium infrastructure and public order arrangements. He did conclude that police operations concerning the match showed some serious weaknesses which helped to bring about the disaster. However, the report also recognized the fact that the design of the turnstiles, the construction of the entry systems, and unique crowd conditions played a role as well. Eventually, in the Hillsborough case none of the operational police commanders and policymakers involved was prosecuted – whereas in the Heysel case several gendarmerie commanders and soccer federation officials were found guilty of criminal negligence. Part of this crucial difference in the post-hoc political and judicial evaluations in these two cases can, in other words, be explained by perceived differences in the quality of the policymaking process, the context in which the policymakers operated, and the possible alternative courses of action that had been open to them.

This brief case comparison suggests a number of key questions for further analysis. How do negative events come about? To what extent are they caused by human or organizational actors who play a part in the policymaking process? To what extent are they the product of misfortunes and circumstances beyond the control of policymakers? These are questions about agency, about pinpointing the locus of failure, the second of the four layers of meaning-making about controversial policy episodes discussed in chapter 1. To answer them, we need somehow to move into the metaphorical "black box" of policymaking and look at the ways in which decisions are made and actions planned and executed. We need to do away with unitary conceptions of "the government" and "the bureaucracy," and instead penetrate into the fragmented world of multiple, disjointed, and sometimes competing actors and agencies.

Two different levels of analysis are involved here. First of all, there is the empirical matter of identifying actors who possibly might have played a role in bringing about the negative events. Who might qualify as the main characters in the policy drama? Underneath that lies the ontological issue of delineating public policymaking as a social phenomenon. The biases and analytical difficulties involved here are the subject of this chapter. The second level of analysis is philosophical, the key issue being the problem of "fate or folly." Once we have indentified candidates for the main parts of the causal chain in a particular case, the next question is: under which conditions and to what extent can policy failures be said to be a matter of policymakers having had bad luck. This question is dealt with in the next chapter.

Therefore, the crucial thing to be identified first is the course of the policy process and the ways in which the conduct of this process might have contributed to outcomes that have come to be judged as catastrophic. Yet what do we mean exactly when we talk about a policy process? What are its boundaries? Which actors, actions, and communications does it involve? In other words, what exactly should we study when we start looking for the causes of policy failure?

In our view, these questions are often left unanswered in fiasco studies. The ontological status of policy processes is problematic, yet seldom discussed. The myth of the black box is indeed a pervasive one, but it helps us little in coming to terms with the problem of identifying the agents and reconstructing the development of a particular policy. Stepping into the black box one cannot help but be overwhelmed by the complexity of what one encounters. The analyst will soon come to conclude that the policy process is ontologically complex and indeterminate. The sources of this complexity and indeterminacy are many, but let us by way of example elaborate two of them at somewhat greater length:

- Institutional complexity: the kinds of policies studied here by definition involve the behavior of large and complex bureaucratic organizations.
- Temporality: the interconnections between the temporal sequence of events and the organizational process of decision and action are manifold and complex.

Each of these properties of policymaking will be discussed separately in this chapter.

Institutional Complexity

More often than not, those seeking to reconstruct and explain the course of a policy process are outsiders looking at the events in retrospect. Being outsiders and coming "late," they will be confronted with a myriad of people, groups, and organizations that apparently have communicated and interacted in manifold ways. Simple questions like: "who was involved?" suddenly appear to be very difficult to answer. How does one determine what constitutes an "actor" or a "stakeholder?" Do we look for formal status and powers? How does one determine whether a particular actor was indeed "involved?" Do we look for revealed preferences in the form of overt activities? Or do we determine the identity of actors from our own analysis of the interests that are (or have been) affected by the policy, regardless of whether these actors themselves did indeed act?[3]

One particularly complicating feature of public policymaking is that crucial functions of any nonroutine policy process tend to be performed by several or many complex bureaucratic organizations. Complex organizations share certain features that make their activities, and therefore the course of events in a policy process, a highly indeterminate object of research:

- Complex organizations are surrounded by walls of paper and regulations. Looking from the outside in, it is often very difficult to grasp (and to prove) which exact members of the organization were formally or de facto capable of taking a controversial decision or action which (might have) influenced the course of the policy process in a significant way. In many cases authority to decide and act is spread among different parts, bureaus, or officials, and is the subject of ambivalence and controversy among them. To understand what policy emerged and how often requires the investigator to master the complexities of the formal and informal lines of authority along which the ability to influence the substance of policy is distributed.
- It follows that the behavior of an organization differs from the behavior of a private person in that it is far less easily traceable to any particular source. Policy goes through many hands before it is finally adopted.[4] Ideas, proposals, evaluations, and decisions are the product of committee work. They are passed around many different desks before becoming firmly established. In that process they are altered, both in design and during implementation, often involving a different set of organizations and officials at different levels of administrative action. As Simon put it: "Many individuals and units of organizations contribute to every decision. These contributions may be viewed as the preconditions for the final compositie decision and, therefore ... it becomes meaningless to ask 'who really makes the decision?'"[5]
- Moreover, in many professional bureaucratic organizations a great deal of individual mobility exists. Stakeholders and officials come to the policy arena, try to make their mark and get to change things as they see fit, but often leave the arena before their impact has been secured and formalized. The organizational process outlasts many of its prime agents and stakeholders.[6]
- At the same time, and increasingly so in the postindustrial age, the formal structure of organizations and the policy-oriented network configurations between these organizations are constantly undergoing transformations. Bureaucratic reorganizations have become the rule rather than the exception. Once stable networks of policymakers, bureaucrat-

ic agencies and selected client and stakeholder groups jointly making and implementing policy, are increasingly giving way to more volatile and ephemeral arenas, where participants come and go, and ad-hoc coalitions emerge and dissolve quickly. Technological innovations push actors to explore the possibilities for restructuring. Consequently, the "rules of the game" are ambiguous and subject to constant negotiation and reinterpretation.[7]

These ontological features of organizational action are problematic at three different levels. They complicate the task of the investigator seeking to reconstruct the actual course of events, because they make it difficult to pinpoint certain people, groups or units as the "prime movers." In many cases, the deeper the analyst digs, the more actors and linkages between actors inside and outside the focal organization come into view, and the less parsimonious the research effort is likely to be. Also, from an explanatory point of view, it becomes exceedingly hard to establish the relative importance of all these various sub-issues, personalities, interactions, and incidents that have occurred within the organization during the period a policy was made. And, finally, these same factors complicate the task of evaluation. The problem of "many hands" is a major obstacle for the allocation of blame and praise to specific individuals within an organization that is held accountable. The problem of many hands worries lawyers and others who seek to ensure that individual members of complex organizations maintain an active sense of personal responsibility, even though they operate in a setting full of opportunities and pressures to forget or deny it.[8]

A case example may serve to illustrate these points. In the late seventies and early eighties the state of Washington was rocked by an increasingly controversial and desperate situation in its public power supply system. Rate payers in Washington and in parts of the surrounding states were confronted with rate increases due to the catastrophic failure of what must have been one of the largest civilian nuclear projects in history: the construction of five major nuclear power plants undertaken by the state's power agency. This mammoth project had absorbed multi-billion dollar investments in bonds and loans but ran into severe financial, managerial, and construction problems. This eventually caused four of the five plants to be aborted in mid-construction. Bankruptcies, political crisis, and drawn-out legal battles were to follow. Meanwhile, the once cheap utility rates in the region had gone up considerably and would remain high indefinitely. Leigland and Lamb have undertaken the painstaking job of searching for a comprehensive explanation of the failure.[9] What they show is that virtually all of the institutional actors involved in the project contributed to its failure, yet in very different ways that are

extremely difficult to prioritize in terms of importance, let alone to establish in terms of individual responsibility or corporate liability.

The reason for this is threefold. First, the project was initiated and managed by the Washington Public Power Supply System (WPPSS), a public
corporation. The WPPSS organization itself was complex. Apart from
being a Seattle municipal corporation, it was also a joint operating agency of the state of Washington, whose membership included nineteen public utility districts and four cities in the region. Consequently, WPPSS's
board consisted of representatives of each of these twenty three partici-
pating agencies.

Moreover, this part-time board did not actually run WPPSS. Instead, it
recruited and supposedly controlled a professional executive, who managed the corporation on a day to day basis. In its turn, WPPSS executive
management was organized around several divisions, including a
Projects Division and a Finance and Administration Division. Leigland
and Lamb clearly show that each of these constituent actors failed to some
degree to perform his job or functions with the degree of professionalism
considered essential for the successful accomplishment of a large-scale
construction project. These performance shortfalls were at the same time
enabled and magnified by weaknesses of communication and interaction
between these various levels of the organization.

But reconstructive and explanatory complications do not stop here. For
one thing, the project was not a matter of WPPSS alone. On the contrary,
it involved local (the hundreds of local utilities involved), state (the state
legislature) and national level agencies (the Bonneville Power
Administration, the Nuclear Regulatory Commission) as well as a large
number of corporate actors, bondholders, and ratepayers. These actors
shaped the legislative and regulatory constraints and opportunities,
served as advocates and counteradvocates of the project, enabled or complicated the financing of the project, and were involved in project implementation. Looked at from this broader interorganizational perspective,
the management of the WPPSS project involved a complex, multilevel,
public-private, and increasingly politicized policy arena, which in itself
was partly shaped by broader macro-economic developments.

From this perspective, the political, financial, public relations, and legal
dimensions of the project come to the fore, all of which harbor a host of
actors and linkages between them. Likewise, a large number of possible
explanations of the project's failure focusing on the interfaces between
WPPSS and its institutional environment become salient. These require
the analyst to look in some detail at how each of these external actors fits
into the picture, to examine their actions and possible rationales for these
actions, and then to face the question whether these actions (or lack of
same) contributed to the failure, how important they were in the broader

context of the project, and whether the central actor (WPPSS) could have prevented or mitigated failure by effective "external" management.

In short, to unravel the organizational and interorganizational patterns, activities, and responsibilities surrounding a single major policy fiasco often is a monumental task. The sheer number of actors and relationships involved make it conceptually hard if not impossible to prioritize any small number of these in what we would regard as a conventional theoretical explanation.[10]

Time: Reconstructing Sequences

Explaining phenomena in terms of cause and effect involves reconstructing temporal sequences. This is evidenced, for example, by the failed attempt of the Carter administration to liberate by military force American embassy personnel held hostage in post-revolutionary Iran, one of the more conspicuous and sombolically powerful fiascoes of Carter's time in office. Although ultimately the drama was a political one, the mission itself required an intricate combination of political and tactical decisions. Looking at those, it is not so easy to pinpoint a single major factor as "the" cause of the mission's failure. For example, the decision to have the helicopters to be used for the Iran rescue mission flown by Marine pilots instead of their normal Air Force pilots, caused these pilots to have to operate helicopters unfamiliar to them. This, in turn, was a major cause of the poor judgment some of them exercised during their night flight across the Iranian desert.[11] These poor judgements made several of them decide to abort their missions because of alleged technical defects that in reality were not that serious. Consequently, an insufficient number of helicopters was available to continue the mission, triggering the decision to abort it entirely. Yet parallel to this another, more or less separate chain of events contributed to turning an aborted mission into a catastrophic one, for example, the events leading up to the collision between one helicopter and a C-130 tanker plane during the pullout operation, resulting in the deaths of eight soldiers, and dramatizing the failure of the operation. Both episodes can be reconstructed in terms of step-by-step sequences of events, with the preceding ones always being a necessary or sufficient cause for the next, and with the two chains of events eventually interacting in unpredicted ways.

In research on man-made disasters, such chains of causes and effects are reconstructed in great detail with the objective of identifying the precise pattern of human error that enabled these disasters to occur. From this research it turns out that even seemingly straightforward accidents tend to be caused by a complex series of factors, many of which impact upon the process long before the actual accident occurs. In fact, in many of these studies, events preceding the accident by numerous years, even decades, are included in the causal chain.[12]

To reconstruct these causal chains is painstaking work, but it can be done relatively convincingly for what one could call "instant" fiascoes: events concentrated in place and time where the evidence of failure is immediate and unmistakeable. Instant fiascoes provide a clear and often dramatic vantage point to identify symptoms of failure. From there, one can start to work one's way back. This is especially true for cases like the Heysel and Hillsborough stadium disasters, the King's Cross station fire, and the sinking of the Herald of Free Enterprise, that have indeed all been analyzed using this type of methodology.[13]

The reconstruction of causal chains is much more difficult with "evolving" fiascoes: more diffuse, spun-out developments that eventually come to be viewed as problematic by a dominant coalition of stakeholders and value judges. Examples of this type of fiascoes are the failure of massive financial government support to rescue the Dutch RSV shipbuilding company; the French blood transfusion scandal evolving around health authorities failing to act decisively to ensure blood banks contained only HIV-tested blood supplies; and the Iran-Contra affair, for example, intiatives by parts of the Reagan administration to secretly sell arms to Iran in exchange for U.S. hostages held by Iran-backed groups in Lebanon, and using the profit to provide illegal aid to the Nicaraguan contra rebels. Evolving fiascoes tend to be less amenable to this sort of methodology because the key manifestations of failure are more ambiguous, opaque, and subject to contestation.

The key question that arises in these cases is: where does the reconstructive chain begin? In chapter 2 we have shown that different people looking at the same policy event may judge it differently, or may judge it a failure but for wholly different reasons. Similarly, in reconstructing the policy process leading up to failures, different observers tend to focus on different types of actors, decisions, or events as possible explanations for these failures. This implies that they may also pick different points in time as crucial. The temporal sequence of fiascoes of the "evolving" type may be particularly hard to reconstruct, because there is no clear and concise starting point that serves as the anchor for reconstruction. Different participants and observers tend to have different views about when exactly a policy went off the rails and became a failure.

In the case of the government subsidies to the RSV shipbuilding conglomerate, for example, the policy pattern was one of repeated and escalating commitments to a fledgling but once powerful and symbolically pivotal part of Dutch industry. These commitments were always entered into not only because of desperation and fear for the employment consequences of witholding financial support, but also because there always seemed to be reasons for optimism about turning points and new ventures that were said to lie ahead. More importantly perhaps, these commitments did not generate negative judgments by members of parliament for many years after they had first been entered into, and hence were not defined as indications of a failing policy. The latter occurred only when political support was finally witheld, bankruptcy was imminent, and journalists began asking questions.

Therefore, the moment and nature of failure in cases like this are politically and not analytically defined. In reconstructing and explaining the RSV debacle, different analysts are likely to select different vantage points from where to start, and may therefore pursue wholly different reconstructive paths. These analytical choices depend on what they see as the key problem to be explained:

- The tenacity of the Dutch Ministry of Economic Affairs in continuing to subsidize what became ever more clearly a losing venture;
- the long-lasting political consensus between government and parliament about what should have been an increasingly controversial policy of support to industries undergoing conjunctural and probably even structural decline;
- the crucial manipulative role of the government in the period prior to the demise of RSV, namely during the reorganization of Dutch shipbuilding industry resulting in the formation of the ill-fated RSV conglomerate;
- the apparent managerial incompetence of the RSV, board of directors which caused a big and potentially viable industry heavily supported by hundreds of millions of public dollars to go bankrupt (RSV's management engaged in some reckless plans and foreign adventures in attempts to diversify its activities, losing millions to con man artists and commercially disastrous projects);
- the lack of effective supervision of RSV on the part of the Ministry of Economic Affairs, given that some of its senior officials occupied a critical watchdog role in the corporate board structure.

There is also a second side to this question, namely: how far back in time should the analysis probe? Since it is assumed by most policy analysts that events can be analyzed in terms of means-ends and cause-and-effect dichotomies, there is always an event that occurred before another event contributing to this second event's occurrence. A rigid interpretation of this assumption would push the analyst towards a reductio ad absurdum, tracing events to such remote and long-gone causes that their explanation may be consistent methodologically but becomes trivial and useless for purposes of policy evaluation and learning. This is the trade-off between analytically powerful and practically manipulable causes in explaining policy fiascoes.

Opening Up the Black Box: The Heysel Case

There are several techniques available to tackle these organizational and temporal complexities. Analysts can, for example, choose between forward and backward logics of event reconstruction and interpretation.[14] The common way of reconstructing and explaining policy events is to follow stage models of the policy process, where a policy is depicted as moving towards a distinct set of phases from inception to termination. But stage models are not only forward-mapping, they also imply a hierarchical view of the organization of the policy process. The analyst starts at the top and examines the initial definitions of the problem, the decision-making process that ensued, and the decisions it resulted in. This focus here tends to be on the policy elites. The next step is to move forward and to look at what happened afterwards during the process of selecting appropriate policy instruments and transforming policy decisions into implementation programs. Finally, one looks at what actually happened during implementation. By that time, the focus has descended to the bottom layers of bureaucracy and society. Using this model, policy failure is something that at once emerges towards the end of the reconstrcuted process and is explained by events and decisions encountered at previous stages. In this first view, the essential problem is the mismatch between strategy and implementation. At its core lie things like technical difficulties in moving from political goals to program objectives, bureaucratic obstacles, problems of coordination and control, street-level bureaucrats charting their own course regardless of official policy, and the balkanization of operational agencies by powerful client constituencies preventing a meticulous implementation of political decisions.

Adopting a backward mapping, "bottom-up" approach, one starts at those actors, decisions, and actions most proximate to the alleged performance failure, and works one's way backward to the more strategic levels of management and politics where the strategic choices shaping the controversial actions in questions have been made. This sort of methodology also allows the analyst to define the problems in terms of a mismatch between the world of implementation and the world of strategy, but the nature of the underlying problems is reversed: Those at the top are insufficiently aware of the harsh realities of day-to-day service delivery, and therefore make uninformed and often mutually contradictory decisions that cannot possibly be implemented successfully, and, in many cases already bear the seeds of failure.

The top-down, forward-mapping mode of reconstruction is the most common one, and its problems and findings are well-documented. This is much less the case for the bottom-up, backward-mapping approach, which has gained prominence only from the late seventies onwards. We shall therefore use the latter to illustrate how temporal and organizational complexities of policymaking are actually intertwined for the analysts.

On May 29 1986, the European Cup soccer final was to be held in the Heysel Stadium in Brussels, Belgium between the teams of Liverpool (England) and Juventus (Italy). Shortly before the match was due to start riots broke out that eventually left thirty-nine, mostly Italian, supporters dead and 450 wounded.

Figure 1 provides a lay-out of the stadium and indicates where the disaster took place. In this case, the decision most proximate to the actual onset of disaster was the belated decision by a Belgian Gendarmerie platoon commander to bypass normal hierarchical procedures and call for urgent reinforcements to come to the Z-section of the stadium (level I in the organization; see figure 2 on p. 68). There he had seen a tragedy unfold before his eyes. Hundreds of Liverpool supporters from the adjacent Y-section had climbed over the fences, ignoring and injuring some of the handful of gendarmes guarding the narrow corridor between the two sections, and were threatening thousands of mostly peaceful Italians in the Z-section. The Italians sought to escape by moving towards the far end of the section, thereby causing a terrible crush of bodies which they then tried to escape by climbing onto the field. Gendarmerie presence in that section of the stadium was insufficiently strong to stop the attack and the Italian panic response. It also took considerable time before the Gendarmes realized the seriousness of the situation. They had been trying by force to push the Italians back on the stands because their instructions were to prevent an invasion of the grounds by "hooligans" at all costs.

The decision to go out and call up reinforcements by himself was an agonizing one for the platoon commander, because in the strict military hierarchy of the Belgian Gendarmerie subordinates are only allowed to operate through their next ranking commander. In this case, that would have been the squadron commander responsible for the policing of the entire X–Y–Z part of the stadium, roughly the western end behind one of the goals (level II). This captain, who had had no previous experience with policing soccer matches, was outside the stadium at the time the riots developed, investigating the alleged robbery of one of the stalls near the entrance. His deputy had responded to the same call and therefore was also outside the stadium. Facing a rapidly escalating situation on the

Figure 1 The Heysel stadium disaster

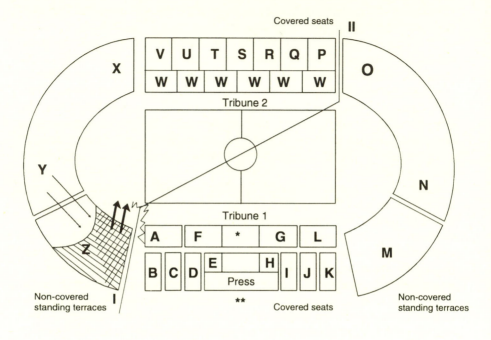

	=	corridor separating sections X-Y and Z
	=	movement of hooligan's attacks
	=	fleeing spectators in section Z
	=	attempts to escape towards pitch
	=	increasing pushing and squeezing in section Z
	=	people crushed against and subsequent collapse of side wall
Sections N and O	=	Juventus supporters
Sections X and Y	=	Liverpool supporters
Sections M and Z	=	"Neutral" spectators
Zone I	=	Gendarmerie
Zone II	=	Minicipal police
*	=	Part of tribune 1 reserved for guests of honor
**	=	Tango-12 communications and command post of fire brigade

ground, the platoon commander had been trying to reach both his immediate superiors for minutes, but communications equipment was faulty, making it impossible to reach persons outside the stands (level I-level II connection).

Confronted with this anomaly, the platoon commander faced the painful choice between observing standard procedures, which implied he should wait until he could get in touch with his squadron commander, at the risk of being completely overrun by the crowd, or showing personal initiative and bypassing his commander to call for reserves higher up the hierarchy in the hope of saving the situation but knowing he was likely to be severely reprimanded for doing so (the Belgian Gendarmerie was an extremely hierarchical organization which tolerated no such improvisation). The choice left him in agony for some time, vainly attempting to reach his squadron commander. This proved to be a costly delay: when he finally decided to forget the rules and go up the hierarchy, the situation had already deteriorated beyond control, and minutes before the reinforcements arrived a wall at the side of the Z-section had collapsed under the pressure of Italians seeking escape from the British onslaught – the crush towards this new escape route left thirty-nine dead and 450 wounded. The pathology of command that became apparent on the night of the Heysel disaster was no isolated incident, however. Going back in time to the period of the Gendarmerie's preparations for the match, some crucial antecedents emerge. First of all, one wonders about the appointment of an inexperienced squadron commander at such a vital position in the crowd-control operation. This appointment was done by the general commander of the Gendarmerie's operation for the match, the chief of the Brussels district, Major Kensier (level III). He picked his man only a few days before the match, partly by default: many more experienced commanders were busy preparing for a forthcoming visit of the Pope scheduled to take place a short time after the European Cup final. In turn, the appointment of this squadron commander was just one element within the broader operational plan made by the commander of the Brussels district and approved by his superiors in the Gendarmerie's General Command (level IV). The rigid command and control procedures he wrote into his plan were nothing unusual. In fact, they were part and parcel of the organizational culture, and reflected a particular view of the nature of large scale public-order policing. The reason he posted relatively few men under an inexperienced commander at what later turned out to be the most dangerous spot in the stadium, was that he did not anticipate any trouble at that spot. The ticket sale arrangements made by the Belgian Soccer Federation were such that, at least in theory, English and Italian fans would be at opposite ends of the stadium (level IV-outside actor interconnection). The Z-section would be filled with neutral, Belgian spectators buying their tickets locally. In the weeks before, however, there had been various signals that the distribution of tickets for the Z-section did not go as planned, and that it was likely that a sizable number of tickets had fallen into Italian hands, making it likely that English and Italians would after all be standing side by side in the Y and Z sections of the stadium. These signals did not reach Major Kensier or their significance was misunderstood.

The next step in the reconstructive chain takes us a little further back in time, and moves the scene from the organizational and operational level to the interorganizational, policy level. Why was the weak and rigid Gendarmerie and not the more flexible municipal police of Brussels responsible for order maintenance in the part of the stadium where the riots took place? This draws attention to the decision process that occurred weeks before the match when it became known who the two finalists would be and it transpired that an English team was involved. In those days, this implied an increased risk of hooliganism and violence. Both of the major police forces operating in the Brussels area claimed the key role in policing the match. The Brussels municipal police based its claim on the fact that the match fell within its assigned territory and asserted that it was perfectly capable of doing the job in and around the stadium with only minor assistance from the Gendarmerie with regard to traffic and patrols throughout the city. At the same time, the Belgian national Gendarmerie pointed to historical precedents whereby its Brussels division too had operated within the stadium during major soccer matches. Public authorities such as the mayor of Brussels and the office of the Minister of the Interior were drawn into the dispute, and finally a compromise was reached (level Va: ad hoc interorganizational policy arena). An imaginary diagonal was drawn dividing the stadium in half (see again figure 1). One half would be policed by the Gendarmerie using its personnel, methods, and command procedures, while the other half would be covered by the municipal police doing likewise. Coordination between the two forces was reduced to the exchange of low-level liaison officers. The pathologies of this arrangement became apparent during the night of the match, when officials from the Belgian soccer federation could find only municipal police commanders to warn them that something was wrong in the Y and Z sections of the stadium. However, these commanders were unable to act in the area of the stadium policed by the Gendarmerie, and the communication arrangements between the two forces were so tenuous and cumbersome that only three out of nine increasingly urgent warning messages from the police reached Gendarmerie commander Kensier at Gendarmerie headquarters. Moreover, coming from "the other side", these urgent warnings were not immediately acted upon (level III-Va interconnection).

The interorganizational conflict between rival police forces that so thoroughly affected the quality of policing at the Liverpool-Juventus match can, however, only be understood if one goes back in time even further – beyond the moment the preparations for the final at the Heysel stadium began. The conflict over who would do what on May 29 was just one among a series of disputes and sensitivities between rival forces policing the same territory with comparable tasks and jurisdictions (level Vb: ongoing interorganizational policy arena). This situation exists throughout Belgium, but usually overt conflict is avoided given the clear superiority of the bigger, better funded and more highly professionalized Gendarmerie. Yet in bigger cities such as Brussels, municipal police forces have sufficient critical mass and expertise to hold their own, which creates a variety of problems. Usually these are solved by pragmatic agreements not to get in one another's way. But the context of a high profile, large-scale event with clear safety risks posed a unique opportunity for grandstanding on both sides. Yet at the same time the task of policing the final required a more intense form of coordination that was unlikely to occur given the broader context of relations between the two forces and the deliberate abstinention from this sensitive area on the part of the responsible political authorities. Figure 2 summarizes these interconnections between temporal and organizational factors, and the analytical issues they entail.

This example makes quite clear that seemingly technical, operational failures like the one at the Heysel stadium tend to be rooted in history and in broader managerial, organizational, and political issues and events.[15] It illustrates that a proper explanation of a policy failure should, indeed, go back in time, but it also testifies to the complexities of doing so.

The reconstructive chain we have drawn for the Heysel case is only one among many that should be looked at if one wants to fully understand why the event happened. For example, other reconstructive chains can be drawn up for

- the Belgian Soccer Federation and the organization and implementation of the ticket sales that led to the unexpected presence of Italians in a section adjacent to the English;
- the role of the European soccer federation in approving a sensitive match at a stadium with clearly deficient infrastructural facilities;
- the role of local and national authorities with respect to limiting the sale of alcohol and the enforcement of rules against public drunkenness and vandalism throughout the day of the match;
- the role of both police forces and private security firms with regard to ticket verification and visitor search procedures at the entrances to the stadium, and so on.

Figure 2 Reconstructing the Heysel stadium tragedy:
temporal and organizational factors

Level of action	Example	Key actor	Time period	Analytical implications
Level I: operator	Decision to turn directly to Major Kensier to request backup units to Z section of stadium	Gendarmerie Platoon Commander Maenhoudt	Just before disaster	Speed and content of decision
Level I+II: operator to direct superior	Repeated attempts to reach Mahieu to obtain back up for riot control in Z section	Gendarmerie Platoon Commander Maenhoudt	Period of several minutes before disaster	Reasons behind decisional conflict
Level III: supervisor	Appointment of captain Mahieu as commander in charge for Z section	General Commander Heysel Major Kensier	A few days before match	Reasons behind appointment of inexperienced commander
Level IV: top of hierarchy	Internal organization and planning national Gendarmerie for Heysel match	General Command Gendarmerie Brussels division	Week to two weeks before match	Reasons behind highly centralized command structure
Level Va: interorganizational ad hoc	Bureaupolitical conflict between local police and Gendarmerie over division of labour at Heysel	Gendarmerie Brussels, Municipal Police Brussels, Ministry of the Interior	Entire match planning period (one month)	Reasons behind peculiar territorial division of responsibility for order maintenance
Level Vb: interorganizational ongoing	Ongoing bureaupolitics between local and national police in Brussels area	Gendarmerie National Command, Municipal Police Brussels, Brussels city government, Belgian Cabinet	Ongoing, with long historical roots	Reasons behind simultaneous policing of Brussels by different and rivalrous police forces

There is, in other words, not a single chain of decisions and actions leading to a policy failure. It is much more likely that there are many separate ones involving different sets of actors and different components of the problem. In most cases these various chains of decisions and actions come together and interact in intricate and unexpected ways, which further complicates the task of the analyst seeking to produce a clear-cut explana-tion.[16] In addition, the very elaborateness of this method and the quantity and quality of data it presupposes make it extremely laborious and diffi-cult to use in comparative analyses covering numbers of cases.

The Epistemology and Politics of Reconstruction

If the ontology of policymaking is characterized by temporal, organiza-tional, and political complexity and ambiguity, analysts and other observ-ers are bound to disagree about the question how it can best be under-stood.[17] Identifying agents in shaping the course and outcomes of the pol-icy process and putting them into an alleged causal chain can be done in different ways, resulting in different explanations of the events.

In the context of policy episodes whose outcomes are controversial, and where in fact many people regard the policy as a failure, the analyti-cal choices made in reconstructing events and identifying agents are bound to have manifest political implications. As mentioned above, the forward-mapping and backward-mapping approaches tend to frame agents and choices in different ways. In the highly charged context of attempts to identify the causes of fiascoes, these different modes of recon-structing the sequence of policy events can prove important tools for pushing blame down (forward mapping) or up (backward mapping) the machinery of government. Forward mapping and top-down analysis is more likely to result in criticism of the process of converting general objectives and decisions into concrete programs and actions – the domain of executive officials, field agencies or bureaus, and operators or street-level bureaucrats. Backward mapping and bottom-up analysis is more likely to be sympathetic to the lower levels of the policmaking machinery, highlighting as it does the constraints on their actions by circumstances not of their own making and decisions taken by higher-ups.

Hence we encounter another political dimension of analyzing contro-versial policy episodes: not only the choice of standards for evaluating policy outcomes but also of the choice of which "process-tracing" meth-odology to use for reconstruction and explanation.[18] This choice and its consequences for the substance of the analysis of agents (the second layer of meaning-making) and causes (the third) tends to have an important impact on how the observer or analyst deals with the problem of allocat-ing responsibilities and attributing blame for what happened, the fourth and politically crucial aspect of constructing fiascoes. In chapter 6, these politics of fiasco analysis will be discussed in greater detail. But before we get there, we first need to reconsider the matter of agency in policy fail-ure somewhat more closely.

Notes

1 Quoted in M.W. McCall and R.E. Kaplan, *Whatever it takes: Decision makers at work*, Englewood Cliffs: Prentice Hall 1985, p. X.

2 See for a comparison: B.D. Jacobs, P. 't Hart, Disaster at Hillsborough Stadium: a comparative analysis, in: D. Parker, J. Handmer (eds.), *Hazard management and emergency planning: Perspectives on Britain*, London: James & James 1990: chapter 10.

3 The latter research strategy is imperative in many of the critical power studies, that focus on the power to keep legitimate stakeholders from penetrating into the decisional arenas and to enforce "non decisions", and on the even more insidious power of preventing people to realize that their interests are negatively affected by certain courses of action preferred by other people. See P. Bachrach and M.S. Baratz, *Power and poverty*, New York: Oxford UP 1970 and S. Lukes, *Power: A radical view*, London: MacMillan 1974.

4 Compare: D. F. Thompson, *Political ethics and public office*, Cambridge, Mass.: Harvard UP, 1987.

5 B.E. Abrahamson, *Bureaucracy or participation*, London: Sage 1977, p. 104 paraphrasing H. Simon's, *Administrative behavior*, New York: Free Press 1976.

6 Studies of complex decision processes show that in many cases, major policy decisions take many years before even reaching the implementation stage. See, for example, D. Hickson et al., *Top decisions*, Oxford: Blackwell 1986; J. Pool, *Sturing van strategische besluitvorming: Mogelijkheden en grenzen* [Steering strategic decisions: possibilities and limitations], Amsterdam: VU publishers 1990.

7 See H. Heclo, *A government of strangers*, Washington: Brookings Institution 1977; J. March and J.P. Olsen, *Rediscovering institutions*, New York: Free Press 1989.

8 See: M.A.P. Bovens, *The quest for responsibility: Accountability and citizenship in complex organizations*, Cambridge: Cambridge UP (forthcoming 1996).

9 J. Leigland, R. Lamb, WPPSS: *Who is to blame for the WPPSS disaster*, Cambridge: Ballinger 1986.

10 Leigland and Lamb forego any attempt at such a form of analysis. They do not depart from any set of theoretical concepts or hypotheses about the causes of such large-scale project failures. Instead, they work inductively and map out the actors and factors in terms of a number of concentric rings of power, influence and responsibility. They emphasize the variety of players that shaped the course of events, and suggest that the actions of all these players were important contributing, if not necessary, causes for the fiasco. In the analytical trade-off between historical and contextual accuracy versus theoretical elegance and parsimony presented by the organizational complexity of the phenomenon under study, Leigland and Lamb have made a clear if implicit choice for the former. This choice comes at a price: while their method certainly matches the positivist requirement of requisite variety, it does not result in any general "explanation" or development of deductive theory and empirical propositions. Nor does it offer a clear and coherent normative framework that can be used for fiasco analysis in general.

11 See R.T. Gabriel, *Military incompetence*, New York: Hill and Wang 1985, pp. 110 ff.

12 B.A. Turner, *Man-made disaster*, London: Wykeham 1978; W.A. Wagenaar, *De oorzaken van onmogelijke ongelukken* [The causes of impossible accidents], Deventer: Van Loghem Slaterus 1987; J. Reason, *Human error*, Manchester: Manchester UP 1990.

13 See, for example, Jacobs and 't Hart (1991), *op. cit.* ; M. Hertogh, The King's Cross station fire, Paper Crisis Case Inventory Project, Crisis Research Team, Leiden University 1991.

14 This methodology is explained by R.F. Elmore, Backward mapping: Implementation research and policy decisions, in: W. Williams (ed.), *Studying implementation*, Chatham: Chatham House 1982.

15 For a similar line of argument, see the Rogers commission's report on the accident with the space shuttle Challenger. See *Report to the President by the Presidential Commission on the Space Shuttle Challenger Accident*, Washington: Government Printing Office 1986, notably chapters 4–6.

16 An interesting question then becomes which analyst picks what chain and for what reasons.

17 If one accepts this proposition, the epistemology of positivism adhered to by the majority of policy analysts becomes problematic, indeed untenable. See M.E. Hawkesworth, *Theoretical issues in policy analysis*, Albany: State University of New York Press 1988 for a cogent critique. See also B. Jennings, Interpretive social science and policy analysis, in: D. Callahan, B. Jennings (eds.), *Ethics, the social sciences, and policy analysis*, New York: Plenum Press 1983, pp. 3–35. The issue will resurface in chapter 5.

18 See M. Scriven, Maximizing the power of causal investigation: The modus operandi method, in: G.V. Glass (ed.), *Evaluation studies review annual*, 1, 1976, Beverly Hills: Sage, pp. 120–139.

CHAPTER 4

Identifying Agents: Misfortune or Mismanagement?

[A]ll agree that policymakers are not to be held responsible for outcomes outside their power to control. The trouble is that the impossible and the inevitable do not come prelabeled in our social world.

Robert Goodin[1]

1   Folly or Fate?

When "policy fiascoes" are publicly exposed and investigated, two typical reactions can be found. Many external observers, such as journalists, oppositional leaders and academicians, show a tendency to stress the role of individual and organizational errors and weaknesses in the making of a fiasco. They often take an implicit neo-rationalist stance as their critique often implies the assumption that the ways of the world can in principle be fully known and controlled by enlightened minds. Put in the context of a particular policy fiasco, this assumption leads these critics usually to conclude that the disastrous outcomes could easily have been avoided if only the main protagonists had not been so ignorant, stubborn, or otherwise deficient.

One representative of this first category of reactions to policy fiascoes is the historian Barbara Tuchman. As argued in chapter 1, Tuchman's *March of Folly* is a clear example of a wisdom after the event bias. However, it also exemplifies another bias which can often be found in intellectual comments on political and administrative processes. The book is a typical representation of a rationalistic, problem-solving focus on policymaking. Quite characteristically, in denouncing the actual workings of past and present governments Tuchman often compares them to the "beautiful solution" of Plato's Republic in which enlightened intellectuals, the philosopher-rulers, exercise all political and administrative power in a wise and rational way.[2] Unfortunately, it can be doubted whether Platonic intellectuals and academicians will be any better at the art of governance than ordinary professional politicians and bureaucrats. Moreover, Plato's "wonderful vision" might not be just unattainable in real life, it is also incompatible with the very notion of liberal democracy because of its highly technocratic and authoritarian character.[3] Judging democratic policymaking by such technocratic, authoritarian, and unattainable standards, "folly" is virtually an automatic and inevitable verdict. No liberal democracy, by its very nature, can ever live up to these expectations. Taking Plato's Republic as one's model, even if only implicitly, leads to a systematic overestimation of the potential of policymaking and of the functional rationality of public administration.

On the other side of the debate stand those who are held accountable for the unfortunate events, the politicians, managers, and administrators. They often show a tendency to blame external circumstances or "bad luck." They have done their utmost, but the cold winds of fate have drifted them on a lee shore. This resembles the fundamental attribution error well-known from cognitive psychology: people tend to ascribe their successes to personal competence and their failures to external contingencies.[4]

A second issue in this second layer of fiasco analysis has to do with the more philosophical debate about voluntarism and determinism in policymaking. To what extent can policy failures be said to have been caused by policy failure? Where, in other words, does misfortune stop and mismanagement begin?

The Concept of Misfortune in Governance

Neo-rationalistic notions of policymaking have been dominant, implicitly or explicitly, in much of the policy analysis literature. The concept of "fate" as an important factor in public affairs has been germane to most of the scholars in the field. A few introductory remarks on terminology are therefore appropriate.

The absence of "fate" in thinking about policymaking is in fact fairly recent. The concept of fate dates back to the ancient notion of *fortuna*, and can in fact be traced throughout the history of Western political, religious, and literary thought up until the Enlightment. Originally a Roman concept, it continued to play a role in the political and military debates after the Roman Empire vanished: "Yet Christian men continued, in one way or another, to be Romans: civic beings, intensely concerned with the events of political history, the civil and military happenings which befell them and of which they from time to time asked God the meaning."[5]

Fortuna is especially prominent in the work of Boethius, a Roman aristocrat in the service of a Gothic king, whose administrative career came to an end when he fell in disgrace, became imprisoned and finally was put to death. With Boethius – and for obvious reasons given his career – *fortuna* has a fatalistic flavor. In his major work, written during his imprisonment and characteristically called *De Consolatione*, *fortuna* is presented as the circumstantial insecurity of political life: "Her symbol is the wheel, by which men are raised to power and fame and then suddenly cast down by changes they cannot predict or control."[6]

In Roman and medieval sources a distinction often is made between *fortuna* and *occasio*, between the inaccessible and insecure rulings of fate on the one hand and the occasional auspicious moments which are granted man on the other – the "windows of opportunity" as they have been called in the modern policymaking literature.[7] Only much later, from the early renaissance onwards, the two concepts amalgamated and *fortuna* also came to be seen as chance, as a contingency to be accommodated and sometimes even commanded. Especially in Machiavelli's writings *fortuna* "represents not a source of ready-made blessings or ineluctable afflictions, but rather a profusion of challenges. As such, Fortune resembles Occasion herself."[8] Machiavelli saw policy outcomes as determined both by political skills and fate – in his terms by *virtù* and *fortuna*:

> I am not unaware that many have thought, and many still think, that the affairs of this world are so ruled by fortune and by God that the ability of men cannot control them. Rather, they think that we have no remedy at all; and therefore it could be concluded that it is useless to sweat much over things, but let them be governed by fate.... Nevertheless, so as not to eliminate human freedom, I am disposed to hold that fortune is the arbiter of half of our actions, but that it lets us control roughly the other half.[9]

We nevertheless prefer to stick to the Roman subtleties and distinguish between *fortuna, occasio and virtù*.[10] With respect to contemporary policymaking, a similar distinction has been made by Dror, who views the future as determined by a variable mix of necessity, chance, and choice.[11] Therefore, in this chapter, "fortune" stands for the occurrence of decisive events, factors, and situations which the main actor is not able, and cannot reasonably be expected, to control. "Control" is understood broadly here, also including anticipation. Fortune thus signifies the unpredictable and uncontrollable events in life. Understood as "fate" or "necessity," fortune has two faces: an ugly one, which is misfortune or bad luck and a pleasant one, which is good luck.

With respect to fate, man, as a private person, politician, or manager, is basically passive. Misfortune and good luck befall a person, regardless of his or her efforts or intentions. *Occasio* on the other hand stands for "chance" or "providence," for the opportunities that present themselves to

those who actively seek them. The bold and the bright – those who poss-
es *virtù* – often manage to bend the course of events a bit in their direction, if only for some time. Here of course we shall be interested primarily in how people construct the ugly face of fortune: to what extent do they
attribute policy failures to plain bad luck, and on what basis? Good luck
and the proverbial "windows of opportunity" will be less important for
our present purposes. However, since fortune is Janus-faced, a description of the discourse about misfortune will, to a certain extent, also give
us a picture of how its counterpart, good luck, is portrayed.

The Modern Faces of Misfortune

How might misfortune manifest itself in the daily lives of contemporary
public policymakers? Given the discussion above, it seems reasonable to
assume that misfortunes are usually conceptualized as negative contingencies that impinge upon a particular policy or project. To qualify as a
misfortune, these setbacks tend to be described in terms of two basic
properties. They should first of all be necessary conditions for the failure
of the policy or project in question. Occasional mishaps that do not fundamentally change the outcomes of a policy are not relevant for us here.
Secondly, these crucial setbacks should, at the time key policy decisions
were made, not be foreseeable or controllable.

Let us formalize this line of argument a little more. The variables of
foreseeability and controllability can be taken as the basis for a typology
of claims about misfortune, rendering three categories of policy situations
where misfortune may be operative and one category in which mismanagement can be said to be the sole cause of policy failures. These four
boxes are displayed in figure 1. Now let us move from abstract deduction
towards practical experiences. What kinds of policy arguments fit the
table's categories? In other words, what faces might misfortune take in
analyses of policy failures? We will give general prototypes and examples
of each category.

Figure 1 A typology of misfortunes in governance

Type I:	Type II:
foreseeable/controllable	foreseeable/uncontrollable
contingencies	contingencies
Type III:	Type IV:
unforeseeable	unforeseeable/uncontrollable
contingencies	contingencies

Type I: Foreseeable and Controllable Contingencies

This box, of course, is empty when it comes to the faces of misfortune. Failure in these cases could, in principle, be attributed to mismanagement or policy errors. There are many situations in which the outcomes of policies or projects can be said to depend almost completely on the mobilization of sufficient resources, expertise, and technology. Many government operations can be planned precisely and many costs and benefits can be projected with reasonable accuracy. Fortune need not play a major role when an organization deals with a problem that can be conceptualized fully, with ready-made and tested policy options and technologies are available.[12] The importance of fortune in policymaking also decreases when the environment of a particular project or policy is stable, uniform, or otherwise predictable and controllable. In those cases, most observers will argue that failure depends to a large extent on the lack of policymaking skills, management capacities, and other resources that should have been available.

Type II: Foreseeable but Uncontrollable Contingencies

The argument changes, however, when claims are made that in the given situation one or more of the crucial parameters for success was clearly beyond the control of the policymakers, even though their occurence might very well be foreseeable at the time the policy or project was decided upon. General types of these arguments might be:

- *The risks that come true argument:* Here it is claimed that policymakers were dealing with a situation in which the risks of a certain policy were knowable, calculated as carefully as possible, and ultimately discounted, but materialized nonetheless. It appears there are many policy contingencies that can be foreseen or even calculated, but never completely eliminated. For example, estimates of the future development of international air traffic were a key factor in bringing about, and generating support for, the airport expansion plans in both Paris and London discussed in chapter 1. When the initial planning began on both projects, these estimates projected a steep rise in passenger traffic, and therefore in the number of flights the airports were required to handle. Adversity struck when planning, and in Paris also construction, was underway. The October 1973 war in the Middle East and the subsequent use of the oil weapon by the OPEC countries eventually resulted in a sharp and apparently lasting rise in fuel prices. This helped to bring about a major economic recession in the Western world, which in turn slowed down severely the growth of internation-

al trade and mobility of goods and people, hence invalidating the original estimates supporting the construction plans in Paris and London.
Surely "fuel prices" and "international economic developments" are
among the foreseeable contingency factors in air traffic estimates, but
the specific turn they would take over the multi-year planning period
required in airport construction, was difficult to predict let alone control for the airport planners or even for the national governments
involved.

• *The tragic choice argument:* Here the policy situation is represented as
  one in which a choice had to be made, but in which the situation was
  framed in such a manner that all of the options realistically available
  would unavoidably, and predictably, have resulted in serious social,
  economic, or normative damage.[13] These catch–22 arguments of
  "damned if you do, damned if you don't" are not uncommon in policy discourse. One can think of the analysis of painful decisions about
  the distribution of scarce medical resources, such as heart or liver
  transplantations; moral and political dilemmas involved in asylum
  and immigration policies; or the impossibility in many hostage crises
  to reconcile the short-term, personal interests of the families involved
  with the long-term policy commitment of making sure that terrorism
  does not pay.

  To some extent, the cases of the HIV-contaminated blood transfusions that occurred in France and, to a lesser extent, in many other
  countries during the early eighties arguably contain elements of tragic choice. In those first years of the AIDS epidemic no tests were available to scrutinize blood that was used for transfusion, nor were safe
  and tested procedures available to decontaminate blood samples. At
  that time, however, it had already been established scientifically that
  blood and blood products might be an important source of contamina-
  tion. The risk of going on without proper testing was therefore foreseeable, although not precisely defined. Given the fact that blood transfusions were absolutely vital for hemophiliacs and for many forms of
  surgery, a case can be made that health authorities were faced with a
  case of tragic choice until the moment tests were available. In the
  absence of tests and decontamination procedures it was foreseeable,
  but even with a strict scrutiny of blood donors not fully controllable,
  that some patients would become HIV-infected trough transfusions.
  On the other hand, witholding transfusions would also jeopardize the
  life of many patients. The structure of the policy situation changed
  dramatically, and lost its "tragic" quality after feasible and conclusive
  tests had become available. Choices made during this second period
  can be said to have had much more to do with considerations of

opportunity costs and institutional interests than with the resolution of inescapable moral trade offs.[14]

- *The tragedies of the commons argument:* This argument pertains to situations in which a common pool of scarce resources is shared by a fairly large number of players acting on the basis of equity. The classic examples include a well in a dry area, a meadow shared by different sheep farmers, or a lake shared by fishermen. In the absence of any kind of effective norms or central authority, the scarcity of the resource tends to trigger strategic behavior (e.g. overconsumption or overutilization) on the part of the actors that results in a loss or severe depletion of the joint resources, ultimately leaving everybody worse off.[15] These negative outcomes usually do not come as a surprise. In fact, the rate and speed of depletion might very well be calculable when the basic parameters of the situation are clear. However, once the dynamics of individual calculation and freeriding are set into motion, it becomes very difficult and often impossible for any of the individual players – be they individual farmers, corporations, or governments involved in regional or global distribution dilemmas – to prevent the depletion. Particularly in the area of environmental policy, many problem situations have this kind of structure.

  One example includes the control of pollution in large international rivers, such as the Rhine and the Danube. In theory, upstream and downstream states have a joint interest in safeguarding the quality of the river's waters by limiting pollutant discharges, but in practice upstream states will tend to let their industrial interests prevail, since in the short run they face few of the negative consequences of pollution. While the states involved engage in protracted negotiations, pollution worsens. Moreover, when agreements to reduce discharges are finally reached, effective means for inducing and monitoring compliance tend to be lacking, since states are reluctant to relinquish part of their sovereignty to international oversight bodies and courts. The net result, at least for the downstream countries, is that they are faced with serious environmental damage that is perfectly foreseeable but, for them, virtually uncontrollable.[16]

- *The dense policy space argument:* This argument focuses on unintended consequences arising during policy implementation. In the course of the implementation process, big gaps may develop between policymakers' intentions and the actual outcomes of policies or programs. These gaps can be caused by different factors, which are predictable in general terms but also extremely difficult to grasp in terms of causes and effects. This makes it virtually impossible to deliberately anticipate or contain their impact.[17] For example, target groups' reactions to the program may fail to meet the predictions, either because they react more or less strongly than expected, or because their reactions are qualitatively different from what had been anticipated. Also, people not targeted by the program may react to it nevertheless, making its implementation more elaborate, complex, and probably more costly than planned for. Thirdly, the particular policy instruments used may generate their own momentum and unintended effects.[18]

On the whole, it is becoming increasingly likely nowadays that setbacks such as those mentioned above occur. This is because new policies or programs are not initiated in a policy vacuum. On the contrary, they are part of an ongoing sequence of attempts to solve social problems by different forms of government intervention. Consequently new programs tend to interact with other policy initiatives developed previously to deal with the same problem or target group differently, or to deal with different but related problems or target groups. Big gaps between intentions and outcomes, even if caused by this complex configuration of at least partly uncontrollable factors, almost automatically lead observers to criticize the way in which a policy was designed and implemented. An example of this is American employment policy, as discussed in chapter 2.

Type III: Controllable but Unforeseeable Contingencies

The third category comprises of arguments that emphasize that the situation at the time the policy or project was decided upon, was such that no reasonable person could have foreseen the specific occurrence, form, or extent of negative circumstances that were to strongly influence the outcomes of the policy. Although these negative factors might not have been altogether uncontrollable, effective mitigation of their negative impact could only have been achieved had adequate foreknowledge been available. Lacking this, control was severely impaired. The following claims fit this category:

- *The erratic developments and constraints argument:* This includes claims that no reasonable person could have foreseen or anticipated that a major condition for the success of a policy or project suddenly or gradually might be compromised or transformed during its implementation.

    An example is presented by the Dutch Deltaproject. After a major flood disaster claimed 1800 lives and created severe disruption in the southwestern part of the Netherlands in the early fifties, an ambitious and comprehensive plan was developed to prevent the recurrence of such a catastrophe. It took thirty years and billions of dollars to build an almost nationwide system of dams, dykes, and locks that would protect the country from future sea floods. It was guaranteed to offer protection even against springtides that would statistically arise only once in every four thousand years. Not long after completion of the project in the eighties, new research suggested that the expected rise of the sea level due to the greenhouse effect might make it necessary to engage in far more extensive waterworks, rendering most of the previous structures obsolete.[19]

- *The erratic consequences argument:* Here the proposition is that in the given situation, no reasonable person could have foreseen or anticipated the negative effects of products used or measures taken. Take for example the recommendation in the sixties to use asbestos to insulate buildings and equipment. It was cheap and reliable. Not long afterwards research became available which suggested asbestos to be highly carcinogenic. Subsequently, asbestos had to be removed from many houses, office buildings, and trains through elaborate and very costly procedures.

  In a recent Dutch case, the dividing line between misfortune and mismanagement when dealing with "erratic" consequences has been specifically set by law. Starting in the late seventies, the issue of polluted soil was pushed on the political and judicial agendas by a number of incidents where parts of completely new suburbs had to be demolished because the soil contained highly toxic substances. Subsequent investigation of old dumping grounds and industrial estates uncovered that hundreds of areas, many since used for housing and public spaces, were heavily polluted. The total cost of the required clean-up operations was estimated to run into hundreds of millions of dollars. As a result, the question of responsibility and liability became pivotal. Recently, the matter was settled by the Dutch Supreme Court which ruled that the perpetrators of all pollution damage that had occurred after 1975 were fully liable. At that time, the Court argued, ample information about the risks to the environment and to public health of dumping or burying unprocessed toxic substances had become available and disseminated. Therefore one might reasonably have expected proper care and caution on the part of individuals, companies, and civil authorities dealing with these substances. Before that time, however, the Court's decision implied, this was not the case. Damages caused by substances disposed of before 1975 were effectively accepted by the Court as having been the product of misfortune, for which no one could justifiably be held responsible.[20]

Type IV: Unforeseeable and Uncontrollable Circumstances

In theoretical terms, this is the most important or "pure" category of misfortune claims, encompassing situations in which the occurrence of certain key contingenies crucial for the success or failure of a policy or project is argued to have been both unforeseeable and beyond the control of
policymakers. Prototypical claims in this category are:

- *The acts of God argument:* The classical tragedies by Sophocles,
  Aeschylus or even Shakespeare, were caused, and eventually solved,
  by some god or demigod – the deus ex machina. The misfortunes
  which the gods brought upon the mortals whom they wanted to test
  or punish, usually materialized in the form of natural adversities:
  unfavorable winds, long droughts, floods, earthquakes, storms, and
  epidemics. Many contemporary policymakers may not reckon with
  the gods anymore, but the concept of act of God remains an important
  policy excuse. Adversities stemming from nature's capriciousness can
  still be a major factor in the making of modern fiascoes as well as disasters. Think of the rise of new, as yet incurable, diseases such as
  AIDS, hurricanes, an earthquake along the San Andreas fault, a light-
  ning strike in a power supply station, or weather-induced crop failures
  in the American Midwest or the Ukraine. Some of these spells of
  nature, which can neither be predicted exactly nor controlled by man,
  can nullify the effects of any policy, however well-conceived.[21]

  This argument might apply to case of the eruption of the
  Pinatubo volcano in the Philippines in 1991. It virtually destroyed
  Clark Air Force Base, the most important U.S. military stronghold in
  the region. This event seriously compromised long-term American
  geopolitical objectives in the area, since it gave the Philippine government momentum in the negotiations about the reduction of the U.S.
  military presence in the Philippines.

- *The negative invisible hand argument:* C. Wright Mills once observed that
  to say that an historical event is caused by fate is to say that it is the
  summary and unintended result of innumerable decisions by innumerable men.[22] In other words, "modern" fate is not limited to the
  whims of demigods or the spells of nature. Modern man also has to
  reckon with many man-made misfortunes. In modern life many situations occur in which none of the individual actors can control the crucial parameters for their actions even though these parameters are
  man-made. These situations often take the form of what one might
  label as negative invisible hand phenomena. The clearest examples of
  these are stock market crashes and many other macro-economic fluc-

tuations, bank runs, and escape panics.[23] Some would also like to include revolutions in this category.[24]

These are modern misfortunes that clearly befall policymakers, be they single individuals or organizations, in the sense that they cannot break away from or control them. They are the result of collective behavior on a local, global, or transnational scale. Likewise, the success or failure of social-economic policies of small and middle-sized nations with open economies strongly depend upon factors that cannot be controlled or predicted by national politicians – if at all. Think of a sudden trade deficit due to a devaluation of the American dollar; the impact of international events such as the demise of Communism and the Gulf War; or of the devastating effects on employment policies of a world-wide recession triggered by a major stock market crash the size of "Black Monday" in October 1987; or the plight of national governments and monetary authorities facing a contagious and worldwide speculation with their currencies, as happened during the European monetary crisis of 1992–93.

- *The force majeure argument:* This argument hinges on the presumption that the success or failure of a particular project or policy may sometimes depend to a great extent upon the personal drive and charisma of key figures within the political or bureaucratic arena. When these crucial figures vanish from the scene, or become less effective, for example due to a sudden change in the configuration of power, illnesses, elections, or other "superior forces," this supposedly makes a crucial difference. Machiavelli provides us with a fine example of this type of reasoning. He develops a two-tiered explanation for the sudden fall from power of Caesare Borgia, the bastard son of Pope Alexander and ruler of Florence. First of all, Borgia fell seriously ill during a crucial military campaign and could no longer command his troops. In addition it so happened that shortly before this event his father had died and a new pope had been elected who withdrew the Roman support for Florence. The combination of both misfortunes led to Borgia's fall from power. Similar observations can be made in modern political and administrative life.[25] Often policies or projects are "killed" or slowly fade away after a key supporter has been replaced after elections, illness, following promotion, or in the course of a reorganization.

For many individual policymakers, misfortune takes the face of an inexperienced, weak, or malevolent superior. For example, according to the Agranat commision investigating the Israeli October 1973 fiasco, the Vice-Chief of Staff of the Israeli Defense Forces Israel Tal was one of the few among the Israeli political and military elites who accurately assessed the danger of possible combined Syrian and Egyptian attack on Israel. Yet his cautionary observations were overruled by his superiors, Chief of Staff Elazar and Minister of Defense Dayan.[26] Similarly, several lower-level officers and intelligence experts who issued critical reports about Israeli defense preparedness in the face of the mounting Arab threat, found themselves rebuked and their reports suppressed by their superiors who firmy believed in the strategic superiority and invincibility of the Israeli forces.

What goes for individuals goes for entire organizations as well. For them, misfortune may manifest itself as a lack of power or influence in the political arena. The case of the Brussels fire brigade is perhaps illustrative. It was the sole agency involved in the preparation of the Liverpool-Juventus match in the Heysel stadium that developed and acted upon a realistic, worst-case type of estimation of the risks involved (see chapter 3). Yet its status within the interagency network operating in the public order and safety domain in Brussels was so low that it was not even invited to the joint planning sessions, let alone that it could persuade other agencies to adopt its risk assessment and upgrade their prevention and preparedness. Although its own contingency planning proved very helpful during the fateful night, the fire brigade was nevertheless forced to confront a major disaster which it had seen coming but had been unable to prevent.[27]

Identifying Misfortune: Analytical Complexity

Although useful heuristically, the neat, static symmetry suggested by the typology of figure 1 may easily obscure the complexities involved in discussing the nature and role of misfortune in contemporary public policy-making. This can be seen in two ways. First of all, misfortune is not a "real," digital phenomenon, which is either present or absent. The extent to which, in a specific historical case, misfortune is said to have affected the course and outcomes of the policy process, is always a matter of judgment. All the defining properties of misfortune – its sine qua non importance on the policy process, its unforeseeability, and its uncontrollability – are a matter of degree, argumentation, debate, and most likely controversy.

For example, in the case of the RSV affair involving the loss of hundreds of millions of guilders in Dutch government subsidies poored into a shipbuilding conglomerate that went under, there is genuine ambiguity when it comes to the assessment of the question "folly or fate?" On the one hand, the case seems to fit our type II category, since a major cause of the fiasco was the global economic recession during the late seventies.

This caused the world market for large tankers and coasters to collapse at the very moment the Dutch industry was being reorganized. The possibility of a worldwide recession is obviously a factor which can and should be incorporated in industrial policymaking, but it cannot be controlled. A larger part of the ailing Dutch shipbuilding industry might have been saved if the recession had come at another time and in another form.

On the other hand, however, detailed study of the case evidence suggests that the policymakers did receive a series of thorough and consistent warnings about the road they were taking. These focused on the blank check they were handing out to RSV's management. In fact, it appears that to a considerable extent, the policy of continuing to subsidize the fledgling industrial giant was motivated by political considerations on the part of subsequent governments (and, as discussed in chapter 2, key members of parliament). To put it bluntly: it had been a matter of money for jobs, albeit only short-term jobs. Hence at least some of the key policymakers seem to have been fully aware that RSV's long-term prospects were gloomy and getting worse, and were willing to accept this. Looked at the case from this perspective, political "risk discounting" seems to have been as much a contributing cause as the uncontrollable forces of the global economy.

In another example, the military fiasco of Dutch defense preparedness against the German surprise invasion of May 1940, the issue of misfortune or mismanagement is equally ambiguous. Again, from one angle, this looks like a classic example of misfortune in governance: the leaders of a small, peaceful, and neutral nation were maneuvered into a no-win situation by the major powers of the day. Lebow might view the Dutch case as a "spinoff crisis," an instance whereby a third country is drawn into a conflict or war for the sole reason of its geographic position or strategic significance.[28] And indeed, for the De Geer cabinet which took office in August 1939 just a few days before the outbreak of the war in Poland, the options were extremely limited. Holland could not even begin to put up a credible deterrent against a possible German invasion, given Germany's overwhelming military superiority. Alternatively, seeking alliance with England and France at this stage of the conflict would give Hitler a clear casus belli, and might well result in an instant German invasion. Yet the final course of action open to the Dutch – continuing to emphasize neutrality – was equally problematic, since they knew German war plans for the Western front had changed dramatically since 1914, when Holland was left uninvolved.

Viewed in this way, the situation was one of tragic choice and the De Geer cabinet can only be blamed for continuing to entertain the illusion that neutrality was a viable option, and not being more decisive in upgrading its military preparations and psychologically preparing the country for war. Viewed from a broader historical perspective and taking a somewhat different level of analysis, however, the voluntaristic elements of the fiasco come to the fore more clearly. In the early thirties, Holland's options were much more open. It could have sought alliance then. It could have reassessed its foreign policy and defense planning. It could have upgraded its military potential. None of these options were seriously pursued, depriving future governments and military leaders of their room to maneuver in an increasingly ominous international environment. The tragic choice situation of 1939–1940 was, therefore, to a considerable extent self-generated.

Most of the other prototypes of misfortune arguments are equally equivocal. Upon closer inspection or by using a different level of analysis, it is often debatable to what extent the crucial paramaters were indeed uncontrollable and unforseeable. Hence misfortune is not a digital phenomenon.

Secondly, misfortune is also not static. The parameters that determine the division between mismanagement and misfortune are not fixed entities. They are subject to change. Stable and transparent environments can become turbulent or opaque. Technology and human interaction can become so complex that their implications move beyond the average policymaker's grasp. New problems, such as the rise of AIDS, can suddenly transform the nature and complexity of public health policymaking.[29] But the parameters can also change for the better. The skills and competences in a particular field can improve and bring a policy issue within the reach of professional computation or even routinization. Research and experiments can increase our knowledge about the environment; reflection can improve our understanding of complicated problems; precautionary procedures and safety valves can reduce the impact of the unpredictable.[30] For example, tragedies of the commons can be overcome by the development of institutions for common pool resource management.[31] And societal vulnerability to erratic developments and consequences is partly a function of the quality of existing early warning systems and contingency plans. Even natural disasters are no longer always viewed as inevitable, and immutable acts of God. Nowadays, a major earthquake in California causes far fewer casualties than even a medium-sized quake in Mexico City or Yerevan – the crucial difference being the quality of dwellings, disaster contingency planning and emergency responses.

In some eras and domains of public policymaking, the role of fortune seems to have been more or less neutralized. In fact, the history of applied policy analysis and public management theory can, in general, be interpreted as a constant struggle to gain ground upon fortune, hence as a constant push to expand box 1 (see figure 1) at the expense of all the others.[32]

This development had at least one important effect relevant to our concerns here: the more this push has come to be regarded as having been successful in a particular society, the lower this society's tolerance for claims that negative policy outcomes are due to the impact of misfortune. Despite this development, arguments will always be made that there will remain a certain class of situations less amenable to rationalization in this optimistic Platonic spirit. Hence, there is still a plausible case to be made for misfortune as agent of failure. The argument made to support this claim runs roughly as follows:

Despite the impressive advances in the technology of public policy-making, there will always be so-called "wicked problems." These are problems that can not be formulated precisely, that have no true-or-false answers, that solicit widespread disagreement among stakeholders, and for which solutions can not be tested under conditions of *ceteris paribus* but have to be experienced in practice. Wicked problems and policies proposed to deal with them will continue to generate series of unpredictable and unprecedented consequences over an extended period of time.[33] Dealing with them also tends to produce a whole class of "impossible jobs" in government. In these projects and positions, public managers have to deal with irresponsible or intractable clients who are competing with other, more legitimate clients for public resources; at the same time there is little public confidence in their professional authority; and the managers lack guidance from strong and well-established policy myths that provide a basis for a degree of policy continuity.[34]

Making policy in these hard cases, the argument continues, resembles what Dror has labelled "fuzzy gambling."[35] Dror stresses the fact that policymaking in general, and in particular under conditions of adversity, is nothing but a "choice between bundles of ill-defined and ill-definable uncertainties and ignorances, with the aim of influencing the probability of alternative possible futures."[36] When dealing with wicked problems, policies often are mere gambles, for outcomes cannot be predicted correctly, nor can risks be calculated in a precise way. And, which is even worse, many of these gambles are very fuzzy since also the very forms of the alternative futures and the dynamics of change are unknown and often unknowable.

This line of argument does not always go down well with policymakers and policy analysts who were taught to think and act as if the world was malleable. In this respect, Dror observes that:

> However obvious in retrospect and despite full recognition of this inescapable feature by many insightful practitioners (e.g., Bismarck) and thinkers (e.g., Machiavelli and Clausewitz), still the statement that statecraft involves a lot of fuzzy gambling is very disturbing and even shocking. This seems to be espe-

cially pronounced in modern cultures, for a variety of reasons including popular misunderstanding of the nature of scientific knowledge, widespread optimism of human control over their fate, and widespread belief in simplistic visions of "progress". The most fundamental conclusion of the proposed perspective, and also one of the most disturbing to present Western Zeitgeist, is a somewhat tragic feeling mingling with hopes accompanying choice. However much we try to do our best, the outcomes of major decisions are largely shaped by variables outside our control, including change.[37]

Our brief survey of the complexities involved in identifying misfortune, suggests that its scope and impact are highly influenced by the specific social, economic, and political context in which policies are made and arguments about misfortune are advanced. There is no straight line from misfortune to fiasco, nor from mismanagement to fiasco. Much, some would say everything, depends on societal predispositions to accept the idea that there are limitations to public policymaking as a comprehensive form of social control.

Conclusion: The Realm of Misfortune as a Social Construction

Claims about misfortune will continue to play an important role in debates about controversial policy episodes. At the same time, it becomes apparent that the salience of misfortune, and the validity of misfortune claims, will decrease when policy issues are manifestedly moving from the realm of "wicked problems," "impossible jobs," and "fuzzy gambling" into the domain of human and organizational control, routinized technology, and intelligent public decision making. Gaining ground upon fortune is, however, a gradual and seldom an irreversible process. Sometimes policymakers have to accept that they are, temporarily or more fundamentally, losing rather than gaining control. This implies that there is no stable and universal dividing line between misfortune and mismanagement. The line shifts in part as technology develops, knowledge expands, and situations change, but also when cultural and political norms about the scope of virtue in public policymaking evolve.

Value judgments will always be necessary in identifying agents of policy failure. These will take different forms. They can be epistemological (what could policymakers have known?), technical (what was feasible?) or moral (what was reasonable?). They can depend on the level of analysis (what is unforeseeable or uncontrollable for individual actors might be within the realm of the organization as a whole) and they depend upon the standards for scrutiny and thoroughness that are applied. Judgments about which agents determine the course and outcomes of public policymaking can and will not be made in a void. Politics, ideology, and culture all play a major role in the identification and evaluation of environmental contingencies as misfortunes. The very act of identifying what is controllable by government, and therefore the notion of misfortune itself, is inherently normative and imbued with ideological predispositions. Consequently, there is no ultimate, in the sense of objective, answer to the question where mismanagement stops and misfortune begins.

This can be illustrated by the different evaluations of Great Hunger in Ireland in the nineteenth century, as discussed by Shklar.[38] To most of the English rulers this was a tragic event, given their firm beliefs that the system of landholding was sacred and that government should not interfere in the economy. From their libertarian point of view the famine was an economic necessity which could not and should not be remedied by public policy. For Shklar on the other hand, and for many of the descendants of the Irish victims, the Great Hunger "is as good an example as any of the uses of ideology in treating passive injustice as misfortune by imposing a sense of tragic inevitability upon events that are in fact entirely amendable to purposive human alteration."[39] Interestingly though, Shklar also makes it clear that the Irish peasants themselves, being deeply devout, in their turn also "'tended to look upon their suffering as a divine visitation and punishment."[40]

This points to an unmistakable cultural and ideological element in the labelling and appreciation of policy failures. Misfortunes are also, and probably foremost, collective constructions. Cultural frames determine whether and which contingencies are construed as fate. The terminoloy and logic of Douglas and Wildavsky's cultural theory (see chapter 2) can be helpful here. For fatalists such as the Irish peasants, fortune will be the main force in life and little can be done to tame her. Hierarchs such as Tuchman, on the other hand, assume that the world is knowable and predictable. For them uncertainty ought to be not more than provisional, a matter for further research and to be tamed by creative problem solving and gradual refinement of technology and decision rules. In the end misfortune is nothing but "wooden-headedness" or the misapplication of proper procedures.

In more individualistic cultures uncertainty is valued much more positively. Knowledge is always provisional since the free exchange of ideas will often serve to discredit traditional beliefs and obsolete practices. Individualists will tend to focus on the bright side of uncertainty and uncontrollability – on windows of opportunity and serendipity. They will emphasize the aspect of choice and chance. Misfortune is a personal problem, to be treated discretely. Wildavksy's argument, in *Searching for Safety*, for a more resilience-based as opposed to a predominantly anticipatory approach to dealing with risky technologies, is grounded in such an individualist orientation.[41]

In a cultural setting that is more inclined towards egalitarianism, condemnation prevails. Misfortunes are injustices that are to be remedied, preferably by the government. Shklar, for example, typically argues along egalitarian lines:

> We ought to direct our sense of injustice less towards the search for possible initiators and the immediate causes of disasters than towards those who do nothing to prevent them or to help the victims.... Our first suspicions should be turned toward governmental and semi-public agencies because it is not unlikely that they could have done more in the past and should do more in the future to ensure our safety.[42]

What matters here are not the specific cultural archetypes. Nor does it matter whether there are four or five or ten different cultural configurations. What is important is the fact that what counts as misfortune is highly dependent on the kind of cultural frame used to interpret events.

This completes our discussion of the second layer of fiasco analysis, which was about identifying the key agents of failure in complex and controversial policy episodes. The analysis of chapters three and four has made it clear that inevitably, the process by which this happens is as much "political" as it is "analytical." Identifying agents requires observers and analysts to explicitize their methodology of dissecting policy processes, and to develop procedures for locating actors and forces in complex organisational settings and protracted policy episodes. It also forces them to consider their own norms and standards about what they regard as the feasible limits of institutional efforts to control social life. This is likely to be no different for the third tier in analyzing fiascoes: developing explanations about why those who have come to be identified as the key policymakers and agencies acted as they did. In chapter five, we will see that explicitizing assumptions has not been a recurrent features of theories of policy failure. This is why the bulk of that chapter will be devoted to developing our own reconstruction of these assumptions, and to showing how different philosophies of policymaking tend to produce divergent explanations of failure.

Notes

1 R.E. Goodin, *Political theory and public policy*, Chicago: University of Chicago Press 1982, p. 126.
2 See for example, Tuchman, *The march of folly: From Troy to Vietnam*, London:

Cardinal/Sphere Books 1990 (1 ed. 1984), p. 6 and p. 479; but also pp. 477 and 481.

3 Compare K. Popper, *The open society and its enemies, part I* London: Routledge 1948.

4 See the work of social and cognitive psychologists on the attribution process, in particular on the fundamental attribution error, R. Nisbett and L. Ross, *Human inference: Strategies and shortcomings of social judgment*, Englewood Cliffs: Prentice Hall 1980; P.E. Tetlock, Accountability: The neglected social context of judgment and choice, in: B.M. Staw and L. Cummings (eds.), *Research in organizational behavior*, vol 11, Greenwich: JAI Press 1985.

5 J.G.A. Pocock, *The Machiavellian moment: Florentine political thought and the Atlantic republican tradition*, Princeton: Princeton UP 1975, p. 36.

6 Pocock (1975), *op. cit.*, p. 38.

7 See J.W. Kingdon, *Agendas, alternatives and public policies*, Boston: Little, Brown 1984.

8 F. Kiefer, *Fortune and Elizabethan tragedy*, London 1983, p. 203.

9 Machiavelli, *The Prince*, edited by Quentin Skinner and Russel Price, Cambridge: Cambridge UP 1988, pp. 84–85.

10 Similar distinctions can also be found in the edition of Skinner, *op. cit.* (see: Appendix B, Notes on the vocabulary of *The Prince*, pp. 108–109).

11 Y. Dror, Fateful decisions as fuzzy gambles with history, *The Jerusalem Journal of International Relations*, 12, 1990, 1–12.

12 This dichotomy is inspired by C. Perrow, A framework for the comparative analysis of organizations, *American Sociological Review*, 32, 1967, 194–208. Compare also the typology of policy problems in R. Hoppe, A. Peterse, *Handling frozen fire: Political culture and risk management*, Boulder: Westview 1993.

13 G. Calabresi, P. Bobbit, *Tragic choices*, New York: Norton; B. Guy Peters, Tragic choices: Administrative rulemaking and policy choice, in: R.A. Chapman (ed.), *Ethics in public service*, Edinburgh: Edinburgh University Press 1993, pp. 43–57.

14 See especially, A.M. Casteret, *L'affaire du sang*, Paris: Éditions La Découverte 1992; M. Lucas, *Transfusion sanguine et SIDA en 1985: Chronologie des faits et des décisions pour ce qui concerne les hémophiles*, Paris: Inspection Générale des Affaires Sociales 1991; see also C. Perrow, J. Guillèn, *The AIDS disaster*, New Haven: Yale UP 1990.

15 See G. Hardin, The tragedy of the commons, *Science*, 162, 13 december 1968, pp. 1243-1248.

16 P.A. Nollkaemper, *The legal regime for transboundary water pollution: Between discretion and constraint*, Dordrecht: Kluwer 1993.

17 See also S.D. Sieber, *Fatal remedies: The ironies of social intervention*, New York: Plenum Press 1981.

18 All this can of course go either way. Implementation in a dense policy space can also be a source of serendipity.

19 Ironically, but less directly relevant for the judgment about the Deltaplan, the greatest problems of flooding in the Netherlands in recent years have not come from the sea at all. They have been caused by the swelling of the big rivers in the country, caused by continuous and torrential rains in upstream countries like Belgium, France, and Germany.

20 H.R. 24 april 1992, N.J. 1993, 643 and 644 (Van Wijngaarden/Staat; Staat/Akzo Resins).

21 Many of these spells of nature are only predictable in general terms. It is a such foreseeable that crop failures in the Midwest or earthquakes along the St. Andrews fault will occur in the future. But it can, as yet, not be predicted specifically what the exact time and place will be.

22 C. Wright Mills, *The causes of World War III*, 4th ed., New York: Ballantine 1963.

23 See for examples J.S. Coleman, *Foundations of social theory*, Cambridge, Mass.: Belknap of Harvard UP 1990, pp. 197–239.

24 R. Dahrendorf, *The modern social conflict: An essay on the politics of liberty*, London: Weidenfeld and Nicholson 1989, p. 2 says about revolutions: 'To be sure, they are man-

made, but men and women act under conditions which they do not wholly control.'

25 Compare F.L. Shiels, *Preventable disasters: Why governments fail*, Savage: Rowman & Littlefield 1991: p. 106. He considers the declining vigor and health of the Persian Shah as one of the unpreventable aspects of the disastrous outcome of the American policy towards Iran in the late seventies.

26 See, for example, Shiels, (1991), *op. cit.*, pp. 26–28, who also tries to dissect preventable and unpreventable aspects of Israel's 'October Surprise' (see pp. 32–46). See also R.K. Betts, *Surprise attack*, Washington: Brookings 1982 and E. Kam, *Surprise attack: The victim's perspective*, Cambridge, Mass: Harvard UP 1988.

27 P. 't Hart, B. Pijnenburg, *Het Heizeldrama: Rampzalig organiseren en kritieke beslissingen*, Alphen aan den Rijn: Samsom 1988.

28 R.N. Lebow, *Between peace and war: The nature of international crisis*, Baltimore: Johns Hopkins UP 1981, chapters 1 and 2.

29 E.F. Lawlor, When a possible job becomes impossible: Politics, public health, and the management of the AIDS epidemic, in E.C. Hargrove, J. Glidewell (eds.), *Impossible jobs in public management*, Lawrence: Kansas UP 1990, pp. 152–176.

30 Compare the pragmatic strategic approach to handling emergent and risky technologies advocated by J.G. Morone, E.J. Woodhouse, *Averting catastrophe: Strategies for regulating risky technologies*, Berkeley: California UP 1986, pp. 121–176.

31 See the examples provided by E. Ostrom, *Governing the commons*, Cambridge: Cambridge UP 1990.

32 Compare J.D. Thompson, A. Tuden, Strategies, structures, and processes for organizational decision, in: J.D. Thompson et al. (eds.), *Comparative studies in administration*, Pittsburgh: Pittsburgh UP 1959, p. 207.

33 H.W.J. Rittel, M.M. Webber, Dilemmas in a general theory of planning, *Policy Sciences*, 4, 1973, 155–169.

34 Hargrove, Glidewell (eds, 1990.), *op. cit.*.

35 Dror (1990), *op. cit.*, pp. 1–12.

36 Y. Dror, *Policymaking under adversity*, New Brunswick: Transaction Books 1986, pp. 167–168.

37 Y. Dror, Statecraft as fuzzy gambling with history, Unpublished mimeo, p. 14.

38 Judith N. Shklar, *The faces of injustice*, New Haven: Yale UP 1990.

39 Shklar (1990), *op.cit.*, p. 70.

40 Shklar (1990), *op. cit.*, p. 69.

41 A. Wildavsky, *Searching for safety*, New Brunswick: Transaction 1988.

42 Shklar (1990), *op. cit.*, p.56.

CHAPTER 5

Explaining Agents' Behavior:
Implicit Frames

There is no such thing as a classification of the ways in which men may arrive at an error: it is much to be doubted whether there ever can be.

Augustus de Moran[1]

Explaining "Errors"

Let us presume for the moment that an argument can be made that an alleged negative event was indeed, if only partially, caused by deliberate actions or omissions on the part of policymaking agents. This leads to the next analytical question, which takes us to the third layer in fiasco construction: how can we explain why policymaking agents acted in the way they did? More precisely, how can we explain why they failed to prevent the negative event from happening? The third layer thus involves an analysis of the causes of policy failure. In keeping with the key in which this book was written, this chapter will not put forward one or several explanatory theories to answer this question. Instead it will examine the frames different people use to go about explaining policy failure. The key question guiding our inquiry can thus be reframed as follows: How have analysts of policy fiascoes tried to cope with the ontological complexities of policymaking in developing theoretical explanations of policy failure? This chapter shows that such coping efforts have taken different forms, and that it is by no means easy to assess which theories are more successful than others in doing so.

In recent years there has been a strong proliferation of conceptual frameworks, propositions, and theories about policy failure (see appendix). Many of these are elegant and creative, yet there is no sign of even a beginning of consensus about these competing explanations. What we are dealing with, in short, is a large set of highly diverse and mostly unrelated yet inherently biased "answers" looking for research opportunities ("questions") to which they might be applied. The literature on fiascoes and government failure shows a striking diversity of approaches, but also a clear lack of knowledge cumulation.[2] Time and again new "propositions," "frameworks," "models," "theories," and "paradigms" are proposed to explain a particular fiasco or categories of them, only to be abandoned and replaced by new ones proposed by people apparently uninformed that highly similar analytical tools had already been proposed elsewhere. It is beyond the scope of this volume to reflect on the sociological and professional reasons for this state of affairs. Here we look at the theoretical content and methodological orientation of these various approaches to see what are the underlying themes and problems.[3] Looking at this body of knowledge from these angles, several common features stand out:

- *Multiple philosophies of governance.* Analysts implicitly or explicitly depart from different sets of assumptions about the normative and factual "essence" of policymaking (we shall call them philosophies of governance), which predispose them to study and evaluate policymaking and its failures in distinctive ways.
- *Multiple foci, multiple biases.* In a significant number of contributions to the literature, policy failures are held to be caused by "errors" or "flaws." They are therefore regarded as unusual phenomena in need of explanation. On the opposite end of the analytical spectrum, there are those who take policy fiascoes as inevitable byproducts of the complex and failure-prone ways in which we have organized (parts of) economic, political, and administrative life.[4] In short, each way of looking at and evaluating the causes of policy failures harbors certain biases. These biases lead analysts to focus on some properties of political and administrative structures and processes while ignoring others.
- *Multiplicity as a problem.* The great majority of fiasco analysts do not make explicit their ontological, epistemological, and methodological assumptions, but many seem to work within the positivist tradition of especially North-American social science. For these theorists, the existence of multiple, apparently incommensurable theoretical approaches and models to explain policy fiascoes presents a potentially debilitating problem for which no adequate solution has been found yet.

Each of these underlying themes tells us something about how policy analysts approach their task of explaining failure, and about the limitations and biases inherent in their ways of going about it.

Implicit Philosophies of Governance

At this point in the book, the existence of a great variety of theoretical approaches to understanding the causes of policy failures should come as no surprise. It is partly because of the complex and indeterminate nature of the object of study, that is, public policymaking. On top of that, we think that the different ways in which analysts seek to explain failures reflect fundamentally different philosophical positions about what constitutes good government and to what extent reality is able to match the ideal.

In our view, it is possible to reconstruct from the fiasco literature (and indeed from the wider literature about public policymaking) a limited number of configurations of normative ideas and empirical claims about the nature, logic of operation, and relative importance of structures and processes of policymaking. With the pushing and shoveling that is inevitable when typologizing complex phenomena, and recognizing that there are several borderline cases and anomalies, we have deduced from the fiasco literature three distinct types of philosophies.[5] They are, in fact, configurations of assumptions, implicit philosophies of governance shaping theorists' views of the policy world.[6] Theorists in these different traditions differ in terms of what they think are the key tasks and functions of governance, the key actors to be reckoned with, and the degree to which good government is attainable and makes a difference. We have called them optimists, realists, and pessimists.

The Optimists

The optimists' philosophy of governance and organization is firmly rooted in the Enlightenment. They believe that, in principle, a modern organization or a government is a powerful means for achieving the common good, and they view these as suitable vehicles for functional rationality. They may have quandaries about what goes on at the political level but they firmly believe in the machinery of governance below that level. Through specialization, research and development, professional training, and the constant improvement of management and decision-making techniques, a highly efficient and rational organization of governance can be achieved in principle. Failures of governance, insofar as they are not caused simply by political wheeling and dealing or by individual aberrations, are therefore the exceptions that need explaining. They must be the product of errors. They are deviations from the normal state of affairs.

Departing from these assumptions, the optimists have produced a host of different theories about what causes these failures. Among the optimists are most of the human error theorists like Wagenaar and Reason.[7]

They are well aware that government is a human enterprise, and that humans, inevitably, make mistakes. In most cases, these mistakes do not matter much because they occur in the context of an essentially sound organization which contains numerous self-correcting mechanisms and buffers against individual slippage. When disaster does occur, a unique configuration of multiple and cumulative errors must have occurred, that needs to be documented by careful reconstruction:

> A basic premise of this framework is that systems accidents have their primary origins in fallible decisions made by designers and high-level ... decision makers. This is not a question of allocating blame, but simply a recognition of the fact that even in the best-run organisations a significant number of influential decisions will subsequently prove to be mistaken. This is a fact of life. Fallible decisions are an inevitable part of the design and management process. The question is not so much how to prevent them from occurring, as how to ensure that their adverse consequences are speedily detected and recovered.[8]

Neo-rationalist approaches to explaining organizational failures and flawed public policymaking are widespread in contemporary policy analysis. In that respect, mainstream policy analysis resembles the mainstream in organization and management theory which has long been dominated by "rationalistic, formalistic and implicitly omniscient" approaches.[9]

Williams's fervent attack on what he calls "the anti-analytic presidency" in the United States is a good example.[10] He charges that political, ideological, and public-relations forces have come to dominate the logic of White House operations and top-level policymaking. These forces have tended to push out, or relegate to secondary importance, professional advisory bodies such as policy-planning units and policy-review boards. Analytical capabilities within the governance apparatus have been slashed or have become increasingly irrelevant. According to Williams, these developments have exacted a high price in terms of highly damaging fiscal and economic policies of the Reagan administration. Similarly, Neustadt and May compare a number of controversial policy failures with what they see as two major successes in U.S. domestic and foreign policy, and conclude that the crucial difference between them was the quality of the reasoning upon which the crucial policy decisions were founded.[11] In particular, the two sets of policy episodes showed a marked difference in the ways in which top-level policymakers made use of historical analogies in interpreting current problem situations, estimating other players in the arena, and evaluating policy options. Their proposals to improve the quality of what Dror calls "thinking-in-history" a neo-rationalist perspective. They strongly focus on the analytic dimension of

the policy process and are based on the assumption that rational procedures of policy deliberation can be inculcated into policymakers and institutionalized in the policy machinery.

Perhaps one of the archetypical, and certainly one of the most influential, optimists in the study of policy failures has been the American
pychologist Irving L. Janis. He has studied a number of major policy failures in government and in the corporate sector. He argues that flawed
decision making, both by individual policymakers and by high-level
groups within organizations, played a crucial role in bringing them about.
In a series of books and articles, he set out to develop a theory of how and
why such decision-making failures occur. The basic position underlying
all this work can be summarized as follows:

> [A]mong the major causes of unsuccessful outcomes is one that is very much
> under the leaders' control: poor quality of the decisionmaking procedures used
> either to arrive at a new policy or to reaffirm the existing policy. Defective pro-
> cedures – entailing, for example, inadequate information search, biased apprai-
> sal of consequences, and lack of contingency planning – do not guarantee that
> a policy decision will turn out to be a fiasco. The net influence of the uncontrol-
> lable, unknown, and chance factors can occasionally result in "good luck." But
> the likelihood of failure is substantially less if sound procedures of information
> search, appraisal, and planning are used.[12]

Notice what good policymaking is about in Janis's view. It is essentially a
matter of information processing and choice, in other words a set of primarily cognitive tasks that policymakers need to perform. How succesful
they are at doing so, Janis argues, depends on a whole range of cognitive,
motivational, social, and organizational factors. These mediate between
the nature of the problems to be solved, and the adequacy of the
policymakers' grasp of them. Empirically, Janis's theory is highly complex and multilayered, but his basic normative views on the nature and
importance of good governance and management are clear: good policymaking (construed as careful information processing and deliberation) in
most cases leads to good policy results, whereas flawed policymaking
heightens the chances of policy failure. How more "optimistic" can one
get? The good guys get the job done, and the careless, lazy, or incompetent ones are destined to fail.[13]

The Realists

The realists conceive of public policymaking and governance as essentially fragile activities. In this view, the complexity of the challenges that policymakers face and of the institutional environments in which they oper-

ate, make failure a definite instead of – as optimists argue – an unusual possibility. Also, theorists in this vein maintain a different view of human nature in government than the optimists do. The latter tend to see administrative men and women as essentially competent, value-neutral if inevitably constrained information processors and decision makers given to strive for the greater good. The realists on the other hand, see man – both within and outside government – as an essentially self-centered, opportunistic, yet often mindless utility maximizer. What needs to be explained, therefore, is not that failures occur, but that they do not occur more often than they do.

The critical factors that stand between this weak-kneed, cognitively limited, egocentric administrative man or woman and the endemic failure of policymaking are checks and balances governing and constraining the use of political and administrative power in society; procedures for elite recruitment and socialization that produce political and bureaucratic leaders capable of exercising good judgment and strong leadership; and a strict enforcement of sophisticated principles of management and communication. These are to provide the safeguards against sloppiness, carelessness, imcompetence, haste, greed, and abuse that lie dormant in every organization. As Landau puts it, "The cost of error runs high in this world, and it is manifestly more sensible to prevent error than to correct it."[14] Research by LaPorte, Weick, Roberts, and others on high-reliability organizations and by Landau, Bendor, and others on the virtues of redundancy and overlap in public administration stands firmly in this tradition.[15] And in quite another fashion, this is the position taken by many constitutional theorists, traditional institutionalists and pluralists like Wilson, Friedrich, Finer, Bentley, Truman, and Dahl – but perhaps most eloquently presented in the Federalist Papers.[16]

A particular branch of realism can be found at the macro-level. This view is popular mainly among rational choice theorists, some sociologists, and particularly public choice economists. Important, if wholly different proponents of this cluster are Hayek, Hirschman, and E. Ostrom.[17] Analysts adhering to this view tend to evaluate and analyze the performance of government in comparison with how other mechanisms produce coordinated social action.[18] Government, in their view, is "nothing special" and should be looked at predominantly from a functional, service-delivery perspective. At a general level, the most important alternative forms of social coordination are the market system and more structured forms of elite bargaining. Macro-level realists tend to evaluate on a case-by-case basis whether government intervention is more effective and efficient or otherwise more desirable than if the activities in question would be performed or coordinated by other mechanisms.

For analysts belonging to this macro brand of realism, policy failures are likely when governments undertake tasks or continue to do things they, by their very structure and logic of operation, are ill-equipped to handle. The emphasis is on the functional analysis of requirements for task performance and proceeds on the basis of general assumptions about the properties and functional (in)capacities of alternative systems of social coordination and public service delivery.

The Pessimists

Finally, the pessimists accept most of the realists' critical diagnosis of the endemic forces that produce policy failures but take it one step further. Talking about particular domains of policymaking, especially those involving the application of high-risk technology or the design and implementation of megaprojects, pessimists discount the last glimmer of Enlightenment hope left in the minds of the realists that good management can save the day. They argue that even in these systems, where the social and political costs of failure tend to be very high, system failures are bound to occur, no matter how elaborate the precautions and "safety valves." The most influential theorist in this tradition is Perrow, whose theory of "normal accidents" has found application beyond the domain of man-made, technological disasters in which it was orginally developed.[19] Although their arguments follow a markedly different route and are far more general in their implications, critical theorists' structuralist explanations of organizational pathologies, state failure, and government overload also fall into this category.[20]

The analysts labelled "pessimists" for the purpose of this study may more or less agree on the structural, inherent nature of policy failures. There is, however, a clear split among its members when it comes to the normative question of how they evaluate this, and what they propose government ought to do about it. Borrowing again from Douglas and Wildavsky's terminology, one can distinguish pessimists with egalitarian and with individualistic inclinations. The "egalitarian" pessimists build upon this analysis to produce an existential critique of existing structures and dominant ideologies of organization and policymaking. Some propose to abandon them and replace them by new, supposedly more humane and less dangerous institutional arrangements. Schumacher's "small is beautiful" school exemplifies this, as do many (neo-)Marxist studies, and anarcho-liberal and neo-libertarian political theorists.[21] Others, like Perrow, are more narrow in the scope of their analysis and therefore also more selective in their proposals. They invite policymakers to reconsider the costs and benefits of engaging in – or allowing private companies to engage in – ventures and projects that cannot but bring major failures and disasters from time to time. An important example often mentioned by egalitarian pessimists concerns the widespread use of nuclear power, and more generally the societal distribution of technological and other forms of risk.[22]

In contrast, "individualistic" pessimists like Wildavsky agree that failures are inevitable but argue that in the long run we had better be prepared to pay that kind of price for technological and social progress.[23] Their reading of the costs and benefits of fiasco-inducing activities is different. They point to the great social costs of anticipatory curtailment of admittedly risky but potentially extremely beneficial if not economically profitable activities. Their logic is one of social experimentation: major failures constitute an inevitable part of a broader process of trial and error. As Wildavsky puts it:

> My objection to current discussions of risk and safety is that they are one-sided, focusing almost entirely on the dangers of risk taking while neglecting, to the detriment of our common safety, opportunity benefits that would be lost by risk aversion .... safety that improves is a quality of institutions that encourage a search so vigorous that no one can be said either to have designed or controlled it .... Safety results from a process of discovery. Attempting to short-circuit this competitive, evolutionary, trial and error process by wishing the end - safety – without providing the means – decentralized search – is bound to be self-defeating. Conceiving of safety without risk is like seeking love without courting the danger of rejection.[24]

If, by not trying, we forestall error, our society as a whole will be worse off because other modes of learning are distinctly inferior.[25] Hence in the view of individualistic pessimists we should, for example, not abandon nuclear energy but learn to make it safer and more profitable, and in the meantime do the utmost to limit the number, scope, and harmful impact of system failures.

From Implicit Philosophies to Analytical Foci

Philosophies of governance constitute the most fundamental patterns of orientations and expectations that provide analysts with a basic set of questions and hypotheses about governance. They are broad enough as to allow for different empirical models and methodological strategies for research on particular aspects and problems of governance and policy-making. In other words, particular philosophies of government inspire particular sets of empirical frameworks and tend towards particular types of evaluation principles, but there is no one-to-one correspondence between one and the other.

This kind of "focused diversity" at the empirical level can also be observed in the field of fiasco analysis. Policy fiascoes have provoked work by policy analysts from very different disciplinary backgrounds, which explains part of the variety and disjointedness in current theorizing. Psychologists, sociologists, system theorists, economists, political scientists, lawyers, philosophers, students of management and public administration have brought to the study of the causes of policy fiascoes wholly different concepts and styles of analysis, different methodologies, and an orientation towards different levels of analysis.

Comparing these various approaches against the backdrop of the underlying philosophies of government, our review of existing fiasco studies does reveal a relatively small number of unifying sets of empirical and methodological assumptions about how to study policymaking and its failures. We call these analytical foci. They are related but not identical to the philosophies of governance. They are related in the sense that the normative concerns and thematic orientations of these philosophies serve to direct analysts' attention to some features of governance and draw it away from others. To a certain extent, each philosophy of governance also leads analysts to prioritize particular levels of analysis over others. In short, the philosophies of governance help to shape the conceptual frameworks and methodological strategies used in empirical-explanatory studies of particular (classes of) policy episodes.

We have derived four major analytical foci that provide the basis for theory-building and the testing of hypotheses about the causes of policy fiascoes.[26]

Figure 1 The structure of fiasco analysis

Philosophies of government	Optimists	Realists		Pessimists
Analytical foci	Problem solving	Management of competing values	Institutional interaction	Coping with structural constraints

Figure 1 shows how the three philosophies of governance relate to four recurrent types of analytical foci in fiasco analysis, which are outlined and exemplified by citing prototypical authors working in each tradition. We shall present these four analytical foci below and will explain that each entails its own particular biases ("selective assumptions," "perceptual filters," "zones of indifference"). Some aspects of the structures and processes of policymaking are deemed essential in understanding policy episodes, while others are left out of the analysis. These biases limit the range and depth of the explanations produced by analysts working in each of these traditions.

Focus 1: Governance as Problem Solving

This focus is strongly embedded in the optimists' philosophy of governance. It is adhered to by many cognitive and social psychologists and mainstream policy scientists. It suggests that the core tasks and activities of government are identifying, thinking through, and ultimately solving public problems. At the core of this problem-solving view of public policymaking lies the notion of "reality testing." Social problems are "out there," as are a number of ways of solving them, each with certain advantages and drawbacks, as well as (undefined) probabilities. The crucial task for policymakers is to arrive at sound and workable definitions of what the problems are, what can realistically be expected of government to diminish or perhaps completely solve them, what specific options (actions, measures, programs) are available, and which (combinations of) options stand the best chance of achieving the desired ends.

Not surprisingly given its origins in Enlightenment thinking, the problem solving focus on public policymaking holds procedural rationality to be the dominant organizing principle. Good policymaking is set in the context of organizational structures and processes that facilitate the effective and efficient conduct of public affairs. This presumes certain given value preferences and/or political ends whose origins and formation are deemed to be outside the key concerns of the empirical policy scientist. The problem-solving focus matches an emphasis on functional rationality with a voluntaristic outlook on policymaking. Its voluntarism is evident from its view that policymaking is a deliberate activity, whose ends can be accomplished by carefully constructed steps and procedures on the part of political and bureaucratic elites, and meticulously implemented by public bureaucracy. Its functional rationality manifests itself by the use of a means-ends framework to understand public policymaking, whereby government actors or agencies are assumed to have set goals or operational program objectives. These goals are taken as given; their origins and sensibility are not subject to analysis in the problem-solving mode. This is because problem-solving analysis rests on a strict distinction between facts and values. Goals and objectives are taken to belong to the latter category and are, therefore, outside the domain of empirical analysis.[27] The focus of analysis thus switches to the means of policymaking, to the ways in which policymakers develop plans and activities that reduce the discrepancies between their goals and the actual state of affairs as they perceive and evaluate it.

Proponents of the problem-solving perspective all believe that good policymaking and good management matter very much. Therefore, in case of policy failure, they are very likely to start to look for clearly iden- tifiable cognitive mishaps and weaknesses. These include: skill-based, rule-based, or knowledge-based individual slips and mistakes; patterns of inadequate information processing caused by an overreliance on heuris- tics, biases and other cognitive simplification mechanisms; and failures in the design and operation of socio-technical systems that induce human error. In addition to these primarily individualistic approaches, many problem-solving analysts look at social and organizational processes, and the extent to which these produce distorted communications and barriers to effective collective decision making and implementation.[28]

The problem-solving approach to understanding public policymaking has long dominated the emerging discipline of policy analysis. During the war, new techniques such as operations research and systems analysis were further developed and widely applied to coordinate wartime pro- duction. The postwar prominence of positivism and behavioralism in the social sciences further strengthened the appeal of a rationalist, scientific approach to making policy and therefore also to explaining it, stimulated by the development of the policy sciences pioneered by Lasswell and oth- ers. Its intellectual influence matched its popularity among policymakers. The most ambitious attempt to import the problem-solving approach into the policymaking process was the short-lived adoption of the Planning, Programming, and Budgeting System (PPBS) in U.S. federal government under President Johnson. Its failure also marked the end of the virtually unchallenged dominance of the problem-solving approach, which has nevertheless continued to exert a significant, and according to some det- rimental, influence.[29]

Focus 2: Governance as the Management of Competing Values

The value dimension of public policymaking is central to the second view, which is most closely allied to the realist philosophy. Public policymak- ing is seen as a social and political process that evolves around the artic- ulation and adjudication of competing values and ideologies. The conflict between these values and ideologies manifests itself in disagreements about the nature, ends, roles, and limits of government in society (consti- tutional level); the nature and form of policy interventions in particular social spheres and policy sectors (collective choice level); and particular issues involved in the implementation of programs, the performance of public agencies, or the conduct of officials (operational management level).[30] In making and implementing policy, public officials and other stakeholders need to keep these conflicts from escalating, so as to permit continued dialogue, cooperation, and compliance. This management of competing values centers on two core features of governance: how government operates (the rules of the game – the conflict resolution process), and what government does or fails to do (the substance of policy – balancing competitive claims).[31]

Whereas the problem-solving approach built on applied mathematics, decision theory, economics, and cognitive psychology, this alternative analytical focus epitomizes the contribution of political science to policy analysis. This is exemplified by the works of as heterogenous a set of analysts as Dahl, Lindblom, J.Q. Wilson, Edelman, Miliband, Goodin, and Fischer.[32] The focus switches from problem solving to conflict management, from a concern with analysis to a concern with distribution and redistribution, and from the centrality of information processing to the selective uses and manipulation of information and other resources in the policy process.[33] In this perspective, the ends of policymaking are not given. They are the subject of a political – some say pluralistic, others disagree – process of articulation, mobilization, and accomodation, in which power and influence play a crucial role. Although political scientists strongly disagree about how power is distributed in society, how it is wielded and used, and how it can best be studied, all agree that power is a crucial currency in the policy process.[34]

At the same time, there is more than just power and process. The other side of the coin are the values and interests that drive the political process, constrain it, yet also are being shaped by it. This brings into view the normative dimension of policymaking and policy analysis. As Brecht has shown, the content, evolution, and impact of values can be studied empirically.[35] Others have gone beyond this view. They argue policy analysis should be able to adjudicate between different competing values and interests by developing a normative discourse in which a reasoned evaluation of different normative claims and justifications becomes possible.[36]

Consequently, the competing values focus emphasizes substantive and political rationality. It stresses the need to contemplate the origins and content of the competing claims that form the stuff of the policy process. In particular, the justification of these claims in terms of the normative arguments offered by various participants becomes the focal point for inquiry and evaluation. Along with that comes a concern for the ways in which these claims are subsequently traded off, integrated, or otherwise dealt with in the policy process. These become the focal point for inquiry and evaluation. As far as the issue of the controllability of policy processes is concerned, competing values theorists avoid the extreme voluntarism of the problem-solving focus. This middle position on the voluntarism-determinism continuum in the explanation of policy outcomes is nicely phrased by competing values theorists Finney and Lesieur:

As applied to the ... phenomenon of organizational crime, we agree that action is progressively narrowed and increasingly "determined," but not in [a] mechanical and theoretically probabilistic manner ... and not without strong countervailing tendencies for new possibilities and changing commitments to develop as action unfolds. As the management of organizations proceeds, decisions or events that rule out certain courses of action open up yet others; and managers frequently "change their minds" as previous guesses about future outcomes turn out differently than expected.[37]

Focus 3: Governance as Institutional Interaction

This view tends to concentrate on the organizational dimension of public policymaking. It breaks with the normative idea of government as an institution seeking to advance the common good and to adjudicate competing claims about what the common good is or requires. Instead it stresses the need to understand government as a conglomerate of complex organizations intricately tied into broader networks and arenas. In those arenas, government agencies interact with groups of clients, suppliers, intermediate organizations, and other institutional stakeholders. More explicitly than in the previous two foci, it is acknowledged that public organizations and policymakers develop and defend their own "local" world views, norms, and values. The fabric of policymaking is, therefore, one in which the interactions and conflicts between all these institutional stakeholders must be adequately regulated by checks and balances.

The institutional interaction focus highlights the contextual nature of rationality. Policymaking is a multi-organizational activity that involves actors operating at different levels of the political and bureaucratic hierarchy inside and outside government. Inevitably, this entails continuous encounters between multiple conceptions of rationality. Sometimes these encounters take the form of clashes, but on other occasions they can be rejoined. In most cases, both the policy process and its outcomes are fairly unpredictable and impenetrable to outsiders. They are non-linear, often poorly coordinated activities with frequent setbacks, reversals, disconnections, and miscommunications. It would, however, be a serious mistake to see this as a perversion of rationality itself, because at its heart lies an interaction between multiple, contextually loaded rationalities.[38]

The voluntarism that characterized the problem-solving perspective is even less prominent in the institutional interaction perspective. It acknowledges that what government actually "does" is an outcome of complex (inter)organizational processes that are only partly amenable to deliberate management and control. In case of policy failures, institutional analysts do not look so much for localized "errors" or "flaws." Instead they will be concentrating on finding out why a particular conflux of actors and events occurred, and how this produced certain unintended negative social consequences. If anything, institutional analysts will take a critical look at the "rules of the institutional game" which enabled such a conflux to occur. Doing so, they may question whether these rules of the game can and must be amended to prevent such cumulations of adversities from recurring.

Therefore, to understand government as a whole, it is necessary to study more carefully how government organizations actually work. This involves analyzing how they are structured and managed, how policy decisions get made, what takes place during implementation and more generally what goes on at the bottom of the organization. Furthermore, one needs to study how different organizations relate to one another, and how they cooperate, bargain, and compete with others.[39] Finally, a policy analyst should examine to what extent interorganizational relationships take the form of regimes or networks with more or less fixed roles and positions for various parties and more or less accepted rules of interaction. In this perspective, the question of political leadership and control over the behavior of such complex organizations and networks then becomes at once a pivotal and controversial one.[40]

Focus 4: Governance as Coping with Structural Constraints

Structural theorists are of two kinds. One group, the "macro-level" theorists, is not so much interested in studying particular policy fiascoes as it is in identifying the structural causes for what they see as generic patterns of governmental failure. These theorists view governance in contemporary Western democracies as a political-economic process beset by tensions and contradictions embedded in the social, economic, and political structures of these societies. The state in the late capitalist system is required to perform two contradictory functions. On the one hand, it is supposed to facilitate and perpetuate the accumulation of private capital in the hands of economic elites, yet on the other it should help legitimate the existing, inequitable social and political order.[41] Patterns of public expenditure and public policy reflect these structural imperatives. The key problem is that the logic of the capitalist economy's capital needs clashes with growing public demands for transfer payments and welfare provision. The basic dilemma is clear-cut: expenditure cutbacks compromise political legitimacy, and yet the failure to curb public spending threatens economic viability (as well as the dominant position of the ruling class, neo-Marxist structuralists would add).[42]

Incumbent political and bureaucratic elites can at best temporarily negotiate, but never escape these tensions, many of which are inherent in the modern capitalist system. These tensions take many forms: overpro-

duction, resource depletion, sharp inequalities in the distribution of economic costs and benefits, mass unemployment, mounting pressure on the
social welfare system, the formation of urban "underclasses." In short: the
structure of society generates a set of developments likely to result in a situation of structural "overload." This in turn compromises the efficacy of
the political and bureaucratic system of the state. The lack of efficacy ultimately destroys the state's legitimacy, making it vulnerable to increasingly powerful advocates of radical change from opposite ends of the political spectrum.[43] More directly relevant to the understanding of the causes
of specific policy episodes and fiascoes is the work of the second group,
the "meso-level" theorists. These also seek to explain policy fiascoes in
structural, systemic terms, but look at structures and systems of governance at a much less general level and in a more detailed way. The relevant
structures that explain particular policy fiascoes are not to be found at the
overall level of the political and economic organization of society, but
rather at the meso level of the particular policy sector, organizational network, or production unit involved. As mentioned before, Perrow's work
on "normal accidents" in various kinds of high-tech systems has been an
important influence here.

The view of policy rationality embedded in the structural constraints
focus is one that concentrates on the overall rationality of the system as a
whole, inherent in its logic of operation. This often comprises a longer
time horizon, and a bigger geographical or social scope than that which is
harbored by any of the stakeholders in any particular policy arena.
Taking this systems view, structural analysis is able to explain or perhaps
rationalize actions and developments in the course of a policy process
that seems incomprehensible or pathological when viewed from a more
narrow, actor, subsystem, or component-level perspective. Conversely,
and perhaps more relevantly in the context of fiasco analysis, the structural perspective seeks to illuminate the vulnerability of a policy or project
that many stakeholders or contemporary observers assume is satisfactory.

In accordance with this emphasis on the system as a whole rather than
on that of any of its parts, the structural perspective tends toward a more
deterministic view of individual policy episodes. Failures are to a large
extent inherent in the structure and logic of operation of the system. It is
virtually impossible for any but the most powerful coalition of stakeholders to amend these features. From a purely structural, system-level view,
individualized instances of policy failure are less interesting a topic for
detailed analysis and evaluation to begin with. Fiascoes only start to provide a challenge to the system when they occur more frequently, inflict
cumulative damage, and pose legitimacy problems for policymakers and
perhaps the political regime as a whole.

From Analytical Foci to Analytical Biases: The Problem of Multiplicity

Theory is selection. Selection, in turn, means bias. Bias is inevitable in any attempt to make sense of complex social events. Biases should be accepted and can be dealt with more effectively when their sources and nature are brought out for everyone to see and take into account. The four analytical foci tend to look at the structures and processes of policymaking in quite different ways, all of which are highly selective. The explanations for policy failures produced by analysts working in these different analytical traditions, cannot but reflect the biases they entail. They cannot, therefore, aspire to be complete or universally valid diagnoses of "what went wrong." The frame-bounded nature of the "causal" models and policy recommendations encountered in the literature constrains their validity and relevance.

A problem with many theories of policy failures is that their biases remain implicit and hidden. Fiasco analyses are often couched in sweeping claims about "the" causes of error in decision making, implementation, or whichever other dimension of policymaking. Unfortunately, unreflective use of theories which by their very nature emphasize some factors and mechanisms at the cost of ignoring others, may produce oversimplified, distorted, and inappropriately generalized explanations. We will therefore revisit the four main types of analytical foci in fiasco analysis presented above, and make explicit which aspects they select "in" and which they select "out" when purporting to explain a single or a particular set of policy failures.

This will be done by applying them to the disaster with the space shuttle Challenger, the most extensively investigated case in the policy fiasco literature. The basic features of that episode were as follows. The Challenger, one of the marvels of American space technology, exploded less than a minute after launch, obliterating a crew of seven, including the first "teacher in space," Christa Mc Auliffe. The immediate cause of the explosion turned out to be a failure in one of the seals in the booster rocket motor. Ostensibly a technical affair, post-disaster investigations quickly revealed it was not. People soon began to question why this technical failure was allowed to occur, and what this revealed about the effectiveness of NASA safety procedures and about the conduct of the launch readiness review process. A special investigation committee appointed by President Reagan and chaired by former Secretary of State William Rogers concluded that although the immediate cause of the disaster was technical, the accident itself was "rooted in history," that is, the organization and management of the space shuttle project, culminating in the fateful decision to launch the Challenger under the unusually low temperatures that triggered the failure of the O-rings in the solid rocket booster.[44] The report and the thousands of pages of documents and public testimony on which it was based have inspired many analysts to develop more coherent theoretical explanations for the disaster, which traumatized the nation and triggered an institutional crisis for NASA and the space shuttle program.

A Problem-Solving Perspective on Policy Failures: Cognitive Incompetence

For analysts employing a problem-solving focus, policy failures are primarily caused by factors which compromise the cognitive competences of policymakers and institutions. Different adherents to this view depart company as to the prime factors which cause these deficiencies in reality testing. Cognitive psychologists like Tversky, Kahneman, Nisbett, Ross, Russo, Schoemaker, Jervis and many others point to inherent limitations in the information-processing capabilities of humans.[45] Motivational psychologists like Etheredge and Dixon assert that powerful and partly unconscious drives and forces limit the cognitive and interpersonal styles of high-level policymakers.[46] Social psychologists like Janis, Nemeth, Tetlock, and Staw look at pathologies in the intragroup and intergroup processes that shape the ways in which policymakers or agencies define problems, identify solutions, and select options.[47] Organization theorists and political scientists like Wilensky, Burke and Greenstein, and George point to flaws and unintended effects of the institutional structures in which policymakers operate and that provide them with intelligence and advice.[48] Cybernetic theorists focus on problems and distortions in the production, transmission, and reception of information and communication within and between agencies involved in the policy processes, that may quickly amplify and compromise the quality of policymaking.[49]

The problem-solving perspective has been applied by many analysts in explaining the causes of the space shuttle Challenger disaster. Problem-solving theorists have tended to concentrate their explanations of the episode on the final decision to launch the Challenger, that was made in a series of teleconferences between NASA officials at different space centers and both engineers and management officials from Morton Thiokol, the supplier of the solid rocket boosters. The key issue during these conferences was whether it was safe to launch under the climatic conditions that were projected for that morning, notably the unusually low temperatures. Some Morton Thiokol engineers had tried to argue for postponement. They were afraid the cold weather might trigger an erosion of the O-rings, which in turn might cause hot gases to leak through the lower joint of the solid rocket booster, which had been designated as a critical component, that is, a failure point that could cause loss of life or vehicle if the component failed. The warnings of the engineers were not heeded, with fatal results.

To explain this, Hirokawa and colleagues argue that the failure to carefully examine the evidence against launching the shuttle at the projected time was due to "the interaction and joint influence of various cognitive, psychological, and social factors present in the decision environment."[50] They point out a number of cognitive biases at work among the NASA officials concerned, which caused them to cling to shared beliefs that the dangers of a launch under the low temperatures projected for January 28, 1986 were minimal, and to engage in questionable reasoning. They also point to a presumption shift effected by senior officials during the teleconference: whereas during its history NASA had always maintained the conservative decision rule that a launch should be canceled if there were any doubt of its safety, this was now reversed into the risk-seeking decision rule that a scheduled launch should proceed unless there was conclusive evidence that it would be unsafe to do so.[51] Others have explained these deficiencies in reality-testing by suggesting that the participants to the teleconferences suffered from groupthink.[52]

A Competing Values Perspective on Policy Failures: Imbalance Conflict Resolution

Taking the second analytical focus as our key instrument of reconstructing and explaining policy failures, they arise in either of two ways. "Substantive" failures occur when the institutions of governance and policymaking fail to resolve political conflict or operate in such a way as to systematically enhance the values, interests, and claims of some legitimate stakeholders and neglect those of others. Arguably, many of the Great Society era case studies of failures of social programs, enduring poverty, injustice, and inequality, fall into this category. The same goes for studies like Schulman's that analyze the political dynamics, risks, and failure propensities of large-scale public projects.[53] Moreover, detailed case studies of political instability, crises, and comparative analyses of the breakdown of regimes as in the classic volume by Linz and Stepan provide numerous ideas about how and why substantive failures of governance come about.[54] "Procedural" failures occur when policymakers or agencies fail to observe widely agreed-upon norms and procedures of proper political and administrative conduct. Most of Friedrich's pathologies of politics exemplify these: corruption, betrayal, excessive govermental secrecy and violence. One can also think of institutional breaches of legally defined standards of conduct dealt with in the broader literature on corruption, fraud, waste, abuse, organizational deviance, and bureaucratic (dis)obedience.[55]

From a competing values perspective, factors other than individual self-deception and destructive group dynamics were involved in the Challenger disaster and the decision to launch it. Analysts working in this tradition have pointed to the latent conflict that had been developing during the months preceding the launch between Thiokol engineers and management officials. Engineers were becoming increasingly concerned that there were serious problems with O-ring erosion, and that these should be reflected in top-priority safety status. At the same time, managers both at Thiokol and NASA were under pressure to keep up a very tight launch schedule and were therefore increasingly reluctant to keep putting safety first. They, in turn, were driven by anxieties about the future of the space program as a whole, which since the days of the Apollo had lost its mythical status and was facing a much more competitive political and budgetary environment (the Star Wars project was a major rival for R&D and defense funding). To keep the program afloat, NASA had to show it was able to deliver another stunning feat of technological wizardry. Moreover, lucrative contracts for payload on shuttle flights (including commercial satellites) were at stake. Continuous cost escalations and repated postponement of shuttle launches were therefore hurting the program's credibility and long-term survival.

External pressures such as these were transmitted down the complex NASA hierarchy, and were mirrored in its main subcontractors, such as Morton Thiokol. In such a politicized environment, the conflict between the engineering ethic of technical feasibility and maximum safety versus managerial imperatives became more manifest. Memos warning about the dangers of O-ring erosion were ignored, and when it transpired during the teleconference that Thiokol engineers were recommending postponement of the launch, NASA managers more or less told their Thiokol colleagues to get their house in order. An internal Thiokol teleconference ensued, during which Thiokol's vice president for engineering was literally invited by his senior colleagues to put off his engineering hat and put on his management hat – in other words to reverse his judgment. This eventually happened, and Thiokol agreed to give the go-ahead sign to NASA. From a competing values perspective, then, the essence of the Challenger case is not captured by concentrating, as problem-solving theorists do, on flawed information processing. Instead, it is argued, we should concentrate on the conflict between professional and organizational ethics versus political and hierarchical pressures for loyalty and compliance:

> The competitive environment and ambiguity concerning O-ring safety provide the background for the Challenger launch decision... Authority structures tightened, and managers issued prospective orders, removing authority from

engineers and vesting it in a very few individuals. Importantly, none of the Thiokol or NASA engineers stepped outside the chain of command to inform someone of the risks inherent in the launch. The hierarchical frame had become dominant.[56]

In the words of Starbuck and Millien, engineers and managers in NASA and Morton Thiokol were pursuing at least partially inconsistent goals, and were engaged in a long-term process of "fine-tuning the odds" of launching space shuttles, until something broke.[57]

An Institutional Interaction Perspective on Policy Failures: Organizational Labyrinths

From an institutional perspective, failures occur when the institutional checks and balances and organizational safeguards that are to prevent the delicate machinery of government from going astray, are lacking or fail for some reason or another. Turner's theory of man-made disasters illustrates this logic of analysis. It stresses a series of socio-cognitive, communicative, managerial, and political factors which, often unwittingly and over a long period of time, erode the ability of organizations to effectively operate systems or conduct projects that entail a risk of (technological) disaster.[58] In most policy settings this may be a rare occurrence, but there are also arenas where severe performance shortfalls are, indeed, endemic and compromise the legitimacy and the very survival of the organization or system as a whole. Examples can be found in studies of corporate failures and organizational decline.[59]

Different branches of institutional analysis tend to produce different interpretations of policy failures. For example, public choice theorists originally focused on the performance of bureaucratic organizations. They sought to show how the organizational structure and rules of conduct of public bureaucracies contain perverse incentives for their members and clienteles, and therefore tend to produce ineffective and inefficient social outcomes. Niskanen, for example, hypothesized that public bureaucracies tend to expand in size and overproduce goods and services beyond what is economically rational and socially desirable.[60] Later on, others turned these arguments into a more fully fledged theory of government failure, akin to the theory of market failure in welfare economics. They identified areas of government activity where inefficiencies and other forms of failure are most likely to occur.[61] Work in the public choice tradition acquired considerable momentum in the late seventies and early eighties. Unfortunately perhaps, it has often been overextended and used for ideological attacks on "big government" and "bureaucracy," instead of inspiring systematic empirical research into the actual causes of failures in public service delivery.

In contrast, the bureaucratic politics school of institutional analysis explains policy failures more explicitly with reference to flaws or break-downs of institutional checks and balances and rules of the policy game. Specifically, in one form or another, the following hypotheses to explain major policy failures are commonly found in this literature:

- disconnections, diverging rationales, and latent conflict between the organizational worlds of policymaking and policy implementation, producing unintended negative social consequences;[62]
- extreme forms of bureau-political conflict, inducing paralysis, inertia, or a disintegration of government action;[63]
- failures of political and bureaucratic leaders to control the bureaucrat-ic apparatus, or to constitute and maintain viable network coalitions capable of anticipating and responding effectively to changing policy predicaments.[64]

An institutional perspective on the Challenger disaster highlights yet other causes than the two previous ones have done. Schwartz, for example, argues that NASA fell victim to its own espoused myths of success, and had come to be an organization in decay, substituted fantasies and rituals for rigor and reasoning in managing its operations and making high-risk decisions. Desensitized by a string of successes yet at the same time facing a less benign institutional environment, organizational narcis-sism reigned. NASA officials were fleeing into fantasy and overconfi-dence, unaware of the pressures they put on one another, and developing collective mechanisms for denying troublesome realities. In this view, the decision process producing the Challenger accident was embedded in a bigger pathology of cultural change within NASA and the Challenger program.[65]

A similar claim that the tragedy of 28 January 1986 was embedded in the institutional setting of the Space Shuttle program is made by Vaughan, who focuses on the interplay between those parts of NASA that were running the program, and various internal and external bodies that were supposed to regulate and monitor its performance.[66] She shows how NASA managed to assert a considerable degree of autonomy, and how the effectiveness of internal regulatory bodies was crippled by their dependence for both information and resources on the agency they were supposed to control. As far as external regulation by Congress was con-cerned, NASA was indeed extremely sensitive to budget cuts, but at the same time it was able to defend its autonomy by exploiting its legal man-date as the national space agency and mobilizing external support for its programs. A similar logic of institutional interdependence complicating oversight and enforcement of performance standards applied to the relationship between NASA and Morton Thiokol: on the one hand Thiokol needed the big NASA contracts, on the other hand it had assumed a strategic position within the program that would be extremely costly and time-consuming for NASA to replace. This held true even after the disaster had taken place: even though it lay at the root of the failure, Morton Thiokol was kept on board of the space program.[67]

A Structural Constraints Perspective on Policy Failures: Systemic Failure

For structural theorists, individual failures are not so much dependent variables in need of explanation and reflection as they are prototypes for some broader, system-level analysis and assessment. Perrow, for example, was dissastisfied with standard explanations of massive technological failures and disasters, and suggested that previous (mostly problem solving) analysts were looking for the wrong things and in the wrong way. What was needed instead were explanations that concentrated:

> on the properties of systems themselves, rather than on errors that owners, designers, and operators make in running them. Conventional explanations for accidents use notions such as operator error; faulty design or equipment; lack of attention to safety features; lack of operating experience; inadequately trained personnel; failure to use the most advanced technology; systems that are too big, underfinanced, or poorly run .... But something more basic and important contributes to the failure of systems. The conventional explanations only speak of problems that are more or less inevitable, widespread, and common to all systems, and thus do not account for variations in the failure rate of different kinds of systems. What is needed is an explanation based upon system characteristics.[68]

Perrow proposed to find such an explanation by looking at the structural properties of the systems in which major accidents occur. These systems are always combinations of technological features that lie at the heart of the particular activity at hand (generation of nuclear power, commercial air and sea traffic, space exploration, DNA-experiments), and human and organizational arrangements put in place to make these technologies work in a purposeful and optimally safe way.

To explain major failures in these systems, Perrow suggested two structural properties of systems were essential: the degree of interactive complexity of the system as a whole; and the degree of (temporal, spatial, and functional) coupling between the various components of the system. Interactively complex systems consist of multiple components that may interact with one another in so many possible ways that those who manage and operate the system cannot always fully see, understand, let alone predict and control all these interactions. In tightly coupled systems the linkages between different components of the system are very direct – if not always foreseeable and controllable. This opens up the possibility of unstoppable chain reactions following an initial disturbance or error.

Structural analysis in the Perrowian fashion does not eliminate the human, organizational, or managerial components in fiasco analysis. Instead, it contextualizes them in terms of the broader structural pattern in which they are set. It regards them as necessary but not sufficient causes of major accidents in particular types of high-risk systems. Nor, should we add, does this kind of analysis only apply to technological high-risk systems. In fact, frameworks such as Perrow's have also been used to explain accidents in predominantly social systems, such as major crowd events, mass shopping malls, and leisure centers.[69]

If, for the proponents of the institutional school, the details of the Challenger launch decision are less important than the broader organizational and interorganizational context in which it was set, structural theorists take this argument one step further. For them, an analysis of the properties of space shuttle technology and the generic features of the production system designed to run it could already have made it clear that major accidents such as the Challenger explosion were bound to happen (even if specific predictions as to their frequency are impossible to make). Perrow, for example, placed space missions in his category of interactively complex, tightly coupled systems, in other words in the category of activities most vulnerable to system accidents. He was particularly concerned that errors in design, which he judged to be virtually inevitable given the complexity of the technology required, would go unnoticed. These would subsequently lead to major problems because, in Perrow's analysis, NASA's rigid system of control and command that governs space missions has deprived itself of the capability for flexible response at the operator level.[70] The technological imperative of a space mission is such that literally thousands of people, components, hard- and software coming from a variety of organizations have to be aligned in time and space to perform complex functions in a nearly error-free way. The evolution of the interorganizational system of the space program into a more competitive arena created conditions unfavorable to this alignment process. This was manifest both at the cultural (lack of a joint commitment to prevent failure, i.e., to maximize safety) and structural (time and budgetary pressures combining to erode organizational slack and redundancies essential for safe operation of high-risk technologies) level.[71] If a high-risk technology is managed by such a loosely coupled, results-driven, partially conflictual organizational configuration, disasters are likely to happen.

The Challenger episode, in this view, was the prototype of a "normal accident."[72]

Problematic Responses to Theoretical Pluralism

What to make of these different assumptive frameworks and sets of analytical biases? How to handle four different accounts of the causes of one and the same event, in this case the Challenger disaster? Following Rein and Schon, we could formulate the challenge as one of finding ways to cope effectively with the existence of multiple conceptual frames in fiasco analysis and the analytical "controversies" to which they give rise.[73] In contrast to Rein and Schon's perspective, however, it should be noted that academic controversies following episodes of policy failure, and indeed in many other fields of public policy analysis, do not always take the form of direct debates and/or stalemates between various stakeholders. In some cases they do, as in the ongoing polemic between rational choice theorists and their critics.[74] But in many other instances, we are simply left with multiple "explanations" of a particular episode that coexist within the social science literature, as evidenced by the multiple accounts of the space shuttle tragedy described above. The effects of this frame plurality and of the absence of a productive dialogue are problematic. They make it impossible to arrive at a joint definition of the situation and to reach joint inferences on how to handle it or learn from it.

Underneath these analytical and normative-philosophical differences on how to explain and evaluate particular policy episodes lie diverging epistemological viewpoints on what constitutes a proper explanation and what should be the relevant criteria for choosing between different theories.[75] Simply asking which theory is "right" – in the sense of which theory best accounts for "the facts" of the case – is likely to be an unsatisfactory way of coping with this kind of diversity. Many of the analysts involved could make a cogent case that this question is in itself questionable, because what "the facts" are and what "best accounts for" means are matters of legitimate dispute. Let us therefore look at the efforts of theorists that have tried to go beyond simple positivist "solutions" to this dilemma and transcend the boundaries of any single frame by developing models of policy failure drawing from different strands of theorizing. They have proceeded in roughly three ways, each of which will be reviewed briefly.

Those we have labelled eclecticists have borrowed from different foci, and have come up with models that typically involve some kind of combination of individual, group, organizational, and interorganizational variables. Their prime concern has been not so much to somehow integrate different substantive theoretical approaches, but to develop explanations which take into accounts factors at different levels of aggregation. These are held to affect the various stages of the policy process: problem definition, information processing, choice, conflict resolution, policy implementation, and policy adaptation. An example of this is Cohen and Gooch's study of major military fiascoes. After a lengthy and pointed critique of existing approaches to explanation, they survey different literatures ranging from disaster theory to business management. They end up with a synthetic matrix of "critical tasks" for succesful military performance on the one axis, and different layers of organizational command and decision on the other. The critical tasks vary from case to case, but may comprise of anything from minute information processing and transmission of warnings to devising an appropriate military doctrine and coordinating large-scale operations. This approach is well-suited for a systematic description of what went wrong in individual cases, but it is not very helpful – other than in a purely inductive way – to develop a coherent theory of military failures. Cohen and Gooch do discern a limited number of typical failure paths (failures to learn, to adapt, to anticipate, and aggregate failure), but it seems these paths may be triggered by a sheer infinite number of factors at different hierarchical levels in the military.[76]

The problem with this eclectic approach is that it blurs research traditions based on different sets of assumptions about how public organizations work and on different normative expectations about how good government ought to work. Also it lumps together variables operating at different levels of analysis without making clear, for example, when and under what conditions individuals or small groups have a decisive impact on the course and outcomes of the policy process. These eclectic models are useful to the extent that they generate a large number of possible and highly different hypotheses about what might have gone wrong in the policy process. They are much less helpful in specifying which of these hypotheses is best supported by the available evidence and how the various "partial" interpretations relate to one another. And they are notoriously weak on the replication side: most eclecticists seem to be bent on fashioning their own idiosyncratic combination of concepts, hypotheses, and theories.

A second strategy of coping with theoretical pluralism is inductivist. Peirce's review of the literature on bureaucratic failure is a useful example here.[77] After defining the phenomenon of bureaucratic failure (as distinct from political failure), he reviews the pertinent literatures in sociology, political science, and economics. He looks for theoretical and empirical clues that suggest how and why political and hierarchical control of and within the bureaucracy may fail, allowing for bureaucratic failures and harmful policy outcomes to occur. The highly disparate findings from these literatures are synthesized into seventyfive hypotheses that are inductively grouped into a number of categories. Eleven brief case studies of U.S. General Accounting Office reports about program failures and other mishaps provide a context for further empirical exploration. In a comparative overview of the case evidence, the seventyfive hypotheses are tentatively related to twentyeight common characteristics of failure found inductively in the cases studied.

Peirce is quick to acknowledge the problems of his approach from the perspective of theory development:

> Although it might be possible to organize the various hypotheses according to the type of government activity cross-classified by environment and type of failure, it seems doubtful that this undertaking would be worth the effort at the present stage of development. The various bodies of literature surveyed have already provided an unmanageably large collection of low-level generalizations. Although the development of a more general framework would simplify analysis, it seems doubtful that greater theoretical refinement is valuable in the absence of a firmer empirical grounding.[78]

Having looked at eleven cases in some detail, Peirce has the same experience as other fiasco analysts: he is bewildered by the sheer number and variety of possible explanations for these failures offered by the literature, and by the impracticality if not the impossibility of progressing beyond this level towards a more consolidated understanding of the roots of failure. The virtue of his methodology is that it carefully spells out the existing variety, but its fundamental problem is that, if anything, it complicates the task of moving beyond "low-level generalizations." As Nelson puts it: "a framework of appreciation that tries to encompass everything will end up effectively encompassing nothing."[79]

It might nevertheless be very profitable to analyze a particular instance of policymaking using notions, hypotheses and research strategies derived from all four of the frameworks that have been discerned here. Instead of blending them in an idiosyncratic melting pot like the eclecticists do or spelling them out in full detail and taking each single one at a time as the inductivists do, one may attempt to regiment them in more or less systematically articulated parallel explanatory models. This third strategy of coping with analytical pluralism we have called multi-modelism. Allison's famous study of the Cuban missile crisis of 1962 is an example of such a multi-model analysis.[80] One might follow his example when attempting to explain a particular policy failure. Dunleavy has done so for the so-called Westland affair. This was a bitter political and bureaucratic dispute in the Thatcher government over the selection of a manufacturer for army helicopters involving unauthorized leaks to the press and a ministerial resignation.

Dunleavy feels very comfortable with such a multi-model approach to explaining policy episodes. While acknowledging that it is difficult if not impossible to validate one or the other model in studying any single case, he strongly supports the multi-model methodology:

> Contrasting theories of the relations between the state and civil society provide the starting points for identifying radically different medium-range accounts of [a particular case]. The search for evidence to support or refute these interpretations enhances the importance of applied research, and generates new empirical insights which would otherwise be neglected. Similarly, looking at multiple interpretations sharpens up the pursuit of rigorous scholarly standards, and makes clear the importance of multiple criteria of theoretical adequacy over and beyond simple descriptive realism. Nor does an emphasis upon comparing interpretations entail lapsing into relativism, or saying that each interpretation is as good as the next or that it all depends what assumptions you start from.[81]

However, to those theorists seeking analytical parsimony and maximum explanatory power, such a juxtaposition of multiple "models" of failures is unsatisfactory. Dunleavy's defense of this method is likely to be seen by them as begging fundamental questions of theory construction. To them, the original question of "how and why did this happen?" can never be properly answered by a multi-model analysis. What such an analysis does, as articulated so well by Dunleavy, is to generate a variety of possible explanations. This, in itself is not a problem. Indeed, it fits these theorists' ideas about the need for competition between hypotheses, which is thought to produce a relentless search for better explanations. Yet this is problematic when these multiple explanations are derived from wholly different assumptive frameworks. In that case, the various hypotheses are rendered incomparable by the fact that they are based on different ontological assumptions about policymaking, use different concepts, focus on phenomena at different levels of analysis, and require different research methodologies.

Dunleavy would probably respond by saying that the problem is methodological and not fundamental. He encourages us to "analyse multiple decisions in a way that allows comparative testing of coherent models."[82] Presumably this would eventually result in a kind of theoretical "survival of the fittest." This seems a sensible methodological strategy. Yet on the substantive side of the argument, one needs metatheoretical criteria to decide which theory "fits" best. Dunleavy leaves us completely in the dark as to how we should measure any particular model's performance in explaining a particular case. In his own work, he evaluates the strengths and weaknesses of each of the four models he used to explain the Westland affair, but does so in an idiosyncratic, quasi-inductive way suggesting which aspects of the case are more or less covered by the model in question and which are not. Lacking clear metatheoretical guidelines as to what one should consider strong or weak points of an explanatory model, any other analyst looking at Dunleavy's case using the same models may come to completely different conclusions.

Moreover, Dunleavy seems oblivious to the fact that the search for "the facts" of any policy episode is – like it or not – theory-driven. It is very difficult to test any particular theory using a data base gathered using the selection criteria and sampling guidelines of another. Hence Dunleavy's proposed solution to the problem of coping with multiple explanatory frameworks in policy analysis – doing multi-model research on a whole series of cases – is primarily a rhetorical one. It does have considerable heuristic potential for policymakers who are being shown the virtues of looking at a single set of events from a variety of perspectives.[82] However, from an analytical perspective the virtues of competitive multi-modelism as a road to integrative theory formation appear to be more limited than its proponents allow for.

Figure 2: Responses to theoretical pluralism in failure analysis

The Problem:	Theoretical pluralism in explaining policy failure		
Coping attempts:	Eclecticists: (Cohen and Gooch: Military failures)	Inductivists: (Peirce: Bureaucratic failure)	Multi-modelists: (Dunleavy: Westland affair)
Resultant problems:	Indeterminacy	Overload	Incommensurability

In sum, as illustrated in figure 2, three types of responses to analytical pluralism in fiasco analysis have been followed. While serving to synthesize and to some extent integrate elaborate and often disparate bodies of literature, each of these three responses leaves us with problems. Eclecticism leaves too much room for arbitrariness and therefore for indeterminacy of the "explanations" it generates. Inductivism is much more intersubjectively verifiable but does not lead to well-integrated frameworks. On the contrary, it tends to generate an overload of ad-hoc explanations. Finally, the multi-model approach avoids both extremes but ultimately cannot overcome fundamental problems of incommensurability between the various models discerned.

Consequences for Understanding Policy Fiascoes

What, if anything, can we learn from this meta review and "deconstruction" of the policy failure literature? The present state of the field of failure analysis seems to suggest we have reached a critical juncture. Although there are many different concepts, models and theories purporting to explain policy failures, the degree of cross-fertilization and cumulation between them is disappointing. We have shown that underlying these diverse approaches are different ontological and normative assumptions about the essence of governance. In other words, the diversity of existing explanatory approaches reflects fundamentally different philosophies about the nature and possibility of "good" government. Given such diversity, there seems to be not much ground for hoping that the current malaise of disjointed framework proliferation will end, and that any sort of integrative approach will rise as a phoenix from the ashes of accumulated parochialism.

Theoretical pluralism, therefore, is a fact of life in the explanation of policy failures. We would argue that pluralism on the level of philosophies of governance is not much of a problem for policy analysis. On the contrary, it is a source of debate in political theory and normative public administration. We should cherish it and nurture more open debate between the various positions. What should be kept in mind, however, is the extent to which the strong adherence to a particular philosophy of governance may predetermine both what one sees (what one takes to be "real" or "crucial") and how one evaluates it. These two, we have tried to show, are usually intertwined in policy analysis.

The problems of pluralism emerge primarily at the empirical level, when the conceptual and normative frames implicit in particular philosophies of government somehow spill over into analytical biases of analytical foci. However, it also presents itself at the prescriptive level where hidden assumptions make for surprising and often implausible recommendations. The problem is not that these biases exist, but that they remain unrecognized and implicit. Consequently, many explanatory frameworks are misleadingly couched in universalistic terms, while in fact they are highly particularistic.

Without fully realizing the particularity of their own philosophical assumptions, observers and analysts of controversial policy episodes alike may rush towards explanation and judgment. In this process, which is often embedded in a political and organizational process of coping with the trauma of failure and determining accountability, it is easy to forget that one's command of "the facts" about what happened and why is biased in important ways. This takes us to the final layer in the process of constructing policy fiascoes: the attribution of blame.

Notes

1 A. de Moran, Formal logic (1847), London 1926, quoted in D.H. Fischer (ed.), *Historians' fallacies: Towards a logic of historical thought*, London: Routledge 1970, p. XVII.
2 Peirce's (1981) careful survey of the literature on bureaucratic failure and his development and preliminary empirical testing of a propositional inventory from this literature being an important exception. W. Peirce, *Bureaucratic failure and public expenditure*, New York: Academic press 1981.
3 The approach of this chapter has been inspired in important ways by Marieke Kleiboer's forthcoming PhD-dissertation *Multiple realities of international mediation*, Leiden: Centre for Law and Policy, Leiden University. We are grateful for her assistance with this chapter.
4 See, on this point, S.D. Sieber, *Fatal remedies*, New York: Plenum Press 1981.
5 For a more deductive approach to typologizing intellectual currents ("paradigms") in sociology, see W.G. Burrell, G. Morgan, *Sociological paradigms and organizational analysis*, London: Heinemann 1979; similar though less deductively coherent typologies in the field of public administration and public policy have been provided by, amongst others, R.T. Golembiewski, *Public administration as a developing discipline*, New York: Dekker 1977; T.A.J. Toonen, Administrative plurality in a unitary state: The analysis of public organizational pluralism, *Policy and Politics*, 11, 1983, 249–271.
6 In some ways these implicit philosophies resemble the "theories of the state" used by Dunleavy. He described them as: "...bridging the gap between normatively based political thought and the eclectic forms of contemporary empirical analysis .... They analyse the interrelationship between governmental institutions broadly defined and civil society; in a way informed by particular moral values and conceptions of human nature; using distinctive methods; and offering consistent and integrated accounts of diverse political processes .... Within every main theory of the state ...., a wide range of applied interpretations .... are possible." See: P. Dunleavy, Reinterpreting the Westland affair: Theories of the state and core executive decision making, *Public Administration*, 68, 1990, p. 30 and the literature cited there.
7 This tradition of research is summarized well in J. Reason, *Human error*, Manchester: Manchester UP 1990.
8 J. Reason (1990), *op. cit.*, p. 203.
9 A. Jarman, A Kouzmin, Crisis decision making: Towards a contingent decision path per-

spective, in: U. Rosenthal, M.T. Charles, P. 't Hart (eds.), *Coping with crises: The management of disasters, riots, and terrorism*, Springfield: Charles Thomas 1989, p. 398.

10 W. Williams, *Mismanaging America: The rise of the anti-analytic presidency*, Lawrence: Kansas UP 1990.

11 R. Neustadt, E.R. May, *Thinking in time: The uses of history for decision makers*, New York: Free Press 1986; cp. Y. Dror, School for rulers, in: K.B. De Greene (ed.), *A systems-based approach to policymaking*, Dordrecht: Kluwer, chapter 5.

12 I.L. Janis, *Crucial decisions: Leadership in policymaking and crisis management*, New York: Free Press 1989, p.4. See also I.L. Janis, L. Mann, *Decision making: A psychological analysis of conflict, choice, and commitment*, New York: Free Press 1977; I.L. Janis, *Groupthink: Psychological studies of foreign policy decisions and fiascoes*, Boston: Houghton Mifflin 1982.

13 In all fairness to Janis and other "optimistic" theorists it should be observed that they do offer some empirical evidence for their position: in two comparative case studies of the linkages between processes and outcomes of foreign policy (crisis) decisions, high positive correlations are found. See G.M. Herek, I.L. Janis and P. Huth, Decisionmaking during international crises: Is quality of process related to outcome?, *Journal of Conflict Resolution*, 31, 1987, pp. 203–226; P.E. Tetlock, R.S. Peterson, C. McGuire, S. Chang, P. Field, Assessing political group dynamics: A test of the groupthink model, *Journal of Personality and Social Psychology*, 63, 1992, 403–425.

14 M. Landau, Foreword, in: E.B. Portis, M.B. Levy (eds.), *Handbook of political theory and policy science*, New York: Greenwood Press 1988, p. VIII.

15 Compare a special symposium of the *Journal of Contingencies and Crisis Management*, 2, 4, 1994 for a pronounced debate between optimists and pessimists in the field of organizational design and safety, with LaPorte and colleagues in a marked role, and the references cited there. See also J. Bendor, *Parallel systems: Redundancy in government*, Berkeley: California UP 1985; M. Landau, D. Chisholm, The arrogance of optimism: Succes oriented vs failure avoidance management strategy in public administration, *Journal of Contingencies and Crisis Management* (1995, 3, 2, 67–80).

16 Compare D.E. Apter, Institutionalism reconsidered, *International Social Science Journal*, nr. 129, 1991 (theme issue on Rethinking Democracy), 463–481.

17 See, for example, F. Hayek, *The constitution of liberty*, London: Routledge 1960; A.O. Hirschman, *The rhetoric of reaction: Perversity, futility, jeopardy*, Cambridge, Mass: Belknap Harvard UP 1990; E. Ostrom, *Governing the commons*, Cambridge: Cambridge UP 1990.

18 A classical statement is R.A. Dahl, C.E. Lindblom, *Politics, economics and welfare*, Chicago: Chicago UP 1953.

19 C. Perrow, *Normal accidents: Living with high risk technologies*, New York: Basic Books 1984. See, for example, C.C. Hood, M. Jackson, The new public management: A recipe for disaster? In: D. Parker, J. Handmer (eds.), *Hazard management and emergency planning: Perspectives on Britain*, London: James and James 1991, pp. 109–126.

20 C. Offe, *Strukturprobleme des kapitalistischen Staates: Aufsätze zur politischen Soziologie*, Frankfurt am Main: Surkamp 1972; S.R. Clegg and D. Dunkerley, *Organization, class, and control*, London: Routledge and Kegan Paul 1980.

21 E.F. Schumacher, *Small is beautiful: A study of economics as if people mattered*, New York: Harper and Row 1973.

22 Perrow (1984), *op. cit.*; U. Beck, *Risikogesellschaft: Auf dem Weg in eine andere Moderne*, Frankfurt: Suhrkamp 1986.

23 A. Wildavsky, *Searching for safety*, Berkeley: Transaction 1988.

24 Wildavsky (1988), *op. cit.*, p. 228.

25 See, for example, S.B. Sitkin, Learning through failure: The strategy of small losses, *Research in Organizational Behavior*, 14, 1992, 231–266.

26 For a different overview, see for example J.E. Lane, *The public sector: Concepts, models and approaches*, London: Sage 1993, pp. 69-106. Also very useful is L. DeLeon, As plain as 1, 2, 3, .. and 4: Ethics and organization structure, *Administration and Society*, 25, 3, 1993,

pp. 293–316.

27 See H. Simon, *Administrative behavior*, New York: Free Press, 3d. ed. 1976, whose fact-value distinction was more rigid than A. Brecht's (in: *Political theory*, Princeton: Princeton UP 1950) value relativism, which did allow for the scientific study of values, albeit in a limited way.

28 W.E. Souder, Causes of crises: the behavioral accident, *Industrial Crises Quarterly*, 2, 1988, 185-194; Reason (1990), *op. cit.*; D. Bell, H. Raiffa and A. Tversky (eds.), *Decision making: normative, empirical and prescriptive interactions*, Cambridge: Cambridge UP 1990. At the policy level, see M.L. Goggin, Ann O'M. Bowman, J.P. Lester, L.J. O'Toole, *Implementation theory and practice: Toward a third generation*, New York: Harper Collins 1990.

29 See especially, O.F. White Jr., C.J. McSwain, The Phoenix project: Raising a new image of public administration from the ashes of the past, in: H.D. Kass, B.L. Catron (eds.), *Images and identities in public administration*, London: Sage 1990, pp. 23–60.

30 This three-level approach is taken from L. Kiser and E. Ostrom, Three worlds of action: a metatheoretical synthesis of institutional approaches, in: V. Ostrom ed., *Strategies of political inquiry*, Beverly Hills: Sage 1982.

31 This is, for example, also a central tenet of most theories of democracy, and is most crucial in Lijphart's politics of accomodation. See A. Lijphart, *Democracy in plural societies*, New Haven: Yale UP 1977.

32 R.A. Dahl, C.E. Lindblom, *Politics, economics and welfare*, Chicago: Chicago U.P. 1953; C.E. Lindblom, *The policymaking process*, Englewood Cliffs: Prentice Hall 1968; R. Milliband, *The state in capitalist society*, London: Weidenfeld and Nicolson 1969; M. Edelman, *The symbolic uses of politics*, Urbana: University of Illinois Press 1964; J.Q. Wilson, *The politics of regulation*, New York: Basic Books 1980; R.E. Goodin, *Political theory and public policy*, Chicago: Chicago UP 1982; F. Fischer, *Technocracy and the politics of expertise*, London: Sage 1990.

33 See also M. Edelman, *Constructing the political spectacle*, Chicago: Chicago UP 1988.

34 See the excellent overview and critique in S. Clegg, *Frameworks of power*, London: Sage 1989.

35 Brecht (1950), *op. cit.*

36 B. Barry, D. Rae, Political evaluation, in: F. Greenstein, N.W. Polsby (eds.), *Handbook of political science*, vol I, Reading: Addison Wesley 1975, pp. 1-50; C.W. Anderson, The place of principles in policy analysis, *American Political Science Review*, 73, 1979, 711–723; F. Fischer, *Politics, values, and public policy*, Boulder: Westview 1980; Goodin (1982), *op. cit.*; D. Stone, *Policy paradox and political reason*, Glenview: Scott Foresman 1988; E.B. Portis, M.B. Levy (eds. 1988), *op. cit.*; P. Wagner, C.H. Weiss, B. Wittrock, H. Wollman (eds.), *Social sciences and the modern states*, Cambridge: Cambridge UP 1991.

37 H.C. Finney, H.R. Lesieur, A contingency theory of organizational crime, *Research in the sociology of organizations*, 1, 1981, pp. 261–262.

38 Hinting at this, but ultimately set in a "problem-solving" key that is critical of the notion of multiple rationalities is P.R. Schulman, The "logic" of organizational irrationality, *Administration and Society*, 21, 1989, 31–53.

39 K. Hanf, F.W. Scharpf (eds.), *Interorganizational policymaking: Limits to coordination and central control*, London: Sage 1978.

40 H.R. van Gunsteren, *The quest for control: A critique of the rational-central rule approach*, New York: Wiley 1976; E. Etzioni-Halevy, *Bureaucracy and democracy: A political dilemma*, London: Routledge 1983; J.E. Lane (ed.), *Bureacracy and public choice*, London: Sage 1987.

41 J. O'Connor, *The fiscal crisis of the state*, New York: St. Martin's Press 1973.

42 J. Gough, *The political economy of the welfare state*, London: MacMillan 1979; C. Offe, *Contradictions of the welfare state*, London: Hutchinson 1984.

43 J. Habermas, *Legitimation crisis*, Boston: Beacon Press 1975.

44 *Report to the President by the Presidential Commission on the Space Shuttle Challenger Accident*, Washington, 6 June 1986, p. 120.

45 R. Jervis, *Perceptions and misperceptions in international politics*, Princeton: Princeton UP 1976; R.J. Russo, P. Schoemakers, *Decision traps*, New York: Simon and Schuster 1988; Bell, Raiffa and Tversky (eds. 1990), *op. cit.*; Z. Maoz, *National choices and international processes*, Cambridge: Cambridge UP 1990.

46 L.S. Etheredge, *Can governments learn?* Oxford: Pergamon 1985; N.F. Dixon, *Our own worst enemy*, London: Jonathan Cape 1987.

47 I.L. Janis, *Groupthink*, Boston: Little, Brown 1982; C.J. Nemeth, B.M. Staw, The tradeoffs of social control and innovation in groups and organizations, *Advances in experimental social psychology*, 22, 1989, 175–210; P. 't Hart, *Groupthink in government: A study of small groups and policy failure*, Amsterdam: Swets and Zeitlinger 1990 (and Baltimore: Johns Hopkins UP 1994); P. Tetlock et al. (1992), *op. cit.*

48 H. Wilensky, *Organizational intelligence*, New York: Free Press 1967; A.L. George, *Presidential decision making in foreign policy*, Boulder: Westview Press 1980; J. Burke, F. Greenstein, *How presidents test reality*, New York: Russel Sage 1988.

49 J.D. Steinbruner, *The cybernetic theory of decision*, Princeton: Princeton UP 1976.

50 R.Y. Hirokawa, D.S. Gouran, A.E. Martz, Understanding the sources of faulty group decision making: A lesson from the Challenger disaster, *Small group behavior*, 19, 4, 1988, 411–433, notably p. 415.

51 Hirokawa et al. (1988), *op. cit.*, p. 423.

52 J.K. Esser, J.S. Lindoerfer, Groupthink and the Space Shuttle Challenger accident: Toward a quantitative case analysis, *Journal of Behavioral Decision Making*, 2, 1989, 167–177; G. Moorhead, R. Ference, C.P. Neck, Group decision fiascoes continue: Space shuttle Challenger and a revised groupthink framework, *Human Relations*, 44, 1991, 539–550.

53 Classics here include: P. Bachrach, M.S. Baratz, *Power and poverty*, New York: Oxford UP 1970; M. Dertick, *New towns in-town: Why a federal program failed*, Washington DC: Urban Institute 1972. On large projects, see P. Schulman, *Large-scale policymaking*, New York: Elsevier 1980; and D. Collingridge, *The management of scale: Big technologies, big decisions, big mistakes*, London: Routledge 1992.

54 Classic contributions include L. Binder et al., *Crises and sequences of political development*, Princeton: Princeton UP 1971; G. Almond, S.C. Flanagan, R.J. Mundt (eds.), *Crisis, choice, and change: Historical studies of political development*, Boston: Little, Brown 1973; J.J. Linz, A. Stepan (eds.), *The breakdown of democratic regimes*, Baltimore: Johns Hopkins UP 1978.

55 C.J. Friedrich, *The pathology of politics*, New York: Free Press 1972. See also J.B. Mc Kinney, M. Johnston (eds.), *Fraud, waste and abuse in government: Causes, consequences and cures*, Philadelphia: Institute for the Study of Human Issues 1986; D.F. Thompson, *Political ethics and public office*, Cambridge: Harvard UP 1987; H. Kelman, V.L. Hamilton, *Crimes of obedience*, New Haven: Yale UP 1989; V.L. Hamilton, J. Sanders, Responsibility and risk in organizational crimes of obedience, *Research in organizational behavior*, 14, New York: JAI Press 1992, 49–90.

56 Hamilton and Sanders (1992), *op. cit.*, p. 76. See also M. McConnell, *Challenger: A major malfunction*, New York: Doubleday 1987; T.L. Cooper, Hierarchy, virtue, and the practice of public administration: A perspective for normative ethics, *Public Administration Review*, 47, 1987, 320–328; R.P. Boisjoly, E.F. Curtis, E. Mellican, Roger Boisjoly and the Challenger disaster: The ethical dimensions, *Journal of Business Ethics*, 8, 1989, 217–230; M.T. Charles, The last flight of Space Shuttle Challenger, in: U. Rosenthal, M.T. Charles, P. 't Hart (eds.), *Coping with crises: The management of disasters, riots, and terrorism*, Springfield: Charles Thomas 1989, pp. 141–168; P. Werhane, Engineers and management: The challenge of the Challenger incident, *Journal of Business Ethics*, 10, 1991, 605–616; J.R. Herkert, Management's hat trick: The misuse of "engineering judgment" in the Challenger incident, *Journal of Business Ethics*, 10, 1991, 617–620; P. Moore,

Intimidation and communication: A case study of the Challenger accident, *Journal of Business and Technical Communication*, 6, 1992, 403–437.

57 W.H. Starbuck, F.J. Milliken, Challenger: Fine-tuning the odds until something breaks, *Journal of Management Studies*, 25, 1988, 319–340.

58 B. Turner, *Man-made disaster*, London: Wykeham 1978.

59 S. Slatter, *Corporate recovery*, Harmondsworth: Penguin 1984 provides detailed examples of corporate decline cases; K.S. Cameron, R.I. Sutton, D.A. Whetten, (eds.), *Readings in organizational declince: Frameworks, research, and prescriptions*, Cambridge: Ballinger 1988.

60 W. Niskanen, *Bureaucracy and representative government*, Chicago: Aldine-Atherton 1971.

61 For example, O. Williamson, *Markets and hierarchies*, New York: Free Press 1975; H. Hanusch (ed.), *Anatomy of government deficiencies*, New York: De Gruyter 1983; C. Wolf, *Markets or governments*, Cambridge: MIT Press 1988.

62 For example, albeit in very different ways the intensive case study by Pressman and Wildavsky, *Implementation*, Berkeley: California UP 1973, and the macro-theoretical overview of S.D. Sieber, *Fatal remedies: The ironies of social intervention*, New York: Plenum Press 1981.

63 U. Rosenthal, P. 't Hart, A. Kouzmin, The bureau-politics of crisis management, *Public Administration*, 69, 1991, 211–233.

64 Compare Y. Dror, *Policymaking under adversity*, New Brunswick: Transaction Books 1986; J. Bryson, B. Crosby, *Leadership for the common good: Tackling public problems in a shared power world*, San Francisco: Jossey-Bass 1992.

65 H.S. Schwartz, On the psychodynamics of organizational disaster: The case of the space shuttle Challenger, *Columbia Journal of World Business*, 22, 1987, 59–67.

66 D. Vaughan, Autonomy, interdepedence, and social control: NASA and the space shuttle Challenger, *Administrative Science Quarterly*, 35, 1990, 225–257.

67 Vaughan (1990), *op. cit.*, pp. 249–250.

68 Perrow (1984), *op. cit.*, p.63.

69 See, for example B.D. Jacobs, P. 't Hart, Disaster at Hillsborough stadium:A comparative analysis, in: J.W. Handmer, D. Parker (eds.), *Hazard management and emergency planning: Perspectives on Britain*, London: James and James 1991, pp. 127–152.

70 Perrow (1984), *op. cit.*, pp. 258–281.

71 Compare G.R. Holt, A.W. Morris, Activity theory and the analysis of organizations, *Human Organization*, 52, 1993, pp. 100–101 (who reconstruct but do not completely agree with the systems-level interpretation of the Challenger offered by Perrowian analysis). See also Landau and Chisholm (1995), *op. cit.*

72 Perrow (1984), *op. cit.*

73 M. Rein, D. Schon, Frame-reflective policy discourse, in: P. Wagner, C.H. Weiss, B. Wittrock, H. Wollmann (eds.), *Social sciences and modern states: National experiences and theoretical crossroads*, Cambridge: Cambridge UP 1991.

74 Compare, for example, J.M. Gillroy, M. Wade (eds.), *The moral dimensions of public policy choice: Beyond the market paradigm*, Pittsburgh: Pittsburgh UP 1992.

75 See Lane (1993), *op. cit.*, pp. 69–70 who nicely outlines the dilemma of evaluating or choosing between different empirical theories of policymaking but then goes on to arbitrarily impose his own ideosyncratic criteria.

76 E.A. Cohen, J. Gooch, *Military misfortunes: The anatomy of failure in war*, New York: Vintage Books 1991.

77 Peirce (1981), *op. cit.*

78 Peirce (1981), *op. cit.*, p. 125.

79 R.R. Nelson, *The moon and the ghetto*, New York: Norton 1977, p. 79.

80 G.T. Allison, *Essence of decision: Explaining the Cuban missile crisis*, Boston: Little, Brown 1971; see also J.D. Steinbruner, *The cybernetic theory of decision*, Princeton: Princeton UP 1974; Toonen (1983), *op. cit.*; H. Linstone (ed.), *Multiple perspectives for decision making*, New York: Elsevier 1984.

81 Dunleavy (1990), *op. cit.*, pp. 56–57.
82 Dunleavy (1990), *op. cit.*, p.59.
83 It is rhetorical in the sense that it dismisses out of hand as "relativists" those analysts who argue that it is a problem to compare multiple explanations of the same policy episode that are based on highly different assumptions about how policies come about and that, as a consequence, might concentrate on actors and forces operating at highly different levels of analysis, different moments in time, and different levels in the organization.

Appendix: Examples of explanatory approaches to policy fiascoes

---

A Single case studies (US cases and illustrative references only)
Vietnam war: Teger (1980); Thompson (1980); Gelb and Betts (1979)
Housing policy: Downs (1974); Welfeld (1992)
Watergate: Raven (1974); Kelman (1976); Janis (1982)
Three Mile Island: Sills, Wolf and Shelanski (eds. 1982); Perrow (1981)
Savings and Loans Scandal: Kane (1989); Calavita and Pontell (1990)
Iran-Contra: 't Hart (1990); Hamilton and Sanders (1992)

B Studies of specific types of fiascoes (selected policy sectors/failure types)
    B1   *Military fiascoes:* Dixon (1979); Gabriel (1980); Betts (1982); Regan (1987);
                Kam (1988); Cohen and Gooch (1990): Shiels (1991)
    B2   *Man-made disasters:* Turner (1978); Miller (1988); Souder (1988);
                Weick (1989); Reason (1990); Wagenaar, Hudson and Reason (1990);
                Groeneweg (1992); Pauchant and Mitroff (1992); Sagan (1993)
    B3   *Corruption and organizational deviance:* Sutherland (1949); Finney and
                Lesieur (1982); Doig, Phillips and Manson (1984); Nas, Price and Weber
                (1986); Morgan (1987); Kelman and Hamilton (1989); Hamilton and Sanders
                (1992); Thompson (1993)
    B4   *Large public projects:* Banfield (1951); Hall (1982); Morris and Hough (1987);
                Collingridge (1992)

C General theories of failure
    C1   *Problem-solving theories:* Janis (1982); Brockner and Rubin (1985); Staw
                and Ross (1987); Russo and Schoemaker (1988); Nutt (1988); Janis (1989);
                't Hart (1990); Vertzberger (1990)
    C2   *Competing values theories:* Friedrich (1972); Linz and Stepan (1978); Rowe
                and Mason (1989)
    C3   *Institutional theories:* Merton (1957); Parkinson (1957); Boyer (1964);
                Crozier (1964); Tullock (1965); Downs (1967); Peter and Hull (1969);
                Niskanen (1971); Goodin (1975); Kaufman (1976); Barton (1980); Peirce
                (1981)
    C4   *Structural constraints theories:* Offe (1984); Perrow (1984); Jacobs and
                't Hart (1991)

CHAPTER 6

Evaluating Agents' Behavior: Analysis as Accusing and Excusing

Disasters that befoul the air and soil and poison the water are generally turned to political account: someone already unpopular is going to be blamed for it.

Mary Douglas[1]

To Explain is to Blame

We have seen in previous chapters that the analysis of policy fiascoes is not a politically neutral activity which can be done by fully detached, unencumbered individuals.[2] The very label of "fiasco" or "failure" entails a political statement. Events are perceived and labelled as "policy fiascoes" when important values and issues are at stake, when societal taboos or sacrosant values have been violated. The labelling of events as a *fiasco* signals that trespassing has occurred. No community can afford to take violations of central values for granted. If this occurs, there tends to be an impulse to maintain and restore social order. Public and political debates about controversial policy episodes should be seen in this light. The identification of failures and the analysis of their causes tend to be part of a process of accounting and blaming. Once events are identified as fiascoes, questions about responsibility and liability force themselves on the public agenda. Who can be held responsible for the damage that has been done to the social fabric? Who should bear the blame? What sort of sanctions, if any, are appropriate? Who should remedy the victims?

Labelling negative events as *policy* fiascoes entails such an act of blaming, often quite deliberately so. It implies holding public officials and agencies (in other words the government) accountable for the damage done. Efforts to understand and explain the genesis of policy fiascoes can, therefore, never be seperated fully from issues of guilt and blame. The specter of political and administrative accountability is always lurking in the background. A full understanding of policy fiascoes requires us to consider the attribution of blame that is an integral part of their construction and evolution.

In the pivotal role of blaming lies the key to understanding why the search for an explanation of controversial policy episodes itself tends to be a highly adversarial process. The politics of blaming start at the very selection and instruction of investigative officials and committees, but it is highlighted especially by the behavior of many stakeholders during the "postmortem period."[3] Many of the officials and agencies involved in an alleged fiasco will engage in impression management, blame shifting, and bureau-political maneuvering. Their reputations are at stake. The odium of failure can ruin their careers and weaken their institutional position. Two examples may illustrate this.

In the aftermath of the Hillsborough disaster some officers of the South Yorkshire police force, which had operational responsibility for crowd control on that occasion, publicly stated that the Liverpool fans were at the root of the tragedy that left ninetyfive people dead and 400 wounded.[4] Immediately a heated debate followed – in the tabloid press, in the political arena, and also between different police forces. The Merseyside police, policing the Greater Liverpool area where most of the fans and victims came from, openly questioned the veracity of the public statements of their South Yorkshire colleagues. It stressed the need for the official inquiry, headed by the Lord Justice Taylor, to "uncover all the facts."[5] The controversy was remarkable in that it brought to the surface disagreements within the ranks of the police at the national level. The different interpretations went beyond professional differences of opinion. They were attempts to shift and reallocate blame for the occurrence of disaster. The bureaucratic agencies, in this sense, represented their own local "constituencies." The South Yorkshire officers wanted to save their force from disgrace and tried to cover up some of the mistakes made. The Merseyside police, on its part, articulated the predominant emotions among the local population and politicians. With this bureaucratic conflict and blaming came different "mythologies" about what had really happened on the day of the disaster, which proved to be very resistant to discrepant information that eventually emerged in the course of the Taylor inquiry. Eventually, intervention by the British Home Secretary was necessary to ask the parties to calm down.

The second example comes from the French blood transfusion scandal. Soon after the start of the prosecution of M. Garetta, the head of the production division of the Centre National de Transfusion Sanguine (CNTS), the French blood transfusion agency, the first two books on what had come to be called *l'affaire du sang* (the blood affair) were published. The first, by a journalist, was written from the perspective of several children who suffered from hemophilia and had been infected by HIV-contaminated blood transfusions. It recorded the history of their illnesses, accused the health authorities of criminal negligence and blamed the government for the deaths of these innocent children. The second book, which appeared soon after, was written by the former director-general of CNTS who had retired after a long career in 1984, not long before the crucial tests became available. His book contains elaborate, justificatory explanations of the technical intricacies involved in the handling of blood products and can be read as a defense of the agency's practices and policies.[6]

Following up on observations made in chapter two, these examples show that the context of fiasco analysis is often highly politicized. Many of the "facts" and accounts of policy episodes available will be biased, and indeed framed specifically to convey certain images about what happened and why, and obscure others. Eventually, the analysts' own statements and reports become part of this process. They may be interpreted by some or all of the parties involved as vehicles for attempts to shift the blame. In other words, fiasco analysts will inevitably feel pressures of this kind building up. They are likely to become both an object and – wittingly or unwittingly – an agent of political processes of framing and blaming.

But the political dimension of fiasco analysis goes beyond opportunistic party politics or bureau-political strife. The very act of fiasco analysis itself is, to a certain extent, inherently political. The pivotal role of accountability and blaming can be felt at each layer of fiasco analysis that has been discussed here. Each of the biases, frames and foci that have been distinguished so far can, in fact, be read as accountability schemes. They imply whether, and to what extent, government is to be held accountable for certain chains of events, and they direct the search for crucial variables in the policy process.

The analysis of policy fiascoes is therefore always wound up in a process of accusing and excusing. Of course many studies of policy fiascoes by academic analysts are not undertaken for the purpose of blaming. Nor are they driven by partisan interests. On the contrary, most of the academic studies of policy fiascoes are motivated by a desire to learn from failure and to improve our insights through detached analysis. However, the work by Mary Douglas and her colleagues on risk analysis suggests convincingly that the interpretation and explanation of policy processes inevitably implies an attribution of blame to some actors and the disculpation of others.[7] This means that, in a broad sense, fiasco analysis is always political. In this chapter we will further investigate these political and forensic aspects of policy analysis. This is best done by returning to each of the four layers of meaning-making in the construction of policy fiascoes that have been discussed in the previous chapters.

Policy Fiascoes as Political Symbols

We saw in the second chapter that the labelling of outcomes as highly negative is biased by cultural frames, temporal, and spatial perspectives and political expediencies. The comparative analysis of policy fiascoes is therefore to some extent a form of political anthropology. Policy fiascoes are important tokens and signposts of particular political cultures. Central tenets of those cultures – whether construed at the national or group level – are revealed by the sort of events that are construed as fiascoes and the sort of explanations of their causes that come to be accepted. The completely different reception of the assault on the Rainbow Warrior in France, New Zealand, and the Netherlands, discussed in chapter 2, is a case in point.

Another remarkable feature of the political side of outcome assessment concerns the strategic impact the labelling of a particular episode as a failure might have. In every political system there appear to be lines that should not be crossed. But these lines are not fixed; they are open to contingent political interpretations. Whose interpretation prevails, depends on many factors. As seen in the examples above, agencies associated with a controversial program switch from assertion to denial and diffusion of responsibility. The political discovery of a policy failure constitutes a critical event, which challenges at least part of the policymaking system as a whole.

If we seek to analyze these political dynamics of failure assessment, we need a theoretical understanding of politics that focuses not so much on its decision making functions, but instead views it as institutionalized drama – as a platform for expressing as well as channeling the heterogeneity of values, perceptions, and interests that inevitably exist in any society.[8] A key aspect of such an understanding are symbols.[9] Narrative stories, figures of speech, and metaphors tend to be used to frame and reframe intricate and often highly technical issues. Budgetary problems can be portrayed as "major overruns" or as "administrative adjustments." Projects that suffer from delay can be depicted as "paralyzed by red tape" or as "in a process of rescheduling." The use of violence by a secret service can be disqualified as "state terrorism" or justified with an appeal to "raison d'état."[10]

Put in this form, policy failures lend themselves to dramatic representation and re-representation in the mass media, in parliament, if need be in the courts. Although particular cultures may evolve typical or preferred symbolic systems, these are not fixed entities: "Our symbol system, then, is not a cage which locks us into a single view of the political world, but a melange of symbolic understandings by which we struggle, through a continuous series of negotiations, to assign meaning to events."[11]

Symbols structure political life and convey important messages. In doing so, they fulfill important functions in the maintenance of political order and stability. In this spirit, March and Olsen have pointed out that the role of rituals and symbolism in politics should not be regarded as some kind of perversity but as part of its essence.[12] Moreover, Edelman has argued repeatedly that the use of political dramaturgy, language, and symbolism serves – intendedly but also unintendedly – to obtain the "consent of the governed" even in the face of great disparities in wealth, status, and power.[13]

The symbolic perspective may help to understand the political construction of policy fiascoes. Policy episodes that are construed as "fiascoes" constitute points of crisis in the symbolic political order. The interpretation of a policy episode as a fiasco implies that, to a certain extent, familiar symbolic frameworks legitimating the preexisting sociopolitical order are compromised.[14]

From a symbolic perspective, several distinctive features of the political construction of policy fiascoes stand out:

- Fiascoes are a perceptual category: for a fiasco to come into being a considerable number of sufficiently influential individuals and groups must perceive important, essentially adverse, changes in their environment.[15]
- Fiascoes are also an affective category: the challenges to previously-held world views that fiascoes bring about, compounded by first-hand or indirect experience of material damages, human suffering, or gross injustice, generate a significant amount of anxiety. Policy fiascoes of major symbolic significance highlighted by prime-time television coverage, such as Watergate, the Challenger space shuttle accident, or the Heysel stadium tragedy, may produce significant degrees of collective stress among mass publics beyond the communities directly affected.
- When a series of events has come to be seen as a policy fiasco, this implies a degree of delegitimation. Fiascoes challenge important myths of politics and governance. They expose acutely that the rationality, morality, power, and competence of incumbent office-holders or bureaucratic agencies is limited, and can lead to adverse effects.[16] From this perspective, fiascoes and fiasco-induced political crises should be viewed as dynamic forces in ongoing, dynamic processes of legitimization, delegitimization, and relegitimization.
- Given this context of fundamental ambiguity, collective stress, and latent or manifest delegitimation, fiascoes provide opportunities for mass mobilization and institutional self-dramatization. This aspect is often overlooked in studies of policy fiascoes. Whilst decision makers

and incumbent policy elites may experience the emergence of collective judgments of their actions as a fiasco as highly threatening, other officials, groups, and organization will harbor the exact opposite interpretation. For them, the very delegitimation of past policies provides an opportunity space to propose new ones.[17]

The Politics of Analysis: Going Back Means Going Up

The seemingly methodological issue which part of the policy process is to be picked for analysis, one of the central concerns of chapter 3, necessitates certain choices that, in actual practice, can have important consequences for the allocation of blame. In many cases, going back in time in reconstructing the roots of failure propels the analyst, whether he applies forward or backward mapping techniques, towards the top of the organizational hierarchy. This connection between time and organization is often overlooked in the reconstructed decision trees of human error studies.

Going back in time to trace the decisions and events that shaped those decisions and actions closest to the onset of failure, often means going up the policymaking ladder. The focus will shift from implementation errors and other operative failures to working conditions, legislative constraints, or faulty policy theories. Investigating committees will not only interview the street level bureaucrats, operators, and field commanders, but will also subpoena heads of agencies, legislators, and senior policymakers.

In doing so, they will find two things. First, the further back one goes, the more likely it is that the impact of the decisions at that point in time and at that level of policy, is mitigated by intermittent events and decisions at lower levels. Secondly, the decisions made at more senior levels of policymaking tend to be more general, and often not explicitly directed at what later became the focus of the fiasco. In the Heyzel case, for example, political nonintervention in the conflict between Gendarmerie and municipal police on the part of the mayor of Brussels and the minister of the Interior can in retrospect be seen as an important contextual factor shaping the cumbersome and vulnerable policing arrangements for the Liverpool–Juventus match. However, it can hardly be understood as deliberately designed to produce the dangerous compromise to divide the section into two separate zones that caused many of the problems later on. Given the ambiguities of reconstructing and interpreting top-level (non)actions and (non)decisions, there is a tendency among investigators to concentrate on the direct, short term, operative causes of mishaps and fiascoes. Analytically, it is much easier to trace and to identify them, and to establish plausible cause-and-effect reconstructions.

The lack of sensitivity to multiple time frames and contextual influences evident from fiasco post-mortems, is only partly due to cognitive biases or analytical expediencies. There is also a political side to these biases. When things go wrong in an organization or with a policy initiative, there will always be a tendency to combine the search for causes with the allocation of blame and – if possible – responsibility. This implies that post-hoc reconstructions of fiascoes are generally defensive, interest-ridden, and political activities. High ranking officials, for example, will have an interest in limiting the search for causes to short-term failures on the operative level as this may help to keep their own role in the genesis of the fiasco off the investigative agenda. Blaming operators and field agencies doesn't rock the ship of state too strongly.

This is especially marked in analyses of "instant failures." These are episodes concentrated in place and time where the evidence of failure is immediate and unmistakable such as industrial accidents, mass transportation disasters, and social breakdowns such as street riots and prison revolts. Many observer reports and official investigations of cases like these focus on human error, and therefore imply a search for individual culprits. This should come as no surprise. Instant failures are almost always events with a high visibility and an immediate threat to life and limb. At least in most Western societies, the violent or accidental death of large numbers of people is considered such a violation of the social order that some degree of social and political scapegoating is inevitable. Someone has to be blamed for the atrocities. In these instances the myth of individual operator failure is particularly expedient for middle managers and higher-level officials. Clinging to it, they avoid having to rethink their own responsibilities for designing, operating, and managing the high-risk systems in which many of such disasters occur. When the organizational and political analysis is nevertheless taken from the operational to the management and policy levels, uncomfortable questions will be asked about the role of high-level officials, policymakers, and indeed also of legislators and supervisory bodies supposedly controlling executive behavior. Many of these may want to avoid such questions from being aired, and will therefore have a vested interest in framing fiasco postmortems in particular ways. It is these political processes of allocating blame and accountability that lie at the heart of what one might call the most attractive failure bias: defensive impulses of stakeholders may result in their nurturing oversimplified negative judgments about the behavior of particular operators, policymakers, and institutions associated directly with the failures.

One example of this process can be seen in the maneuvering on the part of the management of Townsend Thoresen, the company owning the Herald of Free Enterprise ferry which sank near the Belgian port of

Zeebrugge in March 1987, killing almost 200 people and leaving many others wounded and traumatized. It was established soon after the disaster that the ship had gone down because its bow doors had been left open when it took to sea, allowing water to flow onto the car decks and destabilize the vessel. The media were quick to find out that the assistant bosun responsible for monitoring the closing of the ship's bow doors had been asleep when the Herald left for Dover that evening. They also alleged that the ship's captain had a drinking problem (it turned out later that the captain was tested for alcohol and drugs immediately after the disaster, with negative results).

To Townsend Thoresen, the line of reconstruction pursued by the media was convenient, and its senior officials sought to direct, and therefore contain, the official inquiry that followed along these lines. Their position was that the accident was due to an unfortunate, but incidental, lack of oversight on the part of at most a few crew members. This position they sought to maintain throughout the inquiry.

From an opportunistic point of view, they had every reason to; they had a lot to hide. In the course of the inquiry overwhelming evidence was uncovered showing that in the years and months preceding the Herald disaster, various captains of Townsend Thoresen ships had made urgent recommendations to install indicator lights on the bridge that would tell if the bow doors were open or closed. The written record showed that these suggestions had been rebutted, even ridiculed, by management. Also, captains had complained about other safety features of current practices that turned out to be crucial contributing factors in the capsizing of the Herald, such as the inability to establish the ship's draught on any given sailing. In fact, no systematic monitoring of cargo loads and passenger numbers took place. It had been routine procedure to enter fictitious estimates in the log book. Ships that in fact were heavily overloaded and therefore lay deeper into the water were allowed to sail.

All of these facts were initially obscured by Townsend Thoresen's management, even to the point of actively misleading the inquiry. The sheer force of the historical record compromised this strategy, causing one of the company's directors to break down in tears during another round of cross-examination and to confess he had lied to the investigation. The final report of the inquiry shows that this containment strategy had failed, and that another, much more threatening, logic of reconstruction had prevailed. Although the report begins by saying that "at first sight" the disaster was triggered by lapses on the part of the assistant bosun, the chief officer, and the master of the Herald of Free Enterprise, it goes on to state that:

[A] full investigation into the circumstances of the disaster leads inexorably to the conclusion that the underlying or cardinal faults lay higher up in the Company. The Board of Directors did not appreciate their responsibility for the safe management of their ships.[18]

The case of the Herald ferry disaster is no exception; it is a prototype. Strategies of "containment" versus "escalation" in postmortem periods tend to be pursued by the same types of stakeholders across a wide range of cases. The managers and policymakers at the top seek to keep the focus of attention at the bottom of the organization, whereas victims, operators, and critical investigators tend to do the opposite.[19] Legislators and supervisory bodies are caught in the middle of this: on the one hand they can jump at their responsibility to find fault and enforce standards of quality, safety, and integrity; on the other hand, they may anticipate questions being asked why they did not do so earlier, prior to the fiasco, and therefore choose to pursue a more "restrained" line of inquiry.

The Politics of Fate

Misfortunes, so it was argued in chapter 4, are not static things out there. They are not "things out there," because they are construed in social processes. And they are not "static" because what we accept as fortune changes constantly. We have pointed several times to the tensions between a technocratic, choice-oriented approach to policymaking, and some of the political realities of policymaking and evaluation. Recognizing these tensions, one may expect that investing large amounts of time and resources in the prevention of misfortune and effective responses to fateful events will not fully shield politicians and policymakers from blame. The major lesson of a political and symbolic approach to policy analysis is that blaming is the name of the game in the construction of policy fiascoes. In this sense, "misfortune" or "fate" are symbols used in excusing policymakers, just as "mismanagement" or "folly" are symbols that serve to accuse them. Debates about the causes of policy fiascoes inevitably are debates about policy excuses. The crucial – but often implicit – question in these debates is where, when, and how misfortune stops and mismanagement begins.

The acceptability of "bad luck" as an excuse for failures and disasters does not only depend upon evaluations of the actual possibilities and attempts to foresee and control the fatal events. Blaming also depends on the nature of the event. Some failures have such grave consequences or pose such a threat to our worldview or sense of justice that "bad luck," however appropriate in empirical terms, will not be accepted as an explanation. Especially those who have been injured will continue to look for someone to blame. As Shklar puts it:

> To be sure, some fires, floods, storms, and earthquakes are still recognized as natural and unavoidable, but the government is expected to warn, protect and relieve us when they occur. We no longer have childhood diseases and there are so few epidemics that when one does occur – like AIDS – we are aghast and victims blame the government for not being able to stop it. What is perceived in all these cases is that with the technical resources at our command, we should be able to turn all natural disasters into manageable setbacks. Our sense of injustice is deeply aroused when we fail. Our technological expectations are often too high, but given what the last two generations have accomplished, we suspect wrongful indifference or injustice when there is no one to protect us against the still-untamed forces of nature. In fact, it is not the fault of scientists or public officials that little can now be done, nor are they culpably indifferent to the current epidemic. Victims, however, seem to find it easier to bear their misfortune if they can see injustice as well as bad luck.[20]

In many current Western societies, an expansive conception of policy competence has taken hold, which makes it hard to claim that fortune and fate lay at the root of a policy that has turned out badly. Over the past centuries the tolerance for misfortune has decreased exponentially. As Lawrence Friedman, the legal sociologist, has observed: "Slowly people have come to expect more out of government, out of law, out of life. The mechanisms may be obscure, but one key factor is the sense that there are ways to exert control over many of man's ancient contingencies."[21] Consequently, policymakers are expected to eradicate most sources of misfortune, and thus prevent ills from occurring.

In such a cultural and political context emphasizing control and competence, "bad luck" is hardly considered a satisfactory answer to the victims of policy failures. Strict liabilities are therefore accepted in many legal systems, not just to prevent future disasters, but basically to enhance social and retributive justice and, eventually, to prevent the social and political system from disintegrating. Stricter forms of liability are regarded as useful - even when they are clear fictions – to prevent the political system from falling apart. They call upon office-holders to observe their duties and obligations, and are designed to increase the transparency and reliability of government.

In this voluntaristic context, identifying scapegoats and culprits, whether they be persons or institutions, can first of all relieve tensions and clear the air. Through catharsis, it keeps the road to cooperation open in the wake of tragedy, trauma, and crisis.[22] Secondly, political scapegoating in the wake of fiascoes is a way of reestablishing these deeply held convictions (myths) about politics as the realm of rational action, control, and policy choice. The symbolic inference of political accountability can be interpreted as an appeal to establish political control in areas that hitherto have been reigned by the spells of fate.[23] Shklar's analysis exemplifies this line of reasoning: "public agents should not be encouraged to feel that they are in the grip of necessity and personally powerless. They can usually perform better and more responsibly than they do and at the very least be guilty of only passive injustice."[24] Procedural care, commitment, and the reduction of damage therefore are likely to remain the central elements in Western-style efforts to cope with misfortunes for some time to come.[25]

Looking at misfortune and fiascoes from these political and symbolic perspectives, one may speculate that the plight of policymakers in Western countries will increase in the future. Technology and science have been crucial in creating a sense of control over our lives – physical control at first, but gradually also social and institutionalized control. The uncertainties in life have been reduced dramatically over the past two centuries, but with this reduction the disappointments and expectations of compensation of those who suffer from fate have risen correspondingly. In the future people will more than ever look "for someone to blame, and it will probably be the government."[26]

Analytical Frames as Accountability Schemes

The pivotal role of accountability and blame also sheds light on the connection between the philosophies of governance and the identification of crucial process variables and factors which have been discussed in chapter 5. The philosophies of governance can, in fact, be read as accountability schemes. They imply whether, and to what extent, government is to be held accountable for certain chains of events, and they direct the search for crucial variables in the policy process. Roughly, the schemes are as follows: optimists blame people; realists blame organizations; pessimists blame the system as a whole. More specifically, each of the explanatory frames and foci that come with these philosophies offer particular answers to the question which events were within the realm of governance. In the end, the choice of one explanatory frame or another is therefore not a politically neutral one, made by an objective, rational analyst. Every frame implies a particular distribution of blame. And different analytical frames produce different candidates for blame.

Let us return to the Challenger fiasco once more. From a problem-solving perspective, blame lies with the participants to the teleconferences immediately prior to the decision to go ahead with the launch. The prob-

lem-solving analyst looks at the events and sees a distorted decision process and avoidable failures of information-processing. She is likely to
blame NASA managers for not being more probing and attentive to the
possibility that the launch might fail. In addition she will blame Morton
Thiokol managers for not taking the expert judgment of their own engineers seriously enough, and the engineers for not being more persistent
in pressing their case for postponement.

In his turn, the competing values theorist blames not only the individuals involved in the teleconferences but rather NASA's top and middle
management for allowing the organization as a whole to compromise its
commitment to the principle of safety first. Under increasing budgetary
and political pressure, the organization had committed itself to meeting
nearly impossible flight schedules, even if this meant a desperate scram-
ble to prematurely routinize procedures for handling a high-risk technology. In doing so, NASA management violated the spirit if not the letter of
its own flight readiness review procedures, which were obviously
inspired by the idea that preventing a major accident was to be the prime
consideration throughout the project.

An institutional interaction theorist blames NASA as a whole for col-
lectively lulling itself into the narcissistic belief that accidents wouldn't
happen in one of its projects. But he will probably look beyond the NASA
hierarchy and blame regulatory bodies, both internal and external, for not
forcing NASA to face up to the reality of its own vulnerability. In particular, he will find fault with their complacency in relying, in their supervisory role, almost exclusively on information and progress reports provided by NASA management. Similarly, in a switch of roles and responsibilities, NASA might be blamed for not adopting a more hands-on approach
to controlling the performance of its major subcontractors, in particular
Morton Thiokol. The absence of a more proactive and aggressive monitoring strategy on the part of both NASA itself and the regulatory agencies
and groups stands out as a crucial error of omission. In sum, blame in this
perspective becomes divided between NASA's brass and the bodies
responsible for keeping them in check.

Finally, the structural constraints theorist blames not so much NASA
and its regulatory bodies but rather Congress and the Executive for not
recognizing, indeed actively denying or even deliberately obscuring, the
risks associated with manned space missions. Her analysis of the
Challenger incident highlights the inherent instability and error-inducing
character of shuttle technology, compounded by the political and organizational pressures operating at the time of the Challenger launch. The
public had a right to know of these risks in advance. A more explicit political discussion of their acceptability would have been in order. Absent
such public debate, what in fact was a high-risk system was represented

publicly as if it were failure-proof. NASA and its programs were allowed by the ruling elites to become a national myth, thus setting the stage for the "national trauma" that resulted when the Challenger exploded live on televsion.

The four foci thus make for increasingly comprehensive accountability schemes. The problem-solving perspective stays closest to the proximate causes, in other words the operational decisions that are most directly tied to the onset of failure. In contrast the structural constraints perspective digs deepest – going back in time, going sideways in the policy network, and going up the organizational hierarchy – for the people and decisions that shaped the system in which the failure eventually occurred.

These differences also tend to influence the political appeal of each focus. The problem-solving view is likely to be the least controversial. As we have seen above, diagnosing policy failure in terms of human error has its attractions for beleaguered elites. In contrast, the structural contraints scheme may pose the most complete threat to their own position and responsibility, and they will fight it as much they can. The opposite holds for victims and opposition groups. Which of the four accountability schemes becomes the dominant one in any given controversy may of course be partly due the force and ability of the proponents of these various positions. [27]

The Politics of Policy Fiascoes

For a full understanding of the construction of policy fiascoes this fourth, forensic layer of analysis is indispensable. It shows itself in the range, depth, and overall tone of the critical questions that are asked in the wake of adverse events. The "what happened?" of the initial stages soon gives way to the more inquisitive "how could this happen?" This, in its turn, is soon replaced by "what went wrong?" and, eventually, by "who is to pay?" Each of the three preliminary questions bears a relationship to the last one. Together they culminate in the politics of policy fiascoes. Debates about the how, what, and who of controversial policies can only be understood if we realize that they are held against the background of accountability and blame.

In this chapter we have argued that to understand the politics of fiascoes and fiasco analysis, a sensitivity to the uses of political symbols is required. The label "policy fiasco" is one such important political symbol. The use of the term "fiasco" implies that someone ought to pay for a failure, and the prefix of "policy" implies that the bill should be sent to the government.

Having mapped out the four layers of fiasco analysis, we are now in a position to return to the question with which this book began: the marked increase in "policy fiascoes" of the late eighties and early nineties of the twentieth century. If anthropologists are right in suggesting that in most societies someone already unpopular is usually blamed for disasters, we might have a clue for understanding the contemporary ubiquity of policy failure in Western democracies.

Notes

1 M. Douglas, *Risk and blame: Essays in cultural theory*, London: Routledge 1992, p. 5.
2 In this we draw heavily on the work of Mary Douglas on risk, see Douglas (1992), *op. cit.*
3 On the politics of official investigations following out of the ordinary policy events and social crises, compare M. Lipsky, D.J. Olson, *Commission politics: The processing of racial crisis in America*, New Brunswick: Transaction Books 1977.
4 This example has been adapted from U. Rosenthal, P. 't Hart, and A. Kouzmin, The bureau-politics of crisis management, *Public Administration*, 69, 1991, 211–233.
5 The appointment of a judge to investigate the causes of man-made disasters and contro-versial policy episodes is a common British strategy to de-politicize the inquiry process, in contrast to the US and many continental European countries, where there is a tenden-cy for parliament (Congress) to appoint special investigative committees. Although the latter are supposed to be non-partisan, in many cases splits occur during both the inves-tigation and resporting stages between government and opposition factions. In the US, truly major controversies/failures such as Watergate and Iran-Contra may in fact lead to multiple, redundant or openly competing inquiries, e.g. a presidential (in the Iran-Contra case: The Tower Commission), a Congressional (Joint Select Committee), and a judicial (Special Prosecutor Walsh).
6 Anne-Marie Casteret, *L'affaire du sang*, Paris: Éditions La Découverte 1992;
   J.P. Soulier, *Transfusion et SIDA: Le droit à la vérité*, Paris: Éditions Frison-Roche 1992.
7 Compare: B. Wynne, *Rationality and ritual: The Windscale inquiry and nuclear decisions in Britain*, Chalfont St. Giles: Society for the history of science 1982; U. Beck, *Risiko-gesellschaft: Auf dem Weg in eine andere Moderne*, Frankfurt: Suhrkamp 1986; B. Wynne, *Risk management and hazardous waste: Implementation and the dialecties of cred-ibility*, London: Springer 1987.
8 J. Combs, *Dimensions of political drama*, New York: Goodyear 1980.
9 M. Edelman, *The symbolic uses of politics*, Urbana: Illinois University Press 1964. Deborah A. Stone, *Policy paradox and policy reason*, Glenview Ill.: Scott 1988, chapter 6.
10 Framing one's analysis in terms of powerful labels is also a way of establishing one's identity as an analyst. There can, for example, be little doubt about the general thrust of the papers in a collection entitled *Crimes by the capitalist state: An introduction to state crim-inality* (edited by G. Barak, Albany: SUNY Press 1991).
11 D. Kertzer, *Ritual, politics, and power*, New Haven: Yale UP 1988, p. 175.
12 J. March, J.P. Olsen, *Rediscovering institutions*, New York: Basic Books 1989, pp. 49ff.
13 M.J. Edelman, *Political language: Words that succeed and policies that fail*, New York: Academic Press 1977; M.J. Edelman, *Constructing the political spectacle*, Chicago: Chicago UP 1988.
14 Part of this section is based on P. 't Hart, Symbols, rituals and power: The lost dimen-sion of crisis management, *Journal of Contingencies and Crisis Management*, 1, 1, 1993, pp. 36–50.
15 J.K. Schorr, Some contributions German *Katastrophensoziologie* can make to the sociology of disasters, *Journal of Mass Emergencies and Disasters*, 5, 1987, pp. 115–135.

16 Edelman (1977), *op. cit.*, pp.4–5.
17 J.M. Bryson, A perspective on planning and crises in the public sector, *Strategic Management Journal*, 2, 1981, pp. 181–196.
18 *Report of the formal investigation into the loss of the Herald of Free Enterprise*, London: Her Majesty's Stationary Office 1988, as quoted by J. Cook, *An accident waiting to happen*, London: Unwin 1989, p. 20.
19 It should be noted that the latter strategy can be equally one-sided. Investigators begin by assuming management was inept, corrupt, callous, or self-serving. This may lead them to overlook the complexity, ambiguity and constraints managers faced, which amounts to an emotionally or politically driven version of the wisdom after the event (hindsight) bias.
20 J. Shklar, *The faces of injustice*, New Haven: Yale UP 1990, p. xxx.
21 L.M. Friedman, *Total justice*, New York: Russel Sage 1985, p. 51.
22 Douglas (1992), *op. cit.*
23 H. R. van Gunsteren, *Denken over politieke verantwoordelijkheid*, Alphen aan den Rijn: Samsom 1974.
24 Shklar (1990), *op. cit.*, p. 65.
25 Needless to say, this policy pattern tends to be quite different in other cultures and political systems.
26 Shklar (1990), *op. cit.*, p. 64.
27 The acceptability of policymakers, government bureaucracies, or the entire policy system as the key culprits for failure may to a large extent depend on their more general political legitimacy at the time. Compare Easton's multi-level analysis of legitimacy (the political community, the regime, the authorities), in D. Easton, A *systems analysis of political life*, New York: Wiley 1965, pp. 171–220.

CHAPTER 7

Epilogue:
Making Sense of Policy Fiascoes

In our culture failure is anathema. We rarely hear about it, we never dwell on it and most of us do our best never to admit to it...

Sam B. Sitkin[1]

Rethinking the Ubiquity of Failure: Consequences for Understanding Fiascoes

In drawing the conclusions of this study, we stand with Thorstein Veblen, who once wrote that "the outcome of any serious research can only be to make two questions grow where one question grew before."[2] We hope he was right, since what this book has done mainly is to reframe exisiting questions about policy failure and generate new ones. It was the apparent increase in policy fiascoes in most Western democracies throughout the eighties that provided us with the initial puzzle of this study. Seven years later, what has this effort taught us about the apparent ubiquity of policy failure? Perhaps the main lesson to be learned is that the original question – why are there so many policy fiascoes nowadays? – is not very helpful. Especially if one takes a historical perspective, the answer to that question is straightforward and uninformative: moving through time, there is simply more and more policy to go wrong. In other words, because governments have spun an ever wider and more intricate web of policies, programs, and projects, the chances of major mishaps have increased. The increasing number of policy fiascoes thus becomes a matter of statistics. From this point of view, the only major bone of contention concerns the rate of this increase: is it proportional to the increasing scope of government activities, or does it rise exponentially, perhaps due to problems associated with "policy overstretch?"[3]

In our view, a more productive line of inquiry follows if one reframes the original question to read as: why have we become more inclined to understand public events and policy episodes as fiascoes? Why has societal tolerance for misfortune, unintended negative consequences of public policies, and bureaucratic failure decreased? How and why did fiascoes become prime-time news topics and political peak events? Whose agendas were served by this development? Our analysis suggests that the alleged ubiquity of failure is as much a product of social expectations and political ideology as it is due to substantive failures of public service-delivery. The expanding scope of public policy in the postwar era has generated a paradox of rising expectations: the more we became accustomed to a comprehensive and relatively successful welfare state, the more critical we became of it. Even if government was doing better, we were feeling worse about it. We became more sensitive to the unintended consequences of government intervention, such as the bureaucratization of public service delivery, the displacement rather than the resolution of social problems, and the escalating costs of many welfare state provisions.

Eventually, this latent discomfort became more articulate as a result of a paradigm shift in economic and political thought. Throughout the seventies and eighties, but particularly in the latter decade, we have come to look at government first and foremost from an essentially technocratic perspective, driven by an ideology of efficiency. Neoclassical economists and neoconservative political thinkers have succeeded in setting the terms of debate, highlighting individualistic cultural values at the expense of hierarchical and egalitarian perspectives. In many ways, the dominant normative frame for analyzing and judging government has been a "problem-solving" one (see chapter 5), where it had previously been viewed much more in terms of balancing competing values and institutional interaction. Consequently we have tended to judge quite a number of public policies on the basis of standards considerably different from the ones that prevailed at the time when they were conceived. Moreover, these new standards contained a definite bias against "big government" and in favor of market-based institutions for solving social problems. This has tended to cost government, the public sector, and the bureaucracy much of the benefit of the public doubt they once enjoyed in many Western countries. They have lost "diffuse support," and, consequently, their actions (and non-actions) became a readily available object for finding fault.[4]

In other words, by adopting new ways of looking at and evaluating public policymaking, we have ourselves constructed a significant number of the fiascoes we subsequently "observed." Red tape is no longer regarded as merely a nuisance, it has become an evil to be eradicated with every means possible.[5] Cases of government fraud, waste, and abuse are no longer viewed as incidents but as symptoms of a bigger pathology. Unintended negative effects of social programs are no longer taken for granted as problems to be remedied incrementally, but instead have become a sufficent cause for their abolition.[6] Weber's disenchantment of society has now come to pervade one of its own driving forces: the rational system of social control vested in the public bureaucracy. Creeping disenchantment with the limits of bureaucratic rationality in public policy-making has produced an ideological swing that makes us less and less willing to give it a chance at all. The fact that politicians and bureaucrats have in many cases been reluctant to tone down their campaign pledges and institutional rhetoric to the new realities has only reinforced these tendencies.

The disenchantment of government has continued unabated at another level, that is, in our tolerance for fate and misfortune as significant forces shaping our lives and the society we live in. There is a paradox here. At one level, we have grown more disappointed with government as the great societal problem solver. At the same time, however, our expectations concerning a life free from acts of God, nature's capriciousness, and other random forces beyond institutional control have continued to rise. As a result, the tragic dimensions of public life, not so long ago still accepted as an important feature of statecraft and governance, have faded from both popular discourse about politics and from the evaluation designs of policy analysts. Since we no longer accept misfortune as a cause of social ills, someone has to blamed for them. As we have seen in chapter 6, government has become an ever more readily available scapegoat.

Rethinking the Relativity of Failure: Consequences for Policy Analysis

Understanding policy fiascoes poses a tough challenge for policy analysts. We have spent a lot of time in this book documenting the philosophical, conceptual, normative, and ultimately political choices analysts face in moving through the four layers of fiasco analysis. Does this apparent relativity of failure mean that everything is in the eye of the beholder when it comes to understanding policy fiascoes? Is there no such thing as an empirical reality of policy failure? We are reluctant to adopt a fully relativist position. Some physical and symbolic manifestations of policy failure are so powerful as to allow for little if any debate about the question "is this really a fiasco?". This goes both for "instant" and "evolving" fiascoes, for example the explosion of the Challenger space shuttle and the massive increase in homelessness in major American cities throughout the eighties. One could find more cases like these where few analysts would dispute the catastrophic results of the policies pursued. Moreover, when they get around to debating some of these cases they might even come to agree on which are the key factors that contributed to these negative outcomes.

Unfortunately perhaps, our analysis suggests that in the majority of cases this does not happen. It happens more often that analysts find themselves in the midst of ambiguity, indeterminacy, and politicization. In fact, what sets policy "fiascoes" apart as a special category of events is intense public and political arousal. This implies controversy in retrospection among stakeholders, media, outside observers, and policy analysts. Hence the crucial starting point for analysis is to determine who sees what and why when evaluating these episodes. There is very little one can do to isolate policy analysis from the politics of blaming that are inextricably wound up in the construction of policy fiascoes. The problem is felt by many working in this field, for example by students of comparative political scandals and public corruption:

> What really distinguishes the scandalous act from the normally self-seeking is its blatant violation of community norms, of ... the community's conscience collective. This may seem to make the definition of scandal to be as much in the eye of the beholder as is obscenity, and to raise some awful problems of determining community standards. Who would want to be forced to operationalize a definition of that?[7]

Should we, therefore, abandon the quest for a comparative understanding of the dynamics of controversial policy episodes? We think not. But it does require us to be quite specific about what this entails and what not.

In our view, the key challenge for policy analysis in this domain should not be how to save objectivity, validity, and reliability from the twin threats of epistemological relativism and political contestation. This project, we have shown, is doomed to fail. It can only lead to a kind of analytical self-deception: fiasco analysts perfunctory neglecting or "willing away" pivotal philosophical queries and social and political biases. In our view it may be more productive to ask two alternative questions. First, how can fiasco analysis maximize academic rigor without becoming politically irrelevant? Second, how can fiasco analysis be policy relevant without being used politically? The first question deals with the analytical dimension. It requires fiasco analysts to navigate between the Scylla of seemingly robust but irrelevant positivism and the Charybdis of politically astute but philosophically problematic relativism. The second question deals with the applied dimension. It alerts fiasco analysts to the politics of analysis that are such a prominent feature of constructing policy fiascoes and attempts to "learn" from them.

The approach to analyzing policy fiascoes advocated in this book should be viewed within the context of a broader repositioning of policy science that we feel is going on and appropriately so. At the base of this development lies the acceptance of the interpretivist claim that all knowledge about social affairs – including public policymaking – is based on limited information and social constructions. If one does so, the aims and scope of policy evaluation need to be redefined away from current, predominantly positivist, and social-engineering oriented perspectives.[8] In the alternative view that is currently coming to bloom, social science is taken to be a set of conventions aimed at the production and continuous adjustment of more or less systematically derived and verifiable knowledge. Policy science conceived of in this manner is merely one amongst other forms of sense-making, diagnosis, and debate.[9] In this view, policy science does not produce insights that are inherently superior to all other forms of knowledge about policy and politics. Policy science should instead assume that: man is fallible; science is biased; value judgments are crucial; institutions embody values, colour perceptions, and generate biases; and both the substance and the process of policymaking evolve around political interaction. Befitting such a realist framework is the essentially incrementalist view that public policymaking's best bet is to devote the bulk of its efforts to the task of enabling society to avoid, move away from, and effectively respond to what, through pluralistic debate, it has come to recognize as important present and future ills.[10] Policy analysis is supposed to be an integral part of this project, but not in the straightforward manner of science for policy. Instead, the key to policy science's unique contribution lies in its reflective potential. We agree with Majone that

> It is not the task of analysts to resolve fundamental disagreements about evaluative criteria and standards of accountability; only the political process can do that. However, analysts can contribute to societal learning by refining the standards of appraisal and by encouraging a more sophisticated understanding of public policies than is possible from a single perspective.[11]

This also goes for evaluating past policy episodes. Again we cite Majone:

> The need today is less to develop "objective" measures of outcomes – the traditional aim of evaluation research – than to facilitate a wide-ranging dialogue among advocates of different criteria.[12]

Following the logic of this perhaps more modest perspective on the scope for "scientific" policy evaluation, we propose a set of basic, interrelated principles for fiasco analysis which encapsulate most of what we have said so far:

- *Inevitable subjectivity.* It is impossible to develop objectifiable indicators and tools for evaluating controversial policy episodes.
- *Normative pluralism.* In making sense of controversial policies, multiple and different types of norms and standards of evaluation will be deemed relevant by different groups of stakeholders. Within but certainly between different national or subnational political and administrative systems, important variations in value configurations may be found, without the policy analyst being able to make an authoritative choice in favor of one or the other configuration.
- *A more explicit metatheoretical orientation.* In our view, a case study of a particular fiasco begins with the analyst reflecting upon and explicitizing his views on the ontology of the object of study. Based on that, he would adopt a particular epistemological position, that is, he makes clear what sort of knowledge about these events he seeks to generate, how this can be done, to what purpose, and subject to which constraints. He then elaborates his argument, matching his research methodology, data presentation, and conclusions to the epistemological frame adopted. In this way, analysts are more or less forced to face and explicitize the analytical biases and choices inherent to any piece of policy evaluation. In this way, their argument becomes more transparent and verifiable. Its scope and functions in relation to other analyses of the same set of events becomes easier to determine.
- *Taking context seriously.* It is important to view policy fiascoes and other complex policy ventures in their broader historical, ideological, and institutional context. In this context much of the rationale of the problem definitions, strategies, and actions of the policymakers in question can be found. At the same time, we have seen throughout this book that these contextual factors are also essential to reach an understanding of how the outcomes of policies are subsequently perceived and judged in the political system as a whole.
- *Institutionalized intersubjectivity.* This contextual sensitivity in fiasco analysis will be greatly facilitated if different analysts working on a particular episode are routinely induced to compare, and discuss their findings more explicitly than is presently the case. In doing so, they may, firstly, clarify the essential differences between their approaches and become more aware of how these premeditate their conclusions. In other words, they should sit down and communicate when they look, how they look, and what they see when they study the case in question. Secondly, they may attempt to consensually adapt their respective approaches, up to the point of exploring ways in which they might integrate their approaches. Ultimately, this may produce intersubjectively supported interpretations, that presumably take into

account a wider range of values and biases than each single analyst's original approach.

We do not advocate any sort of paradigmatic revolution in policy analysis. First, we do not consider it necessary. Second, scientific revolutions do not happen by design as much as some may want them to. Yet we are inclined to see merit in alternating epistemologies, with a bias towards interpretivism. In this book, we have shown that the predominantly positivist mode of theory formation in fiasco analysis has conduced to a proliferation of adhoc hypotheses and incompatible frameworks. Preferably, these were pitted against one another as if they were knights in a medieval tournament competing for the hand of the fair lady called Truth. This has worked well in the sense of generating a great deal of "requisite variety," collapsed here into four main types of analytical foci. But positivism has been much less successful in generating strategies on how to handle this variety. Since there are definite limits to what a positivist perspective on theory-building can achieve in the way of satisfactory explanations of fiasco episodes, policy analysts need to explore other routes to empirical analysis. In our view, an interpretive approach is well-suited to the features of fiasco analysis described in this book. For example, the interpretive analyst would find it unacceptable to simply "zoom in" on the activities of, say, William Casey and Oliver North during the months of the secret arms deliveries to Iran during the Reagan administration. To understand why they did what they did, as well as why they did it in particular ways foregoing other options, it is necessary to look at what sort of men they were and how their position and status within the Reagan foreign policy establishment were evolving. It is also important to determine how their earlier experiences influenced their definitions of the problem and their preference for a particular way of acting. Furthermore, a historical-institutional analysis may shed more light on the question how it became possible for such a small nucleus of officials to exclude important individuals and organizations in the political and bureaucratic arenas. In performing such an analysis, we may lose deductive rigor and parsimony but gain understanding of how the principal actors interpreted and re-interpreted the evolving situations confronting them, and the behavioral imperatives they derived from those interpretations. Given the importance and uniqueness of the events under study, this should be well worth the effort.

We do not claim the above set of principles for policy analysis provides easy answers to complex normative and epistemological questions. But they do force the analyst to approach the problem of policy fiascoes from multiple perspectives, to take seriously the social and political context in which policy analysis takes place, and to do all of this in a more or less systematic and verifiable manner.

This still leaves us with the problem of theoretical pluralism discussed at some length in chapter five. Much as though some might want it to, theoretical pluralism is not going to go away. It is deep rooted in the nature of the social science project: "Because the personal experiences and evaluative standards of investigators are bound to differ, the embeddedness of social science in value judgments, different personal sensibilities, and political ideology is impossible to avoid."[13] The question is whether we should be worried about this. From the perspective on policy analysis advocated here, pluralism at the level of philosophies of governance is not a major problem for policy analysis. On the contrary, it is a source of debate in political theory and normative discourse on public administration. What our approach calls for is more open debate between the various positions. The problem of multiplicity emerges primarily at the occasion of analyzing a concrete historical case. There, conceptual and normative frames implicit in particular epistemologies, philosophies of governance, and cultural predispositions shape the methodology, substance, and conclusions of the analysis. At this level, too, the problem is not so much that these biases exist, but that they remain unrecognized and implicit. As Nelson observes in an essay in which he juxtaposes political, organizational, and scientific models of policy analysis:

> In addition to their clumsy treatment of value and knowledge (a problem that seems to infect analysis generally), analysts within each of the traditions have had a tendency to combine tunnel vision with intellectual imperialism .... Members of the different traditions have had a tendency to be lulled by their imperialistic rhetoric. This has often led them to provide interpretations and prescriptions that the public, and the political apparatus, rightly have scoffed at.[14]

This is particularly sensitive in the context of debates about policies or programs that, at whatever stage of their development and for whatever reason, have become controversial. The multiple accounts of those episodes offered by different analysts may then easily become ammunition in the process of blaming and accountability, decreasing the likelihood of more dispassionate and ameliorative uses.

Talking not so much about policy analysts but about policy practitioners, Schon and Rein have captured the kind of program for policy analysis advocated here under the heading of "frame-reflectiveness." This implies a willingness on the part of analysts to continuously reflect upon and reassess their own lenses for looking at the world. In addition, they need to make efforts to communicate with and understand analysts using a different set of assumptions.[15] Absent such a reflective orientation, policy analysts may find that they and their conclusions are deemed irrelevant by key players in the political arena. Or they may find themselves set up unwittingly as hired guns in the politics of blaming. They ought to be neither.

Reflective policy analysts may strive for a position as a systematic, well-informed, thoughtful, and fair-minded group provider of inputs to the political process of argumentation, debate, maneuvering, and blaming that characterizes controversial policy episodes. In our view, their effectiveness could be enhanced significantly if they adopt a role conception that befits such a position: explicit about their own assumptions; meticulous in developing their arguments; sensitive to context; and striving to create institutional procedures for open and pluralistic debate. At the same time, since the political world of policy fiascoes in particular is unlikely to be supportive of such frame-reflectiveness, policy analysts need a considerable amount of political astuteness in assessing their own position in the field of forces. It doesn't help much if the analyst has a good story to tell but has nobody influential to listen to him. Hence it is important for analyst to make sure their arguments are heard by who they think are the right people at the right time, and in the right way. This may affect both the substance and the presentation of the analyst's arguments: "Feasibility, rather than optimality, should be the main concern of policy analysts, and ... they should be as preoccupied with political and institutional constraints as with technical and economic constraints."[16]

There is a certain paradox here: the policy analyst who is serious about his role as facilitator of reflection in policy practice, can only succeed if he also understands and utilizes the principles of governmental politics. He needs to be able to penetrate organizational defensiveness and political impulses to manipulate blame for failure. Finding ways to deal creatively with the sometimes opposing requirements of detached reflection and political realism is what the art and craft of policy analysis are all about.

Rethinking the Inevitability of Failure: Consequences for Policymaking

Reflecting many years later upon his experiences as first the celebrated visionary and later the notorious fired architect of the Sydney Opera House, Jorn Utzon observed that perhaps the greatest damage done by the controversy surrounding its construction had been the foregone opportunities for further large-scale architectural experimentation in Australia. The fact that the Sydney experience for many years was portrayed as a policy nightmare to be avoided at all costs, cast a long shadow in Australia. It promoted a distinct conservatism in design and risk aversion in construction management, which deprived the country of its emergent reputation as a venue for innovative architectural ventures. Utzon's observations are obviously biased by his personal involvement in the affair. It is remarkable nevertheless that the desire to avoid adventurous designs requiring new technologies and complex materials was indeed a crucial consideration of the panel selecting the winning design for Australia's New Parliament House, more than a decade after the controversy about the Opera House had reached its peak.[17] Anything smacking of grandiosity in design was sure to elicit criticism, which came out clearly during the debates surrounding the construction of the new High Court building in Canberra some years before.[18] It is also remarkable that the use of fast-track construction management techniques requiring synthetic organization structures has been eschewed for a long time in Australia's public building practices. Those projects where fast-tracking was used, such as the construction of the Westmead Hospital near Sydney, elicited considerable controversy. It took political sophistication, a slick public relations operation, and most of all the on-time delivery of the New Parliament House by the Parliament House Construction Authority (1979–1988) to break the hold of the dominant Opera House analogy that had cast a shadow over all these kinds of projects.

This example shows that the construction of policy fiascoes has a broader significance beyond the politics of blaming and exculpation that focus on the events themselves. Because of their high visibility and drama, policy fiascoes tend to become important analogies for future policymakers, critics, and other stakeholders. If a proposed policy or program has become associated with a major past fiasco, it will have a hard time gaining political, bureaucratic, and communal acceptance. At the same time, it may serve as a powerful source of "don'ts" for those who propose to develop it. In other words, the ways in which policy fiascoes are constructed may have definite implications for future policymaking. To what extent can we uncover some of them on the basis of this study? What does it teach us about the prospects and possibilities for preventing policy fiascoes? Given the current, essentially skeptical if not hostile ideological climate, are policymakers not doomed to be labelled as failures irrespective of what they do and achieve?

This study has focused on public and academic debates about policymaking rather than on policymaking itself. It would therefore be inappropriate and presumptuous to end it with a detailed set of policy recommendations, let alone an operational guide on how to avoid policy fiascoes. We can, however, offer a few preliminary observations. To begin with, we think it is important that policymakers look for ways to come to grips with the contextual, contingent, and occasionally volatile nature of the social and political standards for evaluating public policy. One way to do so might be to engage in forms of context-auditing: To continuously examine what policy predicaments are identified by key players, fora, and insititutions in the community. What kinds of issues come to be framed as problems? What kinds of social expectations with regard to the government's handling of these problems emerge? Mary Douglas has pointed out that standards of accountability are continuously being rene-gotiated in a community, whether policymakers like it or not. This means that certain meanings attached to policies change as policies are enacted. They change in ways that policymakers may not always be able to con-trol, but that they can certainly try to anticipate by engaging in contextu-al auditing. One important example that illustrates the need for such cul-tural auditing by policymakers would be the notion of risk. Douglas sug-gests in most Western societies today, a more expansive conception of personal and societal risk has taken hold. This, in turn, has played an important role in evaluating the behavior of institutions. She observes that

> [A] debate about accountability ... is carried out incessantly in any community. This dialogue, the cultural process itself, is a contest to muster support for one kind of action rather than another. Decisions to invest in more technology, or less, are the result of the cultural dialogue. Decisions to invade, to refuse immi-gration, to license, to withold consent, all these responses to claims need sup-port from institutions of law and justice. The cultural dialogue is therefore best studied in its forensic moments. The concept of risk emerges as a key idea for modern times because of its uses as a forensic resource.... The language of risk is reserved as a specialized lexical register for political talk about the undesir-able outcomes.... The charge of risk is a stick to beat authority, to make lazy bureaucrats sit up, to exact restitution for victims.[19]

Context-auditing may help policymakers anticipate the drift of such social and political developments. These kinds of auditing practices may become even more important if one takes into account the transnational-ization of many policies in both Western Europe and North America with respect to, amongst others, international trade, the environment, and tele-communications. More and more, policymakers will find themselves dealing with and judged by people and institutions harboring cultural predispositions and philosophies of governance that differ markedly from their own. Context-auditing requires policymakers to engage in thought experiments. By shifting time horizons, spatial perspectives, and alternating cultural archetypes, they may continuously probe how a cer-tain proposal, policy, or action on their part might be interpreted by dif-ferent stakeholders and fora. This may help them to anticipate lines of critique they otherwise would not take into account.

Institutionalized forms of context-auditing may serve to upgrade the quality of feasibility analysis during the policy design process. Their impact would be even further increased if they are embedded in a more comprehensive logic of discursive or communicative policy design. The analysis of this study suggests there is much value in Schon and Rein's view of policy design rationality as embedded in ongoing conversations between designers and other stakeholders.[20] There is a case to be made that many policy fiascoes are a form post-hoc "policy backtalk" by stakeholders and communities who found that policies inimical to some of their deep-rooted myths, beliefs, and values had been imposed on them. In this view, policies that solicit opposition and controversy that is left unarticulated or ignored during policy design, will eventually come to haunt their makers during implementation. Policy fiascoes are nothing more and nothing less than a manifestation of the "rhetoric of reaction" generated by unilateral strategies of policymaking.[21] Fiascoes of this kind might be prevented when the design process is opened up to become more iterative, evolving around continuous dialogue about what the problems to be solved look like and what strategies for resolution sollicit the necessary agreement. In this logic of policy design, developing and abiding by more communicative strategies for conflict recognition and conflict resolution become an important challenge for public policymakers.

Coda: From Fiascoes to Successes?

During our research for this study we have been asked many times why we were writing a book about failure rather than about success in public policymaking. Surely that would have resulted in a more "upbeat" and practically useful contribution? It would also have been timely, since it seems the field is turning away from telling policymakers what goes wrong. Policy analysts have started telling the public that policymakers and bureaucrats are doing a much better job than they usually get credit for.[22] Others have followed in the footsteps of private sector management gurus. They have collected examples of excellence, innovation, and success in government, and have built their own recipes for "reinventing government" and "exemplary public management."[23]

We have two rejoinders. Firstly, we think there is a plausible case to be made that at least as much can be learned from studying failure than from studying success. In a culture that takes political order, social welfare, and a high level of public service delivery for granted, failure is much more conspicuous than success. It tends to provide a much stronger institutional impetus to find out what happened and why. It also tends to promote organizational and political forces that advocate change. In contrast, the institutional reinforcement and routinization of successful modes of policymaking have been known to breed future failures through neglect of the differences between past and current situations in which policymaking takes place.[24]

If one succeeds in stripping away or containing the politics of blaming, a controlled strategy of trial and error seems to produce more significant policy learning than reinforcement and imitation of successes.[25] Besides, as Shiels argues "we forget that the greatest success is often the absence of failure. The disaster averted is rarely recognized as such. Small, prudent decisions that avoid a Chernobyl or a space shuttle tragedy almost by definition cannot be measured."[26] The challenge then becomes not only how to bring failures to light, but also how to put them to productive use. As we have argued above, this is both an analytical and a political project.

Secondly and perhaps more importantly, to some extent we have in fact developed a framework for studying policy success, but not quite along the lines of the new apostles of success and excellence in government. In our view, most of what we have written about the dynamics of policy failure as a social and political construct also applies to policy success. Success too is a contextual phenomenon. It is a function of standards and philosophies of government that are variable across time and culture, malleable by political argument and institutional impression management. *Mutatis mutandis*, the analytical scheme of this book about failure can be converted into its mirror image: a set of questions about the construction of policy successes. The emergent literature on success, excellence, and best practices could be analyzed for biases in assessing outcomes, identifying the agents of success (rephrased as "chance or competence?"), explaining their behavior, and evaluating it. The same logic could be applied to scrutinize individual cases of policy success.

Analyzing success in this way would force one to go beyond learning by imitation. The analyst would concentrate instead on critically probing what people mean when they claim this or that policy is a major success, or when a particular agency or administrator is portrayed as examplary. The upshot of this kind of success analysis will probably be a call for caution in embracing the checklists and strategies of the current gurus of public sector success. Like the failure-oriented generation of analysts preceding them, they and their ideas tell us at least as much about the cultural and political context in which they are set, as they do about policy success. This should be taken into account when absorbing their lessons. To be really sure if these are indeed the main conclusions when our framework is applied to understanding policy success, somebody should try and write a book about it. We just might, one day.

Notes

1 S.B. Sitkin, Learning through failure: The strategy of small losses, in: B.M. Staw, L. Cummings (eds.), *Research in Organizational Behavior*, 14, Greenwich: JAI Press 1992, p. 232.

2 T. Veblen, *The place of science in modern civilization*, New York: Russell and Russell 1961, as quoted by C.E. Lindblom, D.K. Cohen, *Usable knowledge: Social science and social problem solving*, New Haven: Yale UP 1977, p. 33.

3 Analogous to Kennedy's notion of "imperial overstretch" in analyzing the breakdown of hegemonic powers in the world system, see P. Kennedy, *The rise and fall of great powers: Economic change and military conflict from 1500 to 2000*, New York: Random House 1987.

4 Compare D. Easton, *A systems analysis of political life*, New York: Wiley 1965.

5 C. Goodsell, *The case for bureaucracy: A public administration polemic*, Chatham: Chatham House 1985.

6 Compare, for example, C. Murray, *Losing ground*, New York: Basic Books 1984.

7 J. Logue, Appreciating scandal as a political art form, or, making an intellectual virtue of a political vice, in: A.S. Markovits and M. Silverstein (eds.), *The politics of scandal: Power and porcess in liberal democracies*, New York: Holmes and Maier 1988, p. 258.

8 Compare H.D. Lasswell and D. Lerner (eds.), *The policy sciences*, Stanford: Stanford UP 1951, H.D. Lasswell, *A pre-view of policy sciences*, New York: Elsevier 1971, and Y. Dror, *Design for policy sciences*, New York: Elsevier 1971 to F. Fischer, *Politics, values and public policy: The problem of methodology*, Boulder: Westview 1980 and G. Majone, *Evidence, argument and persuasion in the policy process*, New Haven: Yale UP 1989. For a useful critique, see P. DeLeon, Reinventing the policy sciences: three steps back to the future, *Policy Sciences*, 27, 1994, 77–95.

9 See J.A. Throgmorton, The rhetorics of policy analysis, *Policy Sciences*, 24, 1991, 153–179.

10 We reject the idea that this role conception implies a conservative view of politics and policymaking: identifying and combatting ills may very well require radical breakthroughs and non-incremental policies. Compare Y. Dror, *Policymaking under adversity*, New Brunswick: Transaction 1986, who uses similar premises.

11 Majone (1989), *op. cit.*, p. 182.

12 Majone (1989), *op. cit.*, p. 183; compare also Throgmorton (1991), *op. cit.*.

13 J.C. Alexander, P. Colomy, Traditions and competition: Preface to a postpositivist approach to knowledge cumulation, in: G. Ritzer (ed.), *Metatheorizing*, London: Sage 1992, pp. 32–33.

14 R.R. Nelson, *The moon and the ghetto*, New York: Norton 1977, p. 19.

15 D. Schon, M. Rein, *Reframing: Toward the resolution of intractable policy controversies*, New York: Basic Books 1994.

16 Majone (1989), *op. cit.*, p. 77.

17 Parliament House Construction Authority, *Project Parliament: Constructing a new parliament house*, Canberra: Government Printing Office 1989.

18 A. Kouzmin, The High Court: The politics of constructing the Court, *Legal Service Bulletin*, 5 (1980): 113–171.

19 M. Douglas, *Risk and blame: Essays in cultural theory*, London: Routledge 1992, p. 24.

20 Schon and Rein (1994), *op. cit.*

21 Borrowing Hirschman's wonderful title: A.O. Hirschman *The rhetoric of reaction: Perversity, futility, jeopardy*, Cambridge: Belknap Harvard UP 1991.

22 Goodsell (1985), *op. cit.* The same can be found in our own country, for example, in A.B. Ringeling, *Het imago van de overheid*, Den Haag: Vuga 1993.

23 Some examples out of a growing stream include D. Osborne and T. Gaebler, *Reinventing government: How the entrepreneurial spirit is transforming the public sector*, New York: Plume Books 1993; T.L. Cooper, *Exemplary public administrators*, San Francisco: Jossey-Bass 1992; R.B. Denhardt, *The pursuit of significance: Strategies for managerial success in public organizations*, Belmont: Wadsworth 1993.

24 Sitkin (1992), *op. cit.*, pp. 234–236; compare also R. Neustadt, E.R. May, *Thinking in time: The uses of history for policymakers*, New York: Free Press 1986.

25 Sitkin (1992), *op. cit.*; see also K.S. Cameron, The effectiveness of ineffectiveness, in: B.M. Staw (ed.), *Research in Organizational Behavior*, 6, Greenwich: JAI Press 1984, p. 235–285. Of course we are aware that the "if" in this sentence is crucial.

26 F.L. Shiels, *Preventable disasters: Why governments fail*, Savage: Rowman and Littlefield 1991, p. 190.

Bibliography

Abrahamson, B.E. 1977. *Bureaucracy or Participation*. London: Sage.

Alexander, J.C., and P. Colomy. 1992. "Traditions and Competition: Preface to a Postpositivist Approach to Knowledge Cumulation." In *Metatheorizing*, edited by G. Ritzer. London: Sage.

Allen, L., et al. 1990. *Political Scandals and Causes Célèbres Since 1945: A Reference Compendium*. Harlow: Longman.

Allison, G.T. 1971. *Essence of Decision: Explaining the Cuban Missile Crisis*. Boston: Little, Brown.

Almond, G., S.C. Flanagan and R.J. Mundt, eds. 1973. *Crisis, Choice and Change: Historical Studies of Political Development*. Boston: Little Brown.

Anderson, C.W. 1979. "The Place of Principles in Policy Analysis." *American Political Science Review* 73: 711–723.

Angel, R.C. 1991. *Explaining Economic Policy Failure: Japan and the International Monetary Crisis of 1969-1971*. New York: Columbia UP.

Apter, D.E. 1991. "Institutionalism Reconsidered." *International Social Science Journal* 129 (theme issue on Rethinking Democracy): 463–481.

Austin, R., and P. Larkey. 1992. "The Unintended Consequences of Micromanagement: The Case of Procuring Mission Critical Computer Resources." *Policy Sciences* 25, 3–28.

Bachrach, P., and M.S. Baratz. 1970. *Power and Poverty: Theory and Practice*. New York: Oxford UP.

Barak, G., ed. 1991. *Crimes By the Capitalist State: An Introduction to State Criminality*. Albany: SUNY Press.

Barry, B., and D. Rae. 1975. "Political Evaluation." In *Handbook of Political Science*. Vol. I, edited by F. Greenstein and N.W. Polsby. Reading: Addison Wesley.

Baume, J. 1967. *The Sydney Opera House Affair*. Sydney: Halstead Press.

Beck, U. 1986. *Risikogesellschaft: Auf dem Weg in eine andere Moderne*. Frankfurt: Suhrkamp.

Bell, D., H. Raiffa and A. Tversky, eds. 1990. *Decision Making: Normative, Empirical and Prescriptive Interactions*. Cambridge: Cambridge UP.

Bendor, J. 1985. *Parallel Systems: Redundancy in Government*. Berkeley: California UP.

Betts, R.K. 1982. *Surprise Attack*. Washington: Brookings.

Binder, L., J.S. Coleman, L. LaPalombara, L.W. Pye, S. Verba and M. Weiner. 1971. *Crises and Sequences of Political Development*. Princeton: Princeton UP.

Blight, J.G., and D.A. Welch. 1989. *On the Brink: Americans and Soviets Reexamine the Cuban Missile Crisis*. New York: Hill and Wang.

Boisjoly, R.P., E.F. Curtis and E. Mellican. 1989. "Roger Boisjoly and the Challenger Disaster: The Ethical Dimensions." *Journal of Business Ethics* 8: 217–230.

Bovens, M.A.P. Forthcoming 1996. *The Quest for Responsibility: Accountability and Citizenship in Complex Organizations*. Cambridge: Cambridge UP.

Brecht, A. 1950. *Political Theory*. Princeton: Princeton UP.

Bressers, H. 1984. "Analyse en Evaluatie van Beleidseffecten." In *Handboek Beleidsevaluatie*, edited by H. Blommesteijn, H. Bressers and A. Hoogerwerf. Alphen: Samsom.

Brewer, G.D., and P. DeLeon. 1983. *The Foundations of Policy Analysis*. Homewood: Dorsey Press.

Bryson, J.M. 1981. "A Perspective on Planning and Crises in the Public Sector." *Strategic Management Journal* 2: 181–196.

Bryson, J., and B. Crosby. 1992. *Leadership for the Common Good: Tackling Public Problems in a Shared Power World*. San Francisco: Jossey-Bass.

Burke, J., and F. Greenstein. 1988. *How Presidents Test Reality*. New York: Russel Sage.

Burrell, W.G., and G. Morgan. 1979. *Sociological Paradigms and Organizational Analysis*. London: Heinemann.

Calabresi, G., and P. Bobbit. 1979. *Tragic Choices*. New York: Norton.

Cameron, K.S. 1984. "The Effectiveness of Ineffectiveness." In *Research in Organizational Behavior*. Vol. 6, edited by B.M. Staw and L. Cummings. Greenwich: JAI Press.

Cameron, K.S., and D.A. Whetten. 1983. "Organizational Effectiveness: One Model or Several?" In *Organizational Effectiveness: A Comparison of Multiple Models*, edited by K.S. Cameron and D.A. Whetten. Orlando: Academic Press.

Cameron, K.S., R.I. Sutton and D.A. Whetten, eds. 1988. *Readings in Organizational Decline: Frameworks Research and Prescriptions*. Cambridge: Ballinger 1988.

Casteret, A.M. 1992. *L'affaire du Sang*. Paris: Éditions La Découverte.

Charles, M.T. 1989. "The Last Flight of Space Shuttle Challenger." In *Coping with Crises: The Management of Disasters, Riots and Terrorism*, edited by U. Rosenthal, M.T. Charles and P. 't Hart. Springfield: Charles Thomas.

Clegg, S.R. 1989. *Frameworks of Power* London: Sage.

Clegg, S.R., and D. Dunkerley. 1980. *Organization, Class and Control*. London: Routledge and Kegan Paul.

Cohen, M.D., J.G. March and J.P. Olsen. 1972. "A Garbage-can Model of Organizational Choice." *Administrative Science Quarterly* 17: 1–25.

Cohen, D.K., and C.E. Lindblom. 1977. *Usable Knowledge: Social Science and Social Problem Solving*. New Haven: Yale UP.

Cohen, E.A., and J. Gooch. 1991. *Military Misfortunes: The Anatomy of Failure in War*. New York: Vintage Books.

Coleman, J.S. 1990. *Foundations of Social Theory*. Cambridge: Belknap of Harvard UP.

Collingridge, D. 1992. *The Management of Scale: Big Technologies, Big Decisions, Big Mistakes*. London: Routledge.

Combs, J. 1980. *Dimensions of Political Drama*. New York: Goodyear.

Comfort, L.K., ed. 1994. Theme issue on risk – Inspired by the work of Aaron Wildavsky. *Journal of Contingencies and Crisis Management* 2: 123–190.

Cook, J. 1989. *An Accident Waiting to Happen*. London: Unwin.

Cooper, T.L. 1987. "Hierarchy, Virtue and the Practice of Public Administration: A Perspective for Normative Ethics." *Public Administration Review* 47: 320–328.

Cooper, T.L. 1992. *Exemplary Public Administrators*. San Francisco: Jossey-Bass.

Crozier, M. 1964. *The Bureaucratic Phenomenon*. Chicago: Chicago UP.

Cyert, R.T., and J.G. March. 1963. *A Behavioral Theory of the Firm*. Englewood Cliffs: Prentice Hall.

Dahl, R.A., and C.E. Lindblom. 1953. *Politics, Economics and Welfare*. Chicago: Chicago UP.

Dahrendorf, R. 1988. *The Modern Social Conflict: An Essay on the Politics of Liberty*. London: Weidenfeld and Nicholson.

DeLeon, L. 1993. "As Plain as 1 2 3 .. and 4: Ethics and Organization Structure." *Administration and Society* 25: 293–316.

DeLeon, P. 1994. "Reinventing the Policy Sciences: Three Steps Back to the Future." *Policy Sciences* 27: 77–95.

Denhardt, R.B. 1993. *The Pursuit of Significance: Strategies for Managerial Success in Public Organizations*. Belmont: Wadsworth.

Derthick, M. 1972. *New Towns in Town: Why a Federal Program Failed*. Washington: Brookings Institution.

Dixon, N.F. 1987. *Our Own Worst Enemy*. London: Jonathan Cape.

Douglas, M., and A. Wildavsky. 1982. *Risk and Culture: An Essay on the Selection of Environmental Dangers*. Berkeley: University of California Press.

Douglas, M. 1992. *Risk and Blame: Essays in Cultural Theory*. London: Routledge.

Dror, Y. 1971. *Design for Policy Sciences*. New York: Elsevier.

Dror, Y. 1986. *Policymaking under Adversity*. New Brunswick: Transaction.

Dror, Y. 1988. "Visionary Political Leadership: On Improving a Risky Requisite." *International Political Science Review* 9: 7–22.

Dror, Y. 1990. "Fateful Decisions as Fuzzy Gambles with History." *The Jerusalem Journal of International Relations* 12: 1–12.

Dror, Y. 1993. "School for Rulers." In *A Systems-based Approach to Policymaking*, edited by K.B. De Greene. Dordrecht: Kluwer.

Dunleavy, P. 1990. "Reinterpreting the Westland Affair: Theories of the State and Core Executive Decision Making." *Public Administration* 68: 29–60.

Easton, D. 1965. *A Systems Analysis of Political Life*. New York: Wiley.

Edelman, M. 1964. *The Symbolic Uses of Politics*. Urbana: University of Illinois Press.

Edelman, M. 1977. *Political Language: Words that Succeed and Policies that Fail*. New York: Academic Press.

Edelman, M. 1988. *Constructing the Political Spectacle*. Chicago: Chicago UP.

Elazar, D. 1993. *The American Mosaic: The Impact of Time, Space, and Culture on American Politics*. Boulder: Westview.

Elmore, R.F. 1982. "Backward Mapping: Implementation Research and Policy Decisions." In *Studying Implementation*, edited by W. Williams. Chatham: Chatham House.

Esser, J.K., and J.S. Lindoerfer. 1989. "Groupthink and the Space Shuttle Challenger Accident: Toward a Quantitative Case Analysis. *Journal of Behavioral Decision Making* 2: 167–177.

Etheredge, L.S. 1985. *Can Governments Learn?* Oxford: Pergamon.

Etzioni-Halevy, E. 1983. *Bureaucracy and Democracy: A Political Dilemma*. London: Routledge.

Feldman, E.J. 1985. *Concorde and Dissent: Explaining High Technology Project Failures in Britain and France*. Cambridge: Cambridge UP.

Feldman, E.J., and J. Milch. 1982. *Technocracy versus Democracy: The Comparative Politics of International Airports*. Boston: Auburn House.

Finney, H.C., and H.R. Lesieur. 1981. "A Contingency Theory of Organizational Crime." *Research in the Sociology of Organizations* 1: 261–262.

Fischer, D.H., ed. 1970. *Historians' Fallacies: Towards a Logic of Historical Thought*. London: Routledge.

Fischer, F. 1980. *Politics, Values and Public Policy: The Problem of Methodology*. Boulder: Westview.

Fischer, F. 1990. *Technocracy and the Politics of Expertise*. London: Sage.

Fischer, F., and J. Forester, eds. 1987. *Confronting Values in Policy Analysis*. Newbury Park: Sage.

Fitzgerald, A. 1989. *The Pentagonists: An Insider's View of Waste Mismanagement and Fraud in Defense Spending*. Boston: Houghton Mifflin.

Friedman, L.M. 1985. *Total Justice*. New York: Russel Sage.

Friedrich, C.J. 1972. *The Pathology of Politics*. New York: Free Press.

Gabriel, R.T. 1985. *Military Incompetence*. New York: Hill and Wang.

Gelb, L.H., and R.K. Betts. 1979. *The Irony of Vietnam: The System Worked*. Washington: Brookings.

George, A.L. 1980. *Presidential Decision Making in Foreign Policy: The Effective Use of Information and Advice*. Boulder: Westview Press.

Gephart, R.P. Jr., L. Steier and T. Lawrence. 1990. "Cultural Rationalities in Crisis Sensemaking: A Study of a Public Inquiry into a Major Industrial Accident." *Industrial Crisis Quarterly* 4: 27–48.

Gillroy, J.M., and M. Wade, eds. 1992. *The Moral Dimensions of Public Policy Choice: Beyond the Market Paradigm*, Pittsburgh: Pittsburgh UP.

Goggin, M.L., A.O.M. Bowman, J.P. Lester and L.J. O'Toole. 1990. *Implementation Theory and*

Practice: Toward a Third Generation. New York: Harper Collins 1990.

Golembiewski, R.T. 1977. *Public Administration as a Developing Discipline*. New York: Dekker.

Goodin, R.E. 1982. *Political Theory and Public Policy*, Chicago: Chicago UP.

Goodsell, C. 1985. *The Case For Bureaucracy: A Public Administration Polemic*. Chatham: Chatham House.

Gough, J. 1979. *The Political Economy of the Welfare State*. London: MacMillan.

Gunsteren, H.R. van. 1974. *Denken over Politieke Verantwoordelijkheid*. Alphen aan den Rijn: Samsom.

Gunsteren, H.R. van. 1976. *The Quest for Control: A Critique of the Rational-central Rule Approach*. New York: Wiley.

Guy Peters, B. 1993. "Tragic Choices: Administrative Rulemaking and Policy Choice." In *Ethics in Public Service*, edited by R.A. Chapman. Edinburgh: Edinburgh University Press.

Habermas, J. 1975. *Legitimation Crisis*. Boston: Beacon Press.

Hall, P. 1982. *Great Planning Disasters*. Berkeley: California UP.

Hamilton, V.L., and J. Sanders. 1992. "Responsibility and Risk in Organizational Crimes of Obedience." In *Research in Organizational Behavior*. Vol. 14, edited by B.M. Staw and L. Cummings. Greenwich: JAI Press.

Hanf, K., and F.W. Scharpf, eds. 1978. *Interorganizational Policymaking: Limits to Coordination and Central Control*. London: Sage.

Hanusch, H., ed. 1983. *Anatomy of Government Deficiencies*. New York: De Gruyter.

Hardin, G. 1968. "The Tragedy of the Commons." *Science* 162: 1243–1248.

Hart, P. 't. 1993. "Symbols Rituals and Power: The Lost Dimension of Crisis Management." *Journal of Contingencies and Crisis Management* 1: 36–50.

Hart, P. 't. 1994. *Groupthink in Government: A Study of Small Groups and Policy Failure*. Baltimore: Johns Hopkins UP.

Hart, P. 't, and B. Pijnenburg. 1988. *Het Heizeldrama: Rampzalig Organiseren en Kritieke Beslissingen*. Alphen aan den Rijn: Samsom.

Hawkesworth, M.E. 1988. *Theoretical Issues in Policy Analysis*. Albany: State University of New York Press.

Hayek, F. 1960. *The Constitution of Liberty*. London: Routledge & Kegan Paul.

Hays, R.A. 1985. "Perceptions of Success or Failure in Program Implementation: The 'Feedback Loop' in Public Policy Decisions." *Policy Studies Review* 5: 51–67.

Heclo, H. 1977. *A Government of Strangers*. Washington: Brookings Institution.

Heineman, R.A., W.T. Bluhm, S.A. Peterson and E.N. Kearny. 1990. *The World of the Policy Analyst: Rationality Values and Politics*. Chatham NJ: Chatham House.

Herek, G.M., I.L. Janis and P. Huth. 1987. "Decisionmaking During International Crises: Is Quality of Process Related to Outcome?" *Journal of Conflict Resolution* 31: 203–226.

Herkert, J.R. 1991. "Management's Hat Trick: The Misuse of 'Engineering Judgment' in the Challenger Incident." *Journal of Business Ethics* 10: 617–620.

Hertogh, M. 1991. "The King's Cross Station Fire." Unpublished paper Crisis Case Inventory Project. Leiden: Leiden University Crisis Research Team.

Hickson, D., R.J. Butler, D. Cray. G.R. Mallory and D.C. Wilson. 1986. *Top Decisions: Strategic Decision-making in Organizations*. Oxford: Blackwell.

Hirokawa, R.Y., D.S. Gouran and A.E. Martz. 1988. "Understanding the Sources of Faulty Group Decision Making: A Lesson from the Challenger Disaster." *Small Group Behavior* 19: 411–433.

Hirschman, A.O. 1991. *The Rhetoric of Reaction: Perversity, Futility, Jeopardy*. Cambridge: Belknap Harvard UP.

Hogwood, B., and L. Gunn. 1984. *Policy Analysis for the Real World*. Oxford: Oxford UP.

Hogwood, B., and B. Guy Peters. 1985. *The Pathology of Public Policy*. Oxford: Clarendon Press.

Holt, G.R., and A.W. Morris. 1993. "Activity Theory and the Analysis of Organizations." *Human Organization* 52: 97–109.

Hood, C.C. 1991. "A Public Management for All Seasons?" *Public Administration* 69: 3–19.

Hood, C.C., and A. Dunsire. 1989. *Cutback Management in Public Bureaucracies*. Cambridge: Cambridge UP.

Hood, C.C., and M. Jackson. 1991. "The New Public Management: A Recipe for Disaster?" In *Hazard Management and Emergency Planning: Perspectives on Britain*, edited by D. Parker and J. Handmer. London: James and James.

Hoogerwerf, A., ed. 1983. *Succes en Falen van Overheidsbeleid*. Alphen: Samsom.

Hoogerwerf, A. 1990. "Policy and Time: Consequences of Time Perspectives for the Contents Processes and Effects of Public Policies." *International Review of Administrative Sciences* 56: 671–692.

Hoppe, R., and A. Peterse. 1993. *Handling Frozen Fire: Political Culture and Risk Management*. Boulder: Westview Press.

Hyatt, C., and L. Gottlieb. 1988. *When Smart People Fail*. Harmondsworth: Penguin.

Ingram, H.M., and D.E. Mann, eds. 1980. *Why Policies Succeed or Fail*. Beverly Hills: Sage.

Jacobs, B.D., and P. 't Hart. 1991. "Disaster at Hillsborough Stadium: A Comparative Analysis." In *Hazard Management and Emergency Planning: Perspectives on Britain*, edited by J.W. Handmer and D. Parker London: James and James.

Janis, I.L. 1982. *Groupthink: Psychological Studies of Foreign Policy Decisions and Fiascoes*. Boston: Houghton Mifflin.

Janis, I.L. 1989. *Crucial Decisions: Leadership in Policymaking and Crisis Management*. New York: Free Press.

Janis, I.L., and L. Mann. 1977. *Decision Making: A Psychological Analysis of Conflict, Choice and Commitment*. New York: Free Press.

Jarman, A., and A. Kouzmin. 1989. "Crisis Decision Making: Towards a Contingent Decision Path Perspective." In *Coping With Crises: The Management of Disasters, Riots and Terrorism*, edited by U. Rosenthal, M.T. Charles and P. 't Hart. Springfield: Charles Thomas.

Jennings, B. 1983. "Interpretive Social Science and Policy Analysis." In *Ethics, the Social Sciences and Policy Analysis*, edited by D. Callahan and B. Jennings. New York: Plenum Press.

Jervis, R. 1976. *Perceptions and Misperceptions in International Politics*. Princeton: Princeton UP.

Kam, E. 1988. *Surprise Attack: The Victim's Perspective*. Cambridge: Harvard UP.

Kaufman, H. 1976. *Are Government Organizations Immortal?* Washington: Brookings Institution.

Kelman, H., and V.L. Hamilton. 1989. *Crimes of Obedience*. New Haven: Yale UP.

Kennedy, P. 1987. *The Rise and Fall of Great Powers: Economic Change and Military Conflict from 1500 to 2000*. New York: Random House.

Kertzer, D. 1988. *Ritual, Politics, and Power*. New Haven: Yale UP.

Kiefer, F. 1983. *Fortune and Elizabethan Tragedy*. San Marino: The Huntington Library.

Kingdon, J.W. 1984. *Agendas, Alternatives and Public Policies*. Boston: Little Brown.

Kiser, L., and E. Ostrom. 1982. "Three Worlds of Action: A Metatheoretical Synthesis of Institutional Approaches." In *Strategies of Political Inquiry*, edited by V. Ostrom. Beverly Hills: Sage.

Kleiboer, M. *Multiple Realities of International Mediation*. PhD thesis in progress. Leiden: Leiden University.

Klose, W. 1971. *Skandal und Politik: Ein Kapitel negativer Demokratie*. Tübingen: Katzmann.

Kouzmin, A. 1979. "Building the New Parliament House: An Opera House Revisited?" In *Working Papers on Parliament*, edited by G. Hawker. Canberra: Canberra Case Series in Administrative Studies, Canberra College of Advanced Education.

Kouzmin, A. 1980. "The High Court: The Politics of Constructing the Court". *Legal Service Bulletin* 5: 113–7.

Kuntz, A. 1988. "From Spiegel to Flick: The Maturation of the West German Parteienstaat."
    In *The Politics of Scandal: Power and Process in Liberal Democracies*, edited by A.S.
    Markovits and M. Silverstein. New York: Holmes and Maier.
Landau, M. 1988. "Foreword." In *Handbook of Political Theory and Policy Science*, edited by E.B.
    Portis and M.B. Levy. New York: Greenwood Press.
Landau, M., and D. Chisholm. 1995. "The Arrogance of Optimism: Succes Oriented Vs
    Failure Avoidance Management Strategy in Public Administration." *Journal of
    Contingencies and Crisis Management* 3: 67–80.
Lane, J.E., ed. 1987. *Bureacracy and Public Choice*. London: Sage.
Lane, J.E. 1993. *The Public Sector: Concepts Models and Approaches*. London: Sage.
Lasswell, H.D., and D. Lerner, eds. 1951. *The Policy Sciences*. Stanford: Stanford UP.
Lasswell, H.D. 1971. *A Pre-View of Policy Sciences*. New York: Elsevier.
Lauer, R.H. 1981. *Temporal Man: The Meaning and Uses of Social Time*. New York: Praeger.
Lawlor, E.F. 1990. "When a Possible Job Becomes Impossible: Politics, Public Health, and the
    Management of the Aids Epidemic." In *Impossible Jobs in Public Management*, edited by
    E.C. Hargrove and J. Glidewell. Lawrence: Kansas UP.
Lebow, R.N. 1981. *Between Peace and War: The Nature of International Crisis*. Baltimore: Johns
    Hopkins UP.
Lebow, R.N., and J. Gross Stein. 1994. *We All Lost the Cold War*. Princeton: Princeton UP.
Leigland, J., and R. Lamb. 1986. *WPPSS: Who Is To Blame for the WPPSS Disaster?* Cambridge:
    Ballinger.
Lijphart, A. 1977. *Democracy in Plural Societies* New Haven: Yale UP.
Lindblom, C.E. 1968. *The Policymaking Process*. Englewood Cliffs: Prentice Hall.
Lindblom, C.E., and D.K. Cohen. 1977. *Usable Knowledge: Social Science and Social Problem
    Solving*. New Haven: Yale UP.
Linstone, H., ed. 1984. *Multiple Perspectives for Decision Making*. New York: Elsevier.
Linz, J.J., and A. Stepan, eds. 1978. *The Breakdown of Democratic Regimes*. Baltimore: Johns
    Hopkins UP.
Lipsky, M., and D.J. Olson. 1977. *Commission Politics: The Processing of Racial Crisis in America*.
    New Brunswick: Transaction Books.
Logue, J. 1988. "Appreciating Scandal as a Political Art Form or Making an Intellectual
    Virtue of a Political Vice." In *The Politics of Scandal: Power and Process in Liberal
    Democracies*, edited by A.S. Markovits and M. Silverstein. New York: Holmes and Maier.
Louis, W.R., and R. Owen, eds. 1989. *Suez 1956: The Crisis and Its Consequences*. Oxford:
    Clarendon Press.
Lucas, M. 1991. *Transfusion Sanguine et SIDA en 1985: Chronologie des Faits et des Décisions pour
    ce qui Concerne les Hémophiles*. Paris: Inspection Générale des Affaires Sociales.
Lukes, S. 1974. *Power: A Radical View*. London: MacMillan.
Machiavelli, N. 1988. *The Prince*, edited by Q. Skinner and R. Price. Cambridge: Cambridge
    UP.
Majone, G. 1989. *Evidence, Argument and Persuasion in the Policy Process*. New Haven: Yale
    UP.
Maoz, Z. 1990. *National Choices and International Processes*. Cambridge: Cambridge UP.
March, J.G. 1972. "Model Bias in Social Action." *Review of Educational Research* 42: 413–29.
March, J., and J.P. Olsen. 1989. *Rediscovering Institutions*. New York: Free Press.
Markovits, A.S., and M. Silverstein, eds. 1988. *The Politics of Scandal: Power and Process in
    Liberal Democracies*. New York: Holmes and Meier.
Markovits, A.S., and M. Silverstein. 1988. "Introduction: Power and Process in Liberal
    Democracies." In *The Politics of Scandal: Power and Process in Liberal Democracies*, edited
    by A.S. Markovits and M. Silverstein. New York: Holmes and Maier.
McCall, M.W., and R.E. Kaplan. 1985. *Whatever It Takes: Decision Makers at Work*. Englewood
    Cliffs: Prentice Hall.

McConnell, M. 1987. *Challenger: A Major Malfunction*. New York: Doubleday.

McKinney, J.B., and M. Johnston, eds. 1986. *Fraud, Waste and Abuse in Government: Causes, Consequences and Cures*. Philadelphia: Institute for the Study of Human Issues.

Milliband, R. 1969. *The State in Capitalist Society*. London: Weidenfeld and Nicolson.

Moore, M.H. 1990. "Police Leadership: The Impossible Dream?" In *Impossible Jobs in Public Management*, edited by E.C. Hargrove and J.C. Glidewell. Lawrence: Kansas UP.

Moore, P. 1992. "Intimidation and Communication: A Case Study of the Challenger Accident." *Journal of Business and Technical Communication* 6: 403–437.

Moorhead, G., R. Ference, and C.P. Neck. 1991. "Group Decision Fiascoes Continue: Space Shuttle Challenger and a Revised Groupthink Framework." *Human Relations* 44: 539–550.

Morone, J.G., and E.J. Woodhouse. 1986. *Averting Catastrophe: Strategies for Regulating Risky Technologies*. Berkeley: California UP.

Morris, P.W.G., and G.H. Hough. 1987. *The Anatomy of Major Projects: A Study of the Reality of Project Management*. New York: Wiley.

Mucciaroni, G. 1990. *The Political Failure of Employment Policy, 1945-1982*. Pittsburgh: Pittsburgh UP.

Murray, C. 1984. *Losing Ground*. New York: Basic Books.

Nelson, R.R. 1977. *The Moon and the Ghetto*. New York: Norton.

Nemeth, C.J., and B.M. Staw. 1989. "The Tradeoffs of Social Control and Innovation in Groups and Organizations." *Advances in Experimental Social Psychology* 22: 175–210.

Neustadt, R., and E.R. May. 1986. *Thinking in Time: The Uses of History for Decision Makers*. New York: Free Press.

Nisbett, R., and L. Ross. 1980. *Human Inference: Strategies and Shortcomings of Social Judgment*. Englewood Cliffs: Prentice Hall.

Niskanen, W. 1971. *Bureaucracy and Representative Government*. Chicago: Aldine-Atherton.

Nollkaemper, P.A. 1993. *The Legal Regime for Transboundary Water Pollution: Between Discretion and Constraint*. Dordrecht: Kluwer.

O'Connor, J. 1973. *The Fiscal Crisis of the State*. New York: St. Martin's Press.

Offe, C. 1972. *Strukturprobleme des Kapitalistischen Staates: Aufsätze zur Politischen Soziologie*. Frankfurt am Main: Surkamp.

Offe, C. 1984. *Contradictions of the Welfare State*. London: Hutchinson.

Osborne, D., and T. Gaebler. 1993. *Reinventing Government: How the Entrepreneurial Spirit is Transforming the Public Sector*. New York: Plume Books.

Ostrom, E. 1990. *Governing the Commons*. Cambridge: Cambridge UP.

Parliament House Construction Authority. 1989. *Project Parliament: Constructing a New Parliament House*. Canberra: Government Printing Office.

Peirce, W. 1981. *Bureaucratic Failure and Public Expenditure*. New York: Academic press.

Perrow, C. 1967. "A Framework for the Comparative Analysis of Organizations." *American Sociological Review* 32: 194–208.

Perrow, C. 1984. *Normal Accidents: Living with High Risk Technologies*. New York: Basic Books.

Perrow, C., and J. Guillèn. 1990. *The Aids Disaster*. New Haven: Yale UP.

Pocock, J.G.A. 1975. *The Machiavellian Moment: Florentine Political Thought and the Atlantic Republican Tradition*. Princeton: Princeton UP.

Policy Sciences. 1992. Theme issue "Perspectives on defense acquisition". 25.

Pool, J. 1990. *Sturing van Strategische Besluitvorming: Mogelijkheden en Grenzen*. Amsterdam: VU publishers.

Popper, K. 1948. *The Open Society and Its Enemies*. Part I. London: Routledge.

Portis, E.B., and M.B. Levy, eds. 1988. *Handbook of Political Theory and Policy Science*. Westport: Greenwood.

Pressman, J.L., and A. Wildavsky. 1984. *Implementation: How Great Expectations in Washington Are Dashed in Oakland*. 3d ed. Berkeley: University of California Press.

Reason, J. 1990. *Human Error*. Manchester: Manchester UP.

Rein, M., and D. Schon. 1991. "Frame-reflective Policy Discourse." In *Social Sciences and Modern States: National Experiences and Theoretical Crossroads*, edited by P. Wagner, C.H. Weiss, B. Wittrock and H. Wollmann. Cambridge: Cambridge UP.

Report of the Formal Investigation into the Loss of the Herald of Free Enterprise. 1988. London: Her Majesty's Stationary Office.

Report to the President by the Presidential Commission on the Space Shuttle Challenger Accident. 1986. Washington: Government Printing Office.

Ringeling, A.B. 1993. *Het Imago van de Overheid*. Den Haag: VUGA.

Rittel, H.W.J., and M.M. Webber. 1973. "Dilemmas in a General Theory of Planning." *Policy Sciences* 4: 155–169.

Rosenthal, U., P. 't Hart and M.T. Charles. 1989. "The World of Crises and Crisis Management." In *Coping with Crises: The Management of Disasters, Riots, and Terrorism*, edited by U. Rosenthal, M.T. Charles and P. 't Hart. Springfield: Charles Thomas 1989.

Rosenthal, U., P. 't Hart and A. Kouzmin. 1991. "The Bureau-politics of Crisis Management." *Public Administration* 69: 211–233.

Russo, R.J., and P. Schoemaker. 1988. *Decision Traps*. New York: Simon and Schuster.

Sabatier, P.A. 1986. "What Can We Learn from Implementation Research?" In *Guidance, Control and Evaluation in the Public Sector*, edited by F.X. Kaufmann, G. Majone and V. Ostrom. Berlin: De Gruyter.

Salomon, L.M. 1979. "The Time Dimension in Policy Evaluation." In *Public Policy* 27: 121–153.

Schmitz, M. 1981. *Theorie und Praxis des Politischen Skandals*. Frankfurt: Campus.

Schon, D., and M. Rein. 1994. *Reframing: Toward the Resolution of Intractable Policy Controversies*. New York: Basic Books.

Schorr, J.K. 1987. "Some Contributions *German Katastrophensoziologie* Can Make to the Sociology of Disasters." *Journal of Mass Emergencies and Disasters* 5: 115–135.

Schulman, P. 1980. *Large-scale Policymaking*. New York: Elsevier.

Schulman, P.R. 1989. "The 'Logic' of Organizational Irrationality." *Administration and Society* 21: 31–53.

Schumacher, E.F. 1973. *Small Is Beautiful: A Study of Economics As If People Mattered*. New York: Harper and Row.

Schwartz, H.S. 1987. "On the Psychodynamics of Organizational Disaster: The Case of the Space Shuttle Challenger *Columbia*." *Journal of World Business* 22: 59–67.

Schwarz, M., and M. Thompson. 1990. *Divided We Stand: Redefining Technology Politics and Social Choice*. London: Wheatsheaf.

Scriven, M. 1973. "Goal-free Evaluation." In *School Evaluation: The Politics and Process*, edited by E.R. House. Berkeley: McCutchan.

Scriven, M. 1976. "Maximizing the Power of Causal Investigation: The Modus Operandi Method." In *Evaluation Studies Review Annual*. 1, edited by G.V. Glass. Beverly Hills: Sage.

Shadish, W.R. Jr., T.D. Cook and L.C. Leviton. 1991. *Foundations of Program Evaluation: Theories of Practice*. Newbury Park: Sage.

Shears, R., and I. Gidley. 1985. *The Rainbow Warrior*. Sydney: Sphere Books.

Shiels, F.L. 1991. *Preventable Disasters: Why Governments Fail*. Savage: Rowman & Littlefield.

Shklar, J.N. 1990. *The Faces of Injustice*. New Haven: Yale UP.

Sieber, S.D. 1981. *Fatal Remedies: The Ironies of Social Intervention*. New York: Plenum Press.

Silverstein, A.M. 1981. *Pure Politics and Impure Science: The Swine Flu Affair*. Baltimore: Johns Hopkins UP.

Simon, H. 1976. *Administrative Behavior*. 3d ed. New York: Free Press.

Simpson, A. 1961. *The Wealth of the Gentry, 1540–1660*. Cambridge: Cambridge UP.

Sitkin, S.B. 1992. "Learning Through Failure: The Strategy of Small Losses." In *Research in Organizational Behavior*. Vol. 14, edited by B.M. Staw and L. Cummings. Greenwich: JAI Press.

Skowronek, S. 1993. *The Politics Presidents Make: Leadership from John Adams to George Bush*. Cambridge Mass: Belknap Press of Harvard UP.

Slatter, S. 1984. *Corporate Recovery*. Harmondsworth: Penguin.

Souder, W.E. 1988. "Causes of Crises: The Behavioral Accident." *Industrial Crises Quarterly* 2: 185–194.

Soulier, J.P. 1992. *Transfusion et SIDA: Le Droit à la Vérité*. Paris: Éditions Frison-Roche.

Starbuck, W.H., and F.J. Milliken. 1988. "Challenger: Fine-tuning the Odds Until Something Breaks." *Journal of Management Studies* 25: 319–340.

Steinbruner, J.D. 1974. *The Cybernetic Theory of Decision*. Princeton: Princeton UP.

Stone, D.A. 1988. *Policy Paradox and Political Reason*. Glenview: Scott Foresman and Company.

Tetlock, P.E. 1985. "Accountability: The Neglected Social Context of Judgment and Choice." In *Research in Organizational Behavior*. Vol. 11, edited by B.M. Staw and L. Cummings. Greenwich: JAI Press.

Tetlock, P.E., R.S. Peterson, C. McGuire, S. Chang and P. Field. 1992. "Assessing Political Group Dynamics: A Test of the Groupthink Model." *Journal of Personality and Social Psychology* 63: 403–425.

Tetlock, P.E., and A. Belkin. 1995. "Counterfactual Thought Exeriments in World Politics: Logical, Methodological, and Psychological Perspectives." *Mimeo*. Berkely: Conference Paper University of California.

Thompson, D.F. 1987. *Political Ethics and Public Office*. Cambridge: Harvard UP.

Thompson, J.D., and A. Tuden. 1959. "Strategies, Structures, and Processes for Organizational Decision." In *Comparative Studies in Administration*, edited by J.D. Thompson, P.B. Hammond, R.W. Hawkes, B.H. Junker and A. Tuden. Pittsburgh: Pittsburgh UP.

Thompson, M., R. Ellis and A. Wildavsky. 1990. *Cultural Theory*. Boulder: Westview Press.

Throgmorton, J.A. 1991. "The Rhetorics of Policy Analysis." *Policy Sciences* 24: 153–179.

Tong, R. 1986. *Ethics in Public Policy*. Englewood Cliffs: Prentice Hall.

Toonen, T.A.J. 1983. "Administrative Plurality in a Unitary State: The Analysis of Public Organisational Pluralism." *Policy and Politics* 11: 249–271.

Tuchman, B.W. 1990. *The March of Folly: From Troy to Vietnam*. London: Cardinal/Sphere Books.

Turner, B.A. 1978. *Man-made Disaster*. London: Wykeham.

Vaughan, D. 1990. "Autonomy, Interdependence, and Social Control: NASA and the Space Shuttle Challenger." *Administrative Science Quarterly* 35: 225-257.

Veblen, T. 1961. *The Place of Science in Modern Civilization*. New York: Russell and Russell.

Wagenaar, W.A. 1987. "Wat Dwaasheid Heet is Wijsheid Achteraf". *Psychologie* 8: 48–52.

Wagenaar, W.A. 1987. *De Oorzaken van Onmogelijke Ongelukken*. Deventer: Van Loghem Slaterus.

Wagner, P., C.H. Weiss, B. Wittrock and H. Wollman, eds. 1991. *Social Sciences and Modern States*. Cambridge: Cambridge UP.

Werhane, P. 1991. "Engineers and Management: The Challenge of the Challenger Incident." *Journal of Business Ethics* 10: 605–616.

White, O.F. Jr., and C.J. McSwain. 1990. "The Phoenix Project: Raising a New Image of Public Administration from the Ashes of the Past." In *Images and Identities in Public Administration*, edited by H.D. Kass and B.L. Catron. London: Sage.

Wildavsky, A. 1987. *Speaking Truth to Power: The Art and Craft of Policy Analysis*. New Brunswick: Transaction Books.

Wildavsky, A. 1988. *Searching for Safety*. Berkeley: Transaction Books.

Wilensky, H. 1967. *Organizational Intelligence*. New York: Free Press.

Williams, W. 1990. *Mismanaging America: The Rise of the Anti-analytic Presidency*. Lawrence: Kansas UP.

Williamson, O. 1975. *Markets and Hierarchies*. New York: Free Press.

Wilson, J.Q. 1980. *The Politics of Regulation*. New York: Basic Books.

Wolf, C. 1988. *Markets or Governments*. Cambridge: MIT Press.

Wright Mills, C. 1963. *The Causes of World War Three*. 4th ed. New York: Ballantine Books.

Wynne, B. 1982. *Rationality and Ritual: The Windscale Inquiry and Nuclear Decisions in Britain*. Chalfont St. Giles: Society for the History of Science.

Wynne, B. 1987. *Risk Management and Hazardous Waste: Implementation and the Dialectics of Credibility*. London: Springer.

Yeomans, J. 1968. *The Other Taj Mahal: What Happened to the Sydney Opera House*. London: Longman.

Index